THE SHAAR PRESS

THE JUDAICA IMPRINT
FOR THOUGHTFUL PEOPLE

A SHAAR PRESS PUBLICATION

Women Talk

Jewish women around the world speak about their lives, challenges, and accomplishments

Debbie Shapiro

First edition – First impression / January 2010

Published by **SHAAR PRESS**
Distributed by MESORAH PUBLICATIONS, LTD.
4401 Second Avenue / Brooklyn, N.Y 11232 / (718) 921-9000

Distributed in Israel by SIFRIATI / A. GITLER
6 Hayarkon Street / Bnei Brak 51127

Distributed in Europe by LEHMANNS
Unit E, Viking Business Park, Rolling Mill Road / Jarrow, Tyne and Wear, NE32 3DP/ England

Distributed in Australia and New Zealand by GOLDS WORLD OF JUDAICA
3-13 William Street / Balaclava, Melbourne 3183 / Victoria Australia

Distributed in South Africa by KOLLEL BOOKSHOP
Ivy Common / 105 William Road / Norwood 2192, Johannesburg, South Africa

ISBN 10: 1-4226-0971-5 / ISBN 13: 978-1-4226-0971-2

Custom bound by Sefercraft, Inc. / 4401 Second Avenue / Brooklyn N.Y. 11232

This book is dedicated to the memories of

MY FATHER,
ASHER LEVINE
ר׳ אשר ב״ר אלכסנדר מענדל הלוי
Who instilled in me a fierce pride in my Jewish roots

MY FATHER-IN-LAW,
DR. HENRY SHAPIRO
ר׳ חיים ב״ר אריה ליב גרשון
A great man who knew how to bring out the greatness in others

MY MOTHER,
ROSE LEVINE
ריזל בת ר׳ מיכאל מאיר
Who taught me to search for the good in others

MY NEIGHBOR,
CHANNAH MONCHARSH
חנה גיטל בת ר׳ יעקב קאפל
Who taught me the life-transforming power of giving

TABLE OF CONTENTS

IN APPRECIATION

I'd like to thank the many wonderful people who helped make this book a reality. They all, in their own, unique way, contributed their special talents to create this volume.

— to my editor, Libby Pheterson, who skillfully enhanced my voice without drowning it. It takes a great writer to make a great editor, and you're both, Libby. Thank you!

— to Miriam Zakon and Shmuel Blitz in ArtScroll's Jerusalem office, for believing in me.

— to my many readers in Lakewood, New Jersey, and to my many dear friends, who responded with such tremendous enthusiasm to the original interviews.

— to Mrs. Judi Dick, for her meticulous editing.

— to Eli Kroen, for the beatiful cover design, and to Mrs. Reizy Ganz, Mrs. Devoiry Biderman, and the rest of the ArtScroll staff, Thank you!

Several hidden *tzaddikim* helped me overcome what appeared to be insurmountable obstacles to publishing this book. Thank you for your advice and assistance, and, most important of all, for being there when I needed you. This book is really yours.

The interviews with Chavie and Bracha originally appeared in *Bina Magazine*; the interviews with Rina Fisch, Meira Fink, and Mrs. Udel Frank originally appeared in the *Voice of Lakewood*. I'd like to thank both of these wonderful publications for so graciously encouraging me to publish this volume.

Writing is never a nine-to-five job. It's while peeling the potatoes for supper or folding that last load of laundry that, suddenly, seemingly out of nowhere, the right words come to mind and they must be put to paper (or rather computer) before they vanish into nothingness, to be lost forever. While rushing to the computer to eternalize my thoughts might make for good writing, it also makes for burnt potatoes and wrinkly laundry. So it's really my family who deserves the biggest kudos for putting up with a wife and mother cum writer. Thank you! And my special thanks goes to you, Dovid, for being there through thick and thin (and I'm not just referring to weight!). May we continue to face our challenges with *emunah* and *bitachon*.

I'd like to thank my delicious grandchildren, each and every one of you, for being the delight of my life, my greatest joy, and the most real, vibrant volume yet to be published (don't say I didn't warn you!).

It's impossible to express my gratitude and admiration to the stars of this book; all those wonderful, open women who allowed me to enter their lives and hear their stories. Each time, as we created that bond of connection that is so unique among women, I felt as if I had discovered a long-lost friend. Thank you for letting me into your hearts. This book is truly yours.

As a youngster, I always dreamed of becoming a writer; as a teenager, of living in Eretz Yisrael; and later on, as a young adult, of marrying a *talmid chacham* and raising a family of *bnei Torah*. I have much to be grateful for, all of my dreams have come true. I am truly undeserving of all His tremendous *chasodim*, and it is to Him, and to Him alone, that I owe my greatest thanks.

INTRODUCTION

It seems that wherever I go, whomever I meet, I discover another story waiting to be told. Why is it that I am always looking for the story within the story? What am I trying to find? I'll answer my question with a Chassidic story:

> Shortly before leaving this world, the holy Baal Shem Tov called for his closest disciples and revealed to each of them his unique mission in life. Some were to lead groups of Chassidim, other were to devote their lives to secret missions of mercy, and to Reb Yaakov, his personal attendant, he whispered, "After my death you are to travel from town to town and wherever you go, repeat my Torah and tell people what I did during my life."
>
> Reb Yaakov was perplexed. "Rebbe, why have you burdened me with a life of wandering and poverty?"
>
> The Baal Shem Tov responded, "My dear Reb Yaakov, don't worry. You will be highly rewarded for your work. And when the time comes for your wandering to end, a sign will be given to you and you will know that you have completed your mission."
>
> Shortly after the Baal Shem Tov left this world, each of his disciples began his assigned task. Reb Yaakov slipped on his backpack, took his walking stick, and began to wander from town to town.
>
> He was warmly welcomed wherever he went. People eagerly gathered to hear him tell inspiring stories about the holy Baal Shem Tov, and since he had been a member of the Chevrah Kadisha, the Baal Shem Tov's inner circle, he knew thousands of sto-

ries. At the inns, he was given free food and lodging. At the shuls, he was given money. So although he did live a life of wandering, he did not live a life of poverty.

After several years of traveling from one town to the next, Reb Yaakov heard about a wealthy Italian Jew who gave a gold ducat for every Baal Shem Tov story that was told to him.

"I will go and tell him all the stories I know," thought Reb Yaakov, "and then I will be a wealthy man."

So Reb Yaakov set out to Rome. Throughout the long journey, he reviewed all the stories he knew about the Baal Shem Tov, as well as the teachings he had heard directly from his Rebbe's holy mouth. In Rome, he was directed to the wealthy man's palace, where he was warmly welcomed.

"Tomorrow night," said the wealthy man, "you can tell us your stories at the Shabbos table."

Friday night, Reb Yaakov was given the seat of honor, right next to the wealthy man. The table was crowded with many guests who had come to hear Reb Yaakov entertain them with stories of the Baal Shem Tov.

When the meal had ended, the wealthy Jew turned to Reb Yaakov with a big smile and said, "Please honor us with a story."

Reb Yaakov tried to speak, but he could not think of a single thing to say. He could not remember anything about the Baal Shem Tov. All the guests were staring at him, waiting for him to say something. Finally he said, "I cannot speak right now."

"Never mind. It is late," said the wealthy man. "We'll hear the stories tomorrow."

But the same thing happened at the second meal, and again at the third meal, and then again, after Havdalah. Reb Yaakov was not able to recall even a single story. After Havdalah he went to his room and began packing his bags.

When the wealthy man saw that Reb Yaakov was preparing to leave, he said, "Reb Yaakov, please stay for a few more days. Perhaps you will remember something." Reb Yaakov agreed.

Reb Yaakov spent the next few days wandering about in the garden, but as hard as he tried, he could not remember a single story. Finally, he told the wealthy man, "I must go."

The wealthy man handed him a small bag of gold coins, and said, "Reb Yaakov, take this. And if you remember anything about the Baal Shem Tov — anything at all — please come back."

Reb Yaakov donned his backpack and set out on the long journey home. Suddenly, after walking for fifteen minutes, he recalled a story. He immediately turned around and raced back to the wealthy man's home.

Reb Yaakov pushed the door open, ran up to the wealthy man's study, and immediately started telling his story, before he would forget. "The strange thing is that the only story that I can remember is one that I had completely forgotten for many years," he began. "I am positive that you never heard it, because I have never told it to anyone."

This is the story that Reb Yaakov told:

Once time, during chol Hamoed Pesach, the Baal Shem Tov asked me to accompany him and several other disciples on a long journey. After a few days of traveling, we arrived at a large city that we had never seen before. The streets were crowded with people dressed for a holiday.

We entered the Jewish ghetto and were shocked to see that the streets were empty, all the doors of the houses were closed shut, and every window was shuttered. Our carriage stopped before one of the houses and the Baal Shem Tov went to the door and knocked. When no one answered, he knocked again, more loudly. Finally, he shouted, "Open up, in the name of Hashem."

From behind the door we heard the voice of what sounded like an elderly woman. "Who is it?" she asked.

"It is Rabbi Yisrael Ben Eliezer," said the Baal Shem Tov. The woman opened the door and quickly let us into the house.

The old woman cried, "Rabbi, do you want to be killed? Today is Easter, and every Easter a Jew is burned alive. If they see you, they'll grab you and burn you."

"Don't be afraid," said the Baal Shem Tov. "Let me do as I must." He walked over to the window overlooking the town square, pulled back the curtains, and opened the shutters. Then he stood there watching what was taking place.

A raised platform had been constructed in the square. Next to it was an enormous wooden stake, with logs piled around the base. A group of pompous priests followed by a large and noisy mob entered the square. A priest wearing a large pointed hat and dressed in scarlet robes stood on the platform.

The Baal Shem Tov pointed to that priest and said to me, "That man is the bishop. Go to where he is standing and tell him that Rabbi Yisrael, the Baal Shem Tov, is waiting for him."

I started to open the door. The woman screamed in hysterics, 'Don't leave this house! You will be dragged to their altar and burned alive!" But I followed the Baal Shem Tov's instructions.

No one noticed me walking through the crowd; it was as if I were invisible. I climbed up onto the platform, and said to the bishop, "Bishop, Rabbi Yisrael Ben Eliezer, the Baal Shem Tov, wants you to come to him immediately."

The bishop was startled. "Go back and tell the Rabbi that I will come in a few hours," he said.

Again, as I walked through the churning crowd, it was as if I were invisible. No one noticed me. Back at the woman's home, the Baal Shem Tov was waiting for me. When I told him what the bishop said, he ordered me to go back to him and tell him to come at once.

The old lady became hysterical. "Don't go," she cried. "They will burn you alive!"

But I obeyed my Rebbe's orders and walked right through the crowd and up to the platform where the bishop was conducting the service. "Rabbi Yisrael Ben Eliezer wants to speak with you, NOW!" I yelled.

The bishop looked at me and whispered, "I will go." To the crowd waiting for him to continue the service he stated, "I will return later to continue."

Back at the house, the Baal Shem Tov opened the door for us and escorted the bishop into another room. Several hours later, the Baal Shem Tov came out of the room alone, and said to me, "It's time to leave." We got into our wagon and began the trip home to Mezibush. And that is as much as I know.

When Reb Yaakov concluded the story, the wealthy man asked, "Reb Yaakov, don't you recognize me?"

Suddenly, Reb Yaakov understood. "You are the bishop," he gasped.

The wealthy man smiled. "That's right," he began. "And you have just saved my soul!"

The wealthy man related his story:

I am descended from a long line of learned and holy rabbis. But as a young man my yetzer hora overwhelmed me and I converted to Christianity. I joined the priesthood and quickly advanced to higher and higher positions in the Church. As I gained greater stature, I became increasingly cruel to other Jews. And the crueler I became, the more I advanced. Finally, I was made bishop, and every Easter I burned a Jew at the stake.

One night I had a vivid dream: A holy tzaddik came to me and said, "Repent, otherwise your soul is doomed." When I asked the holy tzaddik his name, he replied that it was Rabbi Yisrael Ben Eliezer.

This Easter, I went up to the platform determined not to burn a Jew. But then, when I saw the crowd and heard everyone praise me, I promised myself, "This year will be the last time."

Then, when you came, I realized that I must do teshuvah. But first, I wanted to finish the service. I wanted to hear the crowd cheer me one more time. But then, when you came a second time, I realized that I had no choice, that there is no putting off teshuvah.

When I arrived at the old woman's home, the Baal Shem Tov brought me into a private room and asked, "Moshe, are you ready to return to the path of your forefathers and live as a Jew?" I started to cry, and the black cloud covering my soul was suddenly lifted.

The Baal Shem Tov instructed me to sell all my possessions and divide the money into three parts. I was to use one part to buy my freedom from the Church. Another part was to be distributed among the poor. With the third part, I was to travel to a distant country where I could live as a Jew.

"How will I know that my teshuvah has been accepted?" I asked.

The Baal Shem Tov replied, "When a man comes to you and tells you your own story."

The wealthy man continued, "I recognized you at once. When you could not remember even a single story, I understood that my *teshuvah* was not yet complete. I began to do a deeper repentance. When you left, I was sure that I was lost, that my *teshuvah* would never be accepted. I cried from the depths of my soul, begging Hashem to have mercy on me and accept His wayward son. *Baruch Hashem*, you returned."

The wealthy man gave Reb Yaakov half his fortune. Reb Yaakov realized that this was the sign he had been waiting for. He had accomplished his mission, and it was time for him to stop his wandering and return to his family.

Every time I hear another person's story — as I open a window into their inner souls, catch a glimpse of where they've been and how they've gotten to where they are today — it touches within me a chord of recognition that is beyond intellect, and I feel as if I've discovered another aspect of my own self. No, the story that resonates with me is never, thank G-d, as earth shattering as that of the bishop — my challenges were never so dramatic — yet, like the bishop, with each story that I hear I feel as if I've discovered another piece of myself.

The thirty-four noteworthy women whose interviews appear in this volume allowed me a glimpse into their inner world, to hear about their challenges and triumphs, and I can honestly say that I am amazed — and that's because Jewish women really are amazing! We're pulled in so many directions, we have so many responsibilities, and we're constantly prioritizing as we search for the *emes*, the truth, in whatever we do. And it's because of this that we are so incredibly successful in creating a new generation of strong, upright Jews.

Several weeks ago, while visiting the Lauder Yeshurun Beis Zion Yeshiva in Berlin, I attended a class on the "Jewish Home" given by Rebbetzin Talya Rose. She quoted Rabbi Avigdor Miller, *ztz"l*, who points out that Dovid HaMelech defined his essence with the words, "I am Your servant, the son of Your maidservant." He was an *eved Hashem* because he learned the art of being an upright Jew from his mother! It was the *chinuch* that he received from her that made him into the great person he became. That, dear women, is our power. In the words of Chana Jenny Weisberg, one of the women interviewed in this book: "We can change the world, one diaper at a time."

This book contains thirty-four interviews with Jewish women from around the world; ordinary next-door neighbor women, who are using their *chachmas nashim* to become great women. I hope their stories touch something within you, and may all of our stories be wonderful ones.

GROWING UP IN THE MIR

> Our homes were almost a part of the yeshivah; right outside our front door were hooks where the *bachurim* hung their hats."

Leah Breskin

When I was asked to interview Leah Breskin, I was thrilled to have the zechus to speak with a woman who actually grew up in the Mirrer Yeshivah in Yerushalayim, when the Mirrer Yeshivah consisted of only one building instead of the many buildings that dot Bais Yisrael today. Imagine being raised in such an environment!

Until the early 80's the students of the Mirrer Yeshivah learned in a single location. The main entrance was intended for the bachurim, while the side entrance was reserved for the five families who lived in the building. They included:

Mrs. Breskin's cousin, Rav Nachum Peratzovitz, z"l, and his wife, Rebbetzin Ettel (Rav Chaim Shmulevitz's daughter). Their apartment was alongside the yeshivah study hall. Rav Nachum Peratzovitz was Rosh HaYeshivah.

Above them lived Rav Chaim Shmulevitz, z"tl, and his wife, Rebbetzin Miriam, a"h. Rebbetzin Miriam was Mrs. Breskin's aunt. Rav Chaim Shmulevitz was Rosh HaYeshivah.

Across the hall from Rav Chaim's apartment were Mrs. Breskin's grandparents, the Mirrer Rosh HaYeshivah, Rav Eliezer Yehudah Finkel, zt"l, and his wife, Rebbetzin Malka, a"h. After Rav Lazer Yudel passed away in 1965, the apartment was converted into the yeshivah office.

On the second floor lived Mrs. Breskin's uncle, Rav Chaim Zev Finkel, zt"l, and his wife, Rebbetzin Gittel, a"h — R' Chaim Shmulevitz's sister. Rav Chaim Zev was the Mirrer Mashgiach. After Rav Chaim Zev passed away in 1965, Rebbetzin Gittel continued to live in the apartment until she was niftar.

Mrs. Breskin's parents, Rav Moshe Finkel, z"l, and his wife, Rebbetzin Nechama Aidel, a"h, as well as their four children, lived on the floor above Rebbetzin Gittel. Rav Moshe Finkel was the yeshivah's administrative assistant.

The five families, plus the yeshivah office staff, shared one telephone.

I was born in Israel in 1955, and we lived in the Mirrer Yeshivah. It was a lot of fun to grow up in a yeshivah, together with a few hundred *bachurim. [Today, the students number over five thousand, ken yirbu]*. When my aunt wanted something from me or from one of the other kids, she would holler up the steps, and then the *bachurim* would echo it so that we could hear! I remember sitting on the steps as a small child, playing with the *bachurim*. They regarded me as a baby sister. Our homes were almost a part of the yeshivah; right outside our front door were hooks where the *bachurim* hung their hats.

We really were like one enormous family. Sometimes, when the kitchen staff needed help serving the meals, they would ask me. In our home, everything was for the *bachurim* and the yeshivah; the family needs came after that. If one of the *bachurim* was sick, my mother or one of my aunts would prepare toast and rice. But I was never jealous, because we really felt that we were all one family.

Every Shabbos morning at around nine-thirty, when the yeshivah finished *davening*, all the families who lived in the yeshivah, together with the *bachurim*, would pile into Rav Chaim Shmulevitz's apartment to hear *Kiddush*. The women would crowd into the tiny kitchen and schmooze while preparing eggs and onions for the Shabbos *seudah*.

Every Friday, my aunt, Rebbetzin Miriam — Rav Chaim Shmulevitz's wife — went down to the yeshivah kitchen (her own kitchen was tiny) to prepare hard-boiled eggs and *cholent* for all the other families living in the yeshivah building. (The *bachurim* ate the left-over *cholent* at *shalosh seudos*. They waited for it!) She also made a huge pot of gefilte fish for all of her married children, in addition to the families in the yeshivah.

It was my job to deliver the packages of gefilte fish, *l'kavod Shabbos kodesh,* to my aunt's married children, who lived all over Jerusalem.

Every Friday at around noon, my uncle, Rav Chaim Shmulevitz, would go to the *Kosel* with his grandson. I felt as if he was a second father to me. He used to take me for walks in the park. During *sefiras ha'omer* he would ask me to remind him to "*tzel Sefirah.*" Of course he didn't need me to remind him — he recited *sefiras ha'omer* with the yeshivah. But he wanted me to remind him so that *I* wouldn't forget!

One night I was in my cousins' apartment, socializing, when Rav Chaim walked in. He needed quiet to learn, but he did not want me to feel unwanted. So he jokingly asked me if I could learn with him. Of course I got the message, and left so that he could continue learning in peace and quiet.

Rav Chaim knew how to make mitzvos exciting for the children. Every erev Pesach, he would call in all the children to help him with the *bedikas chametz*. When we finished, he would give each of us a *lira* for our help. The following afternoon, my aunt, Rav Chaim's wife, would prepare a meal of lungs, borscht, and mashed potatoes for the family as well as for any *bachurim* who had remained in the yeshivah for Pesach. That way, we weren't starving during the Seder.

On Seder night all the families would get together for a huge Seder at Rav Chaim house. We were at least sixty people. We would open the folding door that divided the living room from the bedroom, and set up a big, long table. Each of the young boys recited the *Mah Nishtanah*. It took an hour to an hour-and-a-half for them to finish! My uncle would listen patiently to every single child's recital. He loved children.

On Pesach we ate machine *matzos meyuchados*. These were

not *shemurah matzos*, but they were more *mehadrin* than regular machine matzos. My parents were always afraid of misusing the yeshivah's funds. *[Rav Moshe Finkel was in charge of the financial aspects of the yeshivah, and, in return, the yeshivah supported the family.]* Because of this, they wouldn't even consider using the yeshivah's money for a *chumrah* such as *shemurah matzos*.

This story happened in 1960, when my older brother, Rav Eliyahu Baruch, *z"l*, was twelve years old. He wanted *shemurah matzos* for the Seder. Since these *matzos* are more expensive than other *matzos*, my father offered to buy him a lottery ticket if he'd eat the machine *matzos meyuchados* without complaining.

Before Pesach, my father's cousin, Rebbetzin Schulman (whose husband was Rosh Yeshivah in Yeshivas Slobodka, Bnei Brak) visited us. When she saw how we were living, she was appalled, and went downstairs to tell the Zaidy, Rav Lazer Yudah. Rav Lazer Yudah explained that our family was living in poverty because we did not want to take any extra money from the yeshivah. Then he started to cry and said a few *pirkei Tehillim*. The following day, my brother won the lottery. The prize was an apartment in Cholon! We were sure that he'd won the prize as a result of my grandfather's *tefillos*. We were too young to understand that our zaidy had recited *Tehillim* for our welfare — but winning a lottery was not the focus of his *tefillos*.

Since the lottery ticket had been purchased with the yeshivah's money, my grandfather said that it really belonged to the yeshivah. My father sold the apartment. He used a small part of the money to purchase necessities for the family, such as proper beds and a refrigerator. But most of the money went to the yeshivah. This is the way my parents lived. Everything was for the yeshivah. The *bachurim* always came first.

Do you remember the Six- Day War?

We all knew that a war would soon break out. There were a thousand tanks and one hundred thousand Egyptian soldiers on the Egyptian-Israel border, waiting for the signal to attack Israel. Prior to the war, *Hagah* — the Israel Civil Defense Unit — set up neighborhood headquarters under the stairs outside the kitchen. This was right next to the yeshivah's dining hall, which served as our neighborhood shelter. They fortified the dining hall's windows with sandbags.

At the beginning of the war, I ran with one of the *Hagah* soldiers to a neighboring building to bring something back to the shelter — and was almost killed by a bomb! That was the last time I left the shelter for the next six days.

The bombing was heavy. One bomb sliced through the yeshivah's upper floor, came out the other side, and landed next to the carpentry shop down the street. We were positive that the building would collapse on us! Today, if you look closely at the main yeshivah building, you can see the stones that were used to repair the hole. They are whiter than the other stones.

What was it like spending six days in the shelter? Ours was the only shelter in the neighborhood, so there were a lot of people there. The women sat on one side, the men on the other. Food was not a problem. After all, the shelter also served as the yeshivah's kitchen and dining room. The yeshivah prepared food for everyone. People slept on the floor. Some *shlepped* mattresses out of the dormitory rooms. Others just slept on their coats, or whatever else they could find. We recited *Tehillim* and *davened* the entire time. The soldiers at Mandelbaum Gate heard our *davening* and told us to continue. Sometimes a few of them would come in to join us.

Prior to the Six-Day War, Mandelbaum Gate — situated on the corner of Shmuel Hanavi and Shivtei Yisrael Streets — was the main crossing point between Jerusalem and Jordon. Much of Jerusalem was within shooting range of the Jordanian soldiers. It was not uncommon for women hanging laundry in Meah Shearim to notice a bullet whiz by — if they were lucky.

When the war was over, I remember standing next to Mandelbaum Gate watching the soldiers change the license plates on the cars (there were very few in those days) coming into Israel from the captured territories. I noticed a group of *Hagah* soldiers walking toward the Old City, and recognized some of them because they had been stationed in the yeshivah. I asked if I could join them, and they agreed. We entered the Old City through *Shaar Shechem* (the Damascus Gate) and walked through the Arab *shuk*. The soldiers bought all sorts of trinkets in the *shuk* at ridiculously low prices. Afterward, we went to the *Kosel*. Then they went up to *Har Habayis*. I walked up to the gate with them. But when I looked inside and saw a beautiful domed building surrounded by an enormous courtyard, I was frightened and didn't go inside. When I told my mother what had happened, she was upset, but grateful that I hadn't gone onto *Har Habayis*. *[Nowadays, it is forbidden for any Jew to step in the main area of the Har Habayis. Unfortunately, many Jews are not aware of the halachah and transgress this prohibition.]*

After the war, Arab women balancing enormous boxes on their heads (I always wondered if they had flat heads) would walk in from East Jerusalem and sit on the curb near the yeshivah, selling figs, grapes, and sabras (prickly pears). The neighborhood women would buy the sabras and eat the succulent fruits one after the other.

At first, the yeshivah hired Arab workers. Then, after the following incident, the administration realized that this could be dangerous, and replaced them with Jewish workers. Walking downstairs to learn in the *beis medrash*, my father noticed a loaf of bread on the floor next to the yeshivah's one and only public telephone (this was before anyone ever dreamed of cell phones!). He picked the loaf off the floor, placed it on a telephone book, and then continued on his way. The following day, my father noticed that the loaf of bread was still there, and asked a *bachur* to bring it down to the yeshivah kitchen. When the *bachur* picked it up, he realized that it was much too heavy to be a simple loaf of bread. There was a bomb hidden inside! Had it exploded, it could have destroyed the entire building .... But Hashem was watching over us, and the timer did not go off.

My parents had incredible *mesirus nefesh* for the yeshivah. They valued *limud Torah* above everything else. In 1965, my father traveled to the United States to collect money for the yeshivah. He remained there for an entire year while my mother remained at home with us children. This was at a time when international phone calls were an unheard-of luxury. It was a very difficult year. We were extremely poor. That summer, while the other kids went to the beach, we stayed at home.

But in those days almost everyone lived in poverty. We all shared one small refrigerator. When we bought a package of butter, we split it between the families. We cooked our meals on a two-burner gas stove. We didn't have an oven, so my mother baked our family's cakes and challahs in the yeshivah oven. She'd run up and down three flights of stairs to put the cake in the oven, and then again to check if it was done — and yet again to remove it from the oven. By the time the cake had cooled off enough to bring it upstairs, half of it would be gone. The smell was too much for the *bachurim* to resist!

My brother, Rav Eliyahu Baruch, used to deliver *shiurim* in our living room. The *bachurim* squeezed into every possible space in our tiny apartment, making my mother a virtual prisoner in the kitchen until they left. It wasn't easy for her, but she did it with *simchah* because the *bachurim* were her life. One time, she noticed one of the *bachurim* sitting on our washing machine. She was really upset! Before the next *shiur*, we taped a note to the machine, stating that it was a washing machine and not a chair! But that's the way my parents' home was — and the homes of all the families who lived in the yeshivah building: open, with people coming in and out. It was simple, busy, and wonderful.

My husband and I moved to Lakewood about thirty years ago, and we live right next to the yeshivah. When I see the *bachurim* racing to yeshivah, I feel as if I am back home, in the Mirrer Yeshivah!

A DIFFERENT PERSPECTIVE

"The doctor admitted me to the hospital for tests, which showed that I had lost 80 percent of my vision. Overnight, I had become legally blind!"

Judith Bron

I first "met" Judith Bron about two and a half years ago, after she submitted an article to the kiruv website where I was editor. I liked the article; it was honest, straightforward, and well written. I accepted it, and wrote Judith a letter asking for personal details to include at the end of the article. That's when I discovered that this very articulate woman is legally blind!

I was fascinated. I spend so much time reviewing my articles, smoothing the language and checking it again and again (and again!) for mistakes. How can a person write without actually seeing what is on the page? And then again, in her letter she wrote that she "reads" our site regularly. How can she possibly read a website if she has impaired sight?

After Judith submitted another article, I needed to clarify certain things and asked her if it would be possible to contact her by phone. She agreed. We immediately clicked. I felt that I had known her forever. I soon discovered a wonderful new friend!

I was born and raised in Buffalo, New York. My family was Conservative. My father insisted that we go to shul on Shabbos morning. We ate kosher, more or less. But our *Yiddishkeit* was cultural rather than halachic. We gave *tzedakah*, but instead of giving for *chinuch* or to help the poor, the money went for things like planting trees in Israel. It was all tradition, without any connection to the Almighty.

After completing high school, I attended SUNY Buffalo, where I graduated cum laude with a BS in social work. Interestingly enough, my elementary school, high school, and university all had the same zip code; I was really not much of a traveler! I was very involved with Hillel (an on-campus center for Jewish students) — I was even president — and met my husband there.

Today my husband is a *chassid* with a long white beard, long white *peyos*, and a shtreimel. But when we first met, he was not at all religious. Originally from Buffalo, his parents sent him to an elite, all-male prep school in Massachusetts. Many of his former schoolmates are famous people today. When he walked into the Hillel House, he looked like Joe College.

But my husband was searching for *emes*. He had read Jewish history and wondered why we are so different from other people. He came to the conclusion that the only reason the Jews had survived as Jews, as opposed to the Greeks, the Babylonians, and the Romans, is because of something called the Torah. He wanted to find out what that Torah was all about.

My husband approached the Chabad rabbi on campus to ask him for help in putting on *tefillin*. The Chabad rabbi was flabbergasted. He'd never dreamed that this typical-looking American guy was Jewish! That rabbi later became our next-door neighbor and a very close family friend.

It was after my husband began studying with the rabbi that we started dating. He was slowly growing in his *Yiddishkeit*, but I was happy the way I was. Once our relationship became serious, however, I also began studying. After our engagement, I learned the basic *halachos* necessary for creating a Jewish home.

Although after we married I followed the three basic mitzvos, I was not committed to the point that I was willing to cover my hair or stop wearing pants. I was still a rebel. The change occurred a few years after our wedding, when my second child was still an infant. One night, while I was window-shopping with a friend (we were at the same level of *frumkeit*), one of the department stores had a huge clearance sale on wigs — $10 apiece! I tried one on, just for the fun of it, and was surprised to discover that I actually looked decent. So I bought it. But I never really intended to *wear* it.

Back home, I modeled the wig for my husband and he *loved* it. I wore it around the house, just to please him. Within a few weeks I was so used to having my hair covered that I couldn't imagine it being otherwise. *Tzenius* had become an integral part of me.

Years later, when I saw pictures of myself in that wig, it suddenly dawned on me that my husband had actually lied to me. The wig was ***ugly*** — but it did the trick. It got me to start covering my hair.

In 1982, I was diagnosed with multiple sclerosis. The symptoms started right before Succos, after I sprayed several cans of insecticide on the swarms of ants that were crawling outside my house. A few days later, on the first day of *Chol HaMoed*, half my face suddenly became paralyzed. But my husband and I were not worried. We assumed the paralysis was nothing more than a side effect of the insecticide, and continued celebrating the Yom Tov. After all, it was Succos and I had a family to take care of. Meals had to be cooked and served and the children needed a mother. We just didn't have the time or energy to worry about it.

But instead of getting better, the symptoms grew worse. After Succos, between PTA meetings and my second son's *upsherin*, I managed to squeeze in an appointment with our family doctor. He referred me to a neurologist.

At the end of the neurologist's examination, I asked the doctor, "What is it?"

He didn't answer me. Instead he said, "Let's wait until I can speak to both you and your husband in my office."

But I wasn't about to wait! "Come on," I said. "I'm a big girl. I can handle it." I expected him to tell me something to the effect of "take two aspirin and call me in the morning." But he didn't.

"Have you ever heard of a disease called multiple sclerosis?" he asked.

Multiple sclerosis? I couldn't even say those words in one breath, let alone spell them!

A few minutes later, my husband and I were sitting in the doctor's office, listening to his dire diagnosis. We must have looked like a bad comic drawing of two ghosts. My first question was, 'Is this hereditary?' It wasn't. I felt as if a huge stone had rolled off my chest. *Baruch Hashem*!

The doctor admitted me to the hospital. Ten days later, I returned home feeling great. I was ready to go on with my life. After all, I had four beautiful children to care for. I didn't have ***time*** to be sick!

When friends of ours in Borough Park heard the diagnosis, they suggested that we go to the Blushever Rebbe, *zt"l*, for a *berachah*. After the Rebbe gave me his *berachah*, I went into the dining room, holding my infant daughter in my arms. The Rebbetzin asked, "Is the baby a boy or a girl?"

"A *maidel,"* I answered.

"May you dance at her wedding," she blessed me.

I responded with a fervent *"Amein."*

The MS really didn't impact my life until four years later, when I woke up one morning and found that I couldn't see. The doctor admitted me to the hospital for tests, which showed that I had lost 80 percent of my vision. Overnight, I had become legally blind!

I remained in the hospital for over a month. Before I was discharged, the doctor came into my room and said, "Mrs. Bron, with an MS exacerbation of this magnitude, you should have ended up in a wheelchair." With those words, I realized the power of Rebbetzin Bronia's blessing. You never know where the blessing originates. *Baruch Hashem*, even though I am legally blind, I am able to cook, bake, work, and write — and, yes, I danced at all five of my children's weddings!

At first, however, I had a lot of difficulty accepting the loss of my eyesight. I was depressed. I thought this was the worst thing that could happen to anyone, and I was unable to reconcile my *emunah* with my new circumstances.

One evening, Rabbi Dr. Abraham Twerski came to Buffalo to lecture at the local Chabad House. He spoke on the topic of living with challenges. Throughout the entire lecture I kept thinking that everything he was saying was fine, but not for someone suffering to the extent that I was! When the lecture was over, I headed to the podium to tell the Rav my horror story. Instead of an outward display of sympathy, he asked, "Are you angry with Hashem?" I responded with an emphatic "Yes!" "That's wonderful," he said. I was shocked! But then he continued, "You can't be angry with Someone that you don't believe exists! So you believe in G-d."

That encounter was the start of a very gradual climb back to acceptance. I slowly learned to recognize my new limitations and go on from there. It wasn't easy, but I began to see myself as normal, despite my handicap. Yes, a good part of my independence had vanished. I could no longer drive a car, read, or even sew on a button. I needed assistance coping with things that I had always taken for granted. A huge chunk of my life was no more and now I had to learn how to live all over again.

In 1987, one year after I lost my vision, we moved to Monsey. We felt that it was important for our family to live in a large, vibrant religious community. In Monsey I was able to phone in my food order to the *frum* grocery store, and know that everything was kosher. *Chalav Yisrael* milk and kosher meat were readily available. My children had lots of *frum* friends to play with.

In 1992, my parents presented me with a typewriter for my birthday. Remember those old-fashioned machines from the dark ages? Using a tape that I had borrowed from the Library for the Blind, I taught myself to touch type. Though unable to read back the text independently, I managed to get my articles published in several papers. In 1995, the New York State Commission for the Blind gave me a computer with an adapted vocal program that actually repeats each character as I type it and then reads back the text that I wrote. Today, thirteen years later, I work on my third adapted computer, and use a very high-tech program called "Jaws" to assist me.

The first couple of articles I wrote were on politics — I'm a political junkie. After they were published, I wrote a few articles on Judaism, and they were also published. To date, I've appeared in sixteen different publications and online magazines! In addition to my writing, I've done some PR work. I've even had my own radio show on a local Jewish radio station in Monsey. That was a lot of fun. I interviewed all sorts of Jewish leaders, politicians, accomplished women, you name it.

I am presently working on a young adult novel about Orthodox Jewish teens, together with my editor, Lorraine Stayer. Since I want to target unaffiliated young Jews, I hope to market it in the mainstream world. Most American Jewish kids think that their Jewish identity consists of nothing more than lighting colored candles and getting presents for eight days each winter, eating a bland flat cracker one night a year, and waving an Israeli flag on a particular day. They deserve to know that there's something more. My book contains all the components anyone would find in a good novel. Good people, bad guys, action, mystery, the celebration of life and yes, death. However, my observant Jewish characters, with our unique lifestyle, will set it apart from the other stuff out there.

I also love cooking and baking, and my grandchildren love eating the things I make. How do I manage that? All my recipes are in the computer, and the computer program reads them out for me. My kitchen cabinets are very well organized, so I don't have to search for the things I need. I also wear magnifying glasses to read the large print on some of the ingredients.

In addition to my work at home, I work as a mentor for other handicapped individuals at the Rockland Independent Living Center. I assist my clients in finding appropriate jobs. I get great pleasure in finally using the education as a social worker, that I received so many years ago, to benefit others."

Judith, you really are an inspiration to me! You seem to have taken this challenge and turned it into wings with which to fly. What would you tell someone who finds himself facing a challenge similar to yours, G-d forbid?

When a person suddenly finds himself a fraction of the person that he had been the day before, the first thing he needs to do is redefine himself. He will have to accept the new definition of self before he can go forward. Learning to perceive himself as a viable, worthy human being again is a very slow and difficult process. Sometimes that means learning new adaptive skills or purchasing adaptive equipment, while at other times it means accepting that certain aspects of the person he'd always been do not exist anymore. The individual is the same person, with the same positive attributes, but his physical limitations force him to define himself in a different way. Although a person in a wheelchair can do many, many things, he cannot dance. So if dancing was an important part of his life, he'll have to find something to replace it.

How does your family cope with your disability?

They were, and still are, extremely supportive. They never stopped loving me, and always accepted me for who I am. To this day, I just keep loving them more and more. When the children were growing up, I often felt guilty that I wasn't able to do the things for them that mothers are supposed to do, such as reading stories to them at night, or shopping with my daughters for their trousseaus. But although I was bothered by it, my children later told me that they never felt bad. They understood that it wasn't that I didn't want to, but rather that I simply couldn't.

I view myself as a normal Jewish woman. I go to shul on Shabbos; a couple of good friends stand next to me during *chazaras hashatz* and quietly whisper the responses for me so that I can join in. Most of my davening, however, is in my own words. I have no doubt that Hashem understands me.

To my grandchildren, I am Bubby with the white cane. They are extremely protective of me. They tell me if there's a stone in the street and help me find the curb. It doesn't even bother them that I mix up their names because I can't always differentiate between them. They just love me the way I am!

But it's not just the grandchildren; I've also come to accept me. It was a difficult road, but I made it!

CHANGING THE WORLD — ONE DIAPER AT A TIME

"I looked in the mirror and saw a loser: nothing but a simple housewife. I had been brainwashed to believe that if a woman is not making money and working outside the home, she's just wasting her life."

Chana Jenny Weisberg

The first time I met Chana Jenny Weisberg was at a N'shei evening that she was hosting in her home — a century-old historic building in the center of Jerusalem. I had read several of her articles and seen her books, Expecting Miracles *and* One Baby Step at a Time, *on display at the local bookstores. I was thrilled to meet another writer and to have an opportunity to "talk shop." I discovered a young woman with a clear mission in life: to make women aware that motherhood is an accomplishment. Or, to put it humorously, "Mothers are changing the world — one diaper at a time!"*

I was thrilled at the opportunity to interview Chana. I found myself naturally gravitating toward her; despite the age difference, I felt a strong affinity with her. I truly admire the way she's making women aware that the floors can wait, the laundry can wait, the cake for Shabbos can wait, but the time spent with a child will never wait. It's like a rainbow or a ray of sunlight, which can never be captured and stored away for a more convenient time. And those precious moments are creating something much more significant than anything else we can do. (I had to remind myself of this when my daughter asked me to pleeeeease watch my granddaughter tomorrow morning, during my precious writing time). Yes, we are privileged to know this intellectually, but we need to be reminded of it again and again — and again. This is especially true in today's world, in which motherhood is frowned upon and intelligent women focus on professional advancement while leaving their children with a babysitter, who, however well qualified, will never substitute (and what mother would want them to?) for a mother's love and care.

I grew up in a high-powered family. Both of my parents are doctors; I went to a private school; I grew up knowing that someday I would have a career. My brother graduated from Harvard Law at the top of his class, so that was what I was aiming for — not to be a lawyer, but that was the general direction. Instead, five years after my college graduation, I found myself a mother.

How did your life path take you from future career woman to full-time mother?

I didn't grow up in a religious home. I wasn't interested in traveling to Israel; I wanted to go someplace exotic, like Nepal. In college, I majored in the Russian language and political science, and was planning to spend my junior year in the Soviet Union. But that year, 1991, the political situation in the Soviet Union was extremely unstable and my mother strongly suggested that I change my plans.

My grandmother had put aside money for each of her grandchildren to travel to Israel. She was a devoted Zionist — in the thirties, she'd taught Hebrew in the New York City public-school system — and wanted us to be connected Jewishly. I thought that if I were to go to Israel, I could use my Russian to work with the new Russian immigrants. I came to Israel and immediately fell in love with the country.

At first I lived with a family friend, but eventually I had to find another place to stay. I went to the Old City and saw a sign for the Jewish Student Information Center — Jeff Seidel's place. I wasn't at all religious at the time, but I thought, "Well, I'm a Jewish student. Maybe they can give me information." I told them that I was looking for a place to live, and they told me that I could stay at Neve Yerushalayim. I was suspicious about studying in an Orthodox place, so I said, "Well, I can't go to any classes. I'm very busy. I go to *ulpan* and I do volunteer work with the Russians." They said that I could live at Neve without taking classes, so I agreed. But once I moved there, I was fascinated — and enrolled as a full-time student.

I eventually met my husband through a mutual friend, and two years after we were married I became a mother. But although I was religious and creating a family, I still very much had the mindset of a professional. I had no idea how to view what I was doing; I felt as if I were a total loser. I looked in the mirror and saw a loser: nothing but a simple housewife. I had been brainwashed to believe that if a woman is not making money and working outside the home, she's just wasting her life.

Interestingly enough, my parents really approve of what I am doing. A few years ago, my mother said to me, "Maybe you'll stay at home until all your children are in first grade." My mother sees that my staying at home is good for my children, and for me too.

To strengthen myself, I became fixated on the topic of motherhood. I began attending lots of classes and reading anything I could get my hands on about the subject. I was totally focused on this one topic, and I still am. Because of that, I started producing articles, and later short videos, to spread the things that I learned.

Before I had my first child, I realized that although I was taking care of my physical needs — taking all the proper blood tests, ingesting the right amount of vitamins — I had no idea of the Jewish way to anticipate a new family member. I looked at other Jewish mothers and thought, "Those women must know something that I don't." So I interviewed women about their experiences. *Expecting Miracles* was the product of those interviews. It's a very popular book and has sold a lot of copies.

What did you glean from the interviews?

Many women spoke about how a woman should work hard on her *middos* and do extra mitzvos, because in that way she impacts her future children's *neshamos*. One of the women I interviewed, a very high- powered Yale graduate and a former lawyer, said that she realized that in becoming a mother, she was more powerful than she had ever been, because she had become a vessel of the A-lmighty.

When I first began writing this book, I was working toward a Master's degree from Hebrew University. I viewed this work as something like a sociological study: I was an outsider looking in. I was an observer, interviewing these curious specimens of a religious society. But as I continued working on the project, I realized that I was getting pulled into it. I realized that I am a *frum* woman, and that these women are me! This totally changed the outlook of the book. It was a very important transition for me, personally. I began to identify myself as part of the community, rather than as an outsider looking in. I learned that my very *being* is a religious person, not just a person who does the mitzvos and wears the long skirts.

After *Expecting Miracles* was published, the natural progression was for me to write about motherhood, the parenting process. I went to parenting classes. That was a whole new world for me. I learned that a mother is a mother forever.

A wise Rebbetzin once told me that a person must do whatever she needs to do to be a better mother. Some women need to get out to work. They need to feel fulfilled in the workplace. Other women are at their best staying home with the children. But whether a woman works or stays home, the main focus should be her family.

It's very important for me to have my creative time in the morning, the few hours that I spend writing my articles or books, or producing the motherhood videos.

Chana sends out a weekly email containing a link to an online video on the joys of motherhood. Usually they're brief, two- to-three-minute interviews with mothers, talking about how they've grown through the challenge of raising a family. Recently, it showed women reciting Tehillim at the Kosel, many of them holding young babies in their arms. The video concluded with the following words: "When parents asked the Steipler Gaon, 'How can we raise wonderful children?' he answered, 'There are two ways. Create peace in your home, and pray.'" This video was to promote the Shelah's special prayer for our children, which is customarily recited on erev Rosh Chodesh Sivan.

How did you become involved in producing videos?

I've been working on producing videos for the last four or five months, and I've received tremendous feedback. One Rebbetzin in New York told me that she had been working with a *baalas teshuvah* who was ambivalent to the idea of having a family. The Rebbetzin told her to watch my videos, and after that, her entire outlook changed! I recently met a mother on the street, and she told me, "We always think that being a mother is just something that we do. But when I watch your movies, I realize that I'm doing something very, very important!"

These films have been viewed over 35,000 times! I don't know if the viewers are religious or not, but even religious people need validation that what they're doing is very, very important. Motherhood needs good PR; after all, it's received terrible PR in the secular world. When most people hear the term "Jewish mother" they think of jokes about an overprotective, bossy woman whose greatest joy is making her children feel guilty. I want to change that. I want people to understand that a Jewish mother is creating a *mikdash me'at*, and through that she is doing the most important thing in the whole wide world!

What are your plans for the future?

I'm not sure, but above my computer I wrote a three-point mission statement: my three goals.

I'll start with the last one first. I want to use my different creative projects to be a *shlichah* for Hashem. I feel that Hashem guides me in the most unforeseen ways. Who would have thought that I would produce videos? But Hashem guided me to it, and it's a wonderful *kiruv* tool.

My second goal it to be connected with those things that are eternal: *Am Yisrael*, *Toras Yisrael*, and Hashem. I am constantly asking Hashem to guide me. I try to figure out what He wants from me;

does He want me to write that article? Am I more interested in making a lot of money or in helping people come close to Hashem?

And my first and foremost goal is to create a thriving, happy, close, and healthy family.

How do you plan to accomplish that?

The most important thing for a happy family is a happy mother. It is crucial that a mother take care of herself; that she figure out what she needs to be happy and to thrive, and then get it *[within reason, of course!]*. Women sometimes feel that, to be good mothers, they must be martyrs. Instead, they should take a step back and ask, "What do I need to be healthy? What do I need to thrive?" When you enter a home with a thriving mother, the atmosphere is positive. But imagine entering a home where the mother is miserable and feels like a victim, like the family servant. What a terrible atmosphere for the children to grow up in! In one of my videos, the mother being interviewed quoted a famous expression, "If Mommy's unhappy, no one is happy." I truly believe that.

We need to take responsibility for our own happiness. That means putting our lives in order and then deciding what we need to be happy. Instead of complaining, "My husband doesn't help me," or "My boss dislikes me," we have to stand up and state what we need, and then make it happen. Make a list of the ten things you need to thrive, and then make every effort to get them!

In raising our families, in doing all the mundane things that we do over and over and over again to keep our homes running smoothly, we are creating something eternal! I know it's difficult. Been there, done that, and am still doing it. Even with grandchildren, I often forget that my reactions and attitude are forming little neshamos. No one expects perfection, just a teensy-tiny baby step in the right direction.

DENVER'S TORAH PIONEERS

> "When I was in the eleventh grade, we learned about the Rocky Mountains ... If someone would have suggested then that someday I'd be living there, I would have thought that person was crazy. But here I am!"

Mrs. Bruria Schwab

At the age of sixteen, I transferred from a public high school in San Francisco, California, to a Bais Yaakov in Denver, Colorado. It was quite a change — from racial riots to color wars; from classes on "alternative lifestyles" to classes on "Building a Jewish Home." Everything was new, and very, very strange — and, as I slowly came to understand — very, very normal!

I'll never forget my first day as a Bais Yaakov student. Surrounded by girls wearing hospital-green striped blouses with matching pleated skirts (our school uniform — ugh!), I suspected that I had landed on another planet. When our Chumash teacher, Mrs. Schwab, entered the class and the girls stood up as a sign of respect, my suspicions were confirmed. Then she opened her mouth and I was even more confused. After all, I had been told the classes were conducted in English, yet every second word was either Hebrew or Yiddish — and I understood neither.

That was over thirty-eight years ago. The lessons that I learned that year literally turned my life around. Whenever I see Rabbi and Mrs. Schwab, I laughingly (although I'm really quite serious) tell them that I must have been their most challenging student. They insist that I was not. I suspect that they're just being polite.

I consider it an extreme privilege to be able to interview one of my role models — to get a glimpse into the person behind the teacher.

I grew up in Tel Aviv in the forties, and learned in the Bais Yaakov there. My father, Rabbi Moshe Chechik, had learned in Radin, under the holy Chofetz Chaim. He immigrated to Eretz Yisrael in 1935 to escape the Polish draft, a move that saved him from the fate that met most of his family during the Holocaust. In Israel, he joined the Chevron Yeshivah in Yerushalayim.

My mother was raised in Yaffo. She had a tremendous love for learning, which has served as an inspiration for me until this day. While still a young girl, she heard of a religious school for girls that had opened in Tel Aviv, and — all on her own! — registered there. Every day she would walk over the sand dunes that later become Tel Aviv for the privilege of attending a religious school.

My father, who later became principal of Ohel Yaakov Boys' School in Tel Aviv, was a *mechanech* in the full sense of the word. My mother was an extraordinary, devoted mother. I had a wonderful childhood, even though times were really difficult. Whenever the sirens sounded during the War of Independence, we would run to hide in the trenches. The bombs landed so close that they sounded as if they were exploding next door. Yet, even there, our family somehow managed to find things to joke about. I even remember making a game of counting the beetles that scuttled about in fear of their unusual guests!

During the "*tzena*," when food was strictly rationed in Eretz Yisrael, people made "apple sauce" out of zucchini and "mock liver" from yeast! Each week we stood in line to receive one tiny chicken for Shabbos. Sometimes, when there were no eggs, we made scrambled eggs from egg powder. But we always had an abundance of bread, and therefore we never went hungry or felt deprived.

After my father passed away in 1978, I discovered his diary and papers. But it was only years later, when my children were already grown, that I had the time to decipher them. I spent an entire year at this labor of love, and learned amazing things about my father, things that I'd never known. The diary, together with my personal memoirs, was later published as a book, entitled, "*Abba: The Father I Knew, the Father I Discovered*" (Targum Press). Writing that book was, for me, an act of closure. I put together the puzzle pieces of his life and received an even deeper glimpse into my late father's greatness.

Mrs. Schwab was kind enough to give me a copy of her father's biography. It's amazing! People often excuse their own behavior by citing circumstances beyond their control — a traumatic childhood, poverty, being far from their family — that forced them to become who they are. Rabbi Chechik's biography is proof that, although we cannot control the circumstances of our lives, we can, and must, control our reactions. As a youngster, Rabbi Chechik lived through pogroms and witnessed atrocities that are beyond my ability to comprehend. Yet he remained a loving and giving individual, with a rock-firm emunah that I, for one, can only hope to emulate.

After graduating from seminary, I taught in Bais Yaakov Tel Aviv for five years. During those five years I married and had a baby. Then we moved to the United States.

That must have been a tremendous culture shock!

Actually, it wasn't. We initially moved to Borough Park, which was full of Israelis. Many of the shopkeepers spoke Hebrew, and I had Hebrew-speaking friends, which made it a lot easier for me to adjust. People in Borough Park lived very simply, so the contrast in values was not as strong as it is today. During our last four years there, I taught the Hebrew language at Esther Schoenfeld High School. During that time I also picked up English.

The most difficult part of living in America was being so far from my family. It pained me that I was unable to attend most of my family's *simchos*. I was able to travel back to Israel for the wedding of only one of my sisters.

When did you move to Denver?

We moved to Denver in 1968 — over forty years ago. The community was an optimistic, growing one, with a dream of becoming a *makom Torah*. There was a Hebrew day school, Hillel Academy, and a yeshivah, Yeshivas Toras Chaim, which had opened the previous year. There was also a large *shechitah* center with many *shochtim*. All the *frum* families there felt like pioneers, creating something that had never existed before. Imagine the feeling of excitement as we anticipated the possibilities that lay before us!

At first, the Bais Yaakov was housed in a shul that was no longer in use. Before the school opened, my husband went with a carpenter to partition the shul into classrooms. He literally stood there and build the Bais Yaakov!

I became friendly with a few of the Israeli women whose husbands were *shochtim*. Having friends who spoke my language made the transition easier for me. (Even now, after so many years of living in America, I read much more quickly in Hebrew than in English.) I also made friends with women who did not speak Hebrew.

When my children were small, I taught part-time. The job — and the responsibilities — grew together with me. Today, I am the *limudei kodesh* principal, and very, very involved with the school. I really spend much more time with teenagers than I do with people my own age! I find it refreshing to work with young adults.

I was worried that my own children would eventually have to leave Denver. I felt that, after moving so far from my family in Israel, I would not be able to bear it if my children lived far from me. But, *baruch Hashem,* two of my children remained here. One teaches in our school. The other is *Rosh Kollel* of the Denver Community Kollel.

Oddly enough, my childhood in Tel Aviv prepared me for teaching in Bais Yaakov Denver, which caters to a wide variety of girls from many different backgrounds. When I went to school in the forties, *frum* schools were for everyone: Litvish, Chassidish, Sefardi, Ashkenazi — we all learned together. Being friends with girls from such a wide variety of backgrounds taught me to appreciate different types of people. My children, as well, tell me that they gained tremendously through going to school together with so many different types of girls.

How does Bais Yaakov Denver differ from other schools?

We are still pioneers! When Bais Yaakov Denver was founded in 1968, many of the big Bais Yaakovs that exist today hadn't opened. Our school initiated many things that today are a given, such as dividing *limudei kodesh* classes by level rather than by grade, and the opportunity to accumulate college credits while still in high school. But the main thing is that we were, and still are, a small school with a strong bond between the students and the teachers. Because we are such a small school, there is a very warm, family-like feeling. And then, our teachers are really outstanding. Each one of them is a role model.

Could you tell me about some of the girls who attended your school?

In our early years, many of our girls came from really unusual backgrounds. In those days there was no dormitory, so the girls lived with local families. We often had girls living with us, and of course we became very close with them.

One of the girls who lived with us came from a home where the father wasn't a Jew. She attended the Jewish day school in the eighth grade, after her mother became the school's cook. She loved Day School, and after graduation chose to continue on in Bais Yaakov Denver. Today she is a real *tzadekes*, with a large family and many married children. Thirty years ago, when I told my father about this girl, he said, "I never understood why you had to move so far away. But now that you've told me about this girl, I understand."

Another time, a girl came to an interview wearing shorts. She had no idea that this is inappropriate attire for a Bais Yaakov student. Today, she's the principal of a *frum* school and married to a *Rosh Yeshivah*!

In recent years my husband traveled to Russia to hand-pick girls to come to our school. He would ask the girls, "What does it mean to be a Jew?" The answers showed how little they knew of *Yiddishkeit*: "To be a good student"; "The *goyim* hate us"; "Jews don't drink." When my husband asked one girl if her mother believes in Hashem, she answered, "No, but my grandmother does. But whenever I ask her about it, she says that she doesn't want to talk about it." That's because, under the Communists, if she did, would have been put in jail.

One of our Ukrainian-born students returned home for a visit after spending two years in our school. Her father told her, "I am embarrassed to walk through the streets with you dressed like that." The girl answered, "Papa, the Queen of England would never give up her crown even though it's very heavy. I am a Jewish princess, and this is my royal garb." Her father never commented on her dress again.

In my office I have a black-and-white picture of some little boys with long, curled *peyos*. People ask me if this picture was taken before the Holocaust. But they are the sons of one of our Russian students! This girl had scoliosis. The doctors in Denver said that she would be handicapped for life, and that she would never be able to have any children. The Shriner's organization paid for her to go to Salt Lake City for spinal surgery. They even paid for her mother to come from Russia to be with her! This girl translated several chapters of *Tehillim* into Russian for her mother to recite during the surgery. Today this girl has a wonderful Yiddishe family.

We've had girls from Pinsk and from Baranowitz. I personally found this extremely moving, and it gave me a sense of closure. As a youngster, my father lived in Pinsk, and before learning in the Chofetz Chaim's yeshivah in Radin, he learned in Baronowitz.

But our school is not, and never has been, a "*baalas teshuvah*" school. Girls from very strong backgrounds — daughters of *rabbeim, roshei yeshiah,* and *frum baalei batim* — send their daughters to Bais Yaakov Denver. Today many of our former *talmidos* living in other cities want their daughter to have the Denver experience, and send their daughters to us.

Many members of our staff have been with us for years. Rabbi Schwab is the dean; I'm *limudei kodesh* principal, Mrs. Melamed is secular-studies principal. And several of our alumnae who live in Denver teach in our school.

In addition to our regular staff, every year we bring in three girls straight from seminary to serve as dorm counselors and *limudei kodesh* teachers. They come for one or two years, and we train them. The girls love it; for years after they leave, they continue to send me amazing letters.

Denver is a special city. The weather is ideal, it's very beautiful, and it's quiet: no crowds, no pushing in the stores. You can easily find a parking spot, and the people are friendly. Although some people would wish it were otherwise, I like the fact that there are no pizza shops. The blue skies and the proximity to the famous Rocky Mountains enhance our quality of life in a very real way.

I really love teaching in a small school. Since it's so small, I really get to know each girl. The girls have a chance to be heard, to ask questions, and to be answered. Because everyone is responsible for some aspects of running student activities, they learn to become leaders.

The results are wonderful! The girls are so positive and confident. They — themselves, without our asking or prodding — requested that I give a *shiur* on the topic of *tzenius*. It's held on Shabbos, after another *shiur* that is hosted by a different Denver family each week. On Shabbos, the out-of-town girls eat with families in the community. They see how we raise our children, and have real role models for building their own families.

Many of the girls stay in touch after graduation. Some phone me every year before Shavuos and jokingly ask if I saved any cheesecake for them — it's a *Yekkishe* minhag that someone who completes *sefiras ha'omer* with a *berachah* is rewarded with a piece of cheesecake on Shavuos. Every year I bake several cheesecakes to give to the girls who were *zocheh*! The girls invite us to their children's bar mitzvahs and weddings — and that, of course, gives us tremendous nachas.

How do you relate to the non-religious parents?

Most of our communication is directly with the girls, not with their parents. So, on a day-to-day basis, there's no problem. But sometimes we have parents — even religious parents — who smother their children, who don't allow them to grow, and that can be very difficult. One time, for example, we paid from our own pocket to send one of our students — a phenomenal girl! — to a seminary in Eretz Yisrael, with the understanding that at the end of the year she would return to teach in our school. But when she came back her parents refused to let her teach in a Bais Yaakov, as it's too "limiting." They insisted that she attend college instead. These incidents are very painful for us.

Did you ever imagine that you would be where you are today?

I always knew I'd be a teacher. My father was principal of a boys' school, and my three sisters also became teachers. But I never imagined that I would be teaching American teenagers — and in Denver, Colorado, of all places! When I was in the eleventh grade, we learned about the Rocky Mountains. I remember thinking, "Who cares?" If someone would have suggested then that someday I'd be living there, I would have thought that person was crazy. But here I am!

What are your plans for the future?

I don't make any plans; I just hope to be able to continue teaching for many more years — Hashem should help.

I can only add a resounding, "Amein."

FRUM IN BAVARIA

"I loved Israel and the Jewish people, and I was marrying a Jewish man. I thought that was enough to be accepted by the *beis din* as a sincere convert. After all, what else was there to being Jewish?"

Michal Evenari

I first met Michal Evenari about two years ago, when a neighbor invited me to a Shabbos afternoon get-together in honor of her conversion to Judaism. It was a privilege to welcome a new Yiddishe neshamah to Am Yisrael. At the get-together, I listened spellbound as Michal told us her amazing story. So last week, when my former next-door neighbor mentioned that Michal was visiting, I jumped at the opportunity to interview her. I hope that you will be as inspired by her story as I am.

I was born on September 1, 1934, in Gevelsberg, a small town in northern Germany. My father was a worker. Before Hitler, *yemach shemo*, came into power, my father, together with a large percentage of the German working class, was out of work. As my stepmother later told me, we ran up a huge bill in the grocery store. Hitler, *yemach shemo*, provided the German people with jobs, which is one of the reasons so many of them supported him.

I was five years old when World War II erupted. At the very beginning of the war, the German government sold highly subsidized radios so that everyone would be able to listen to their "beloved" Fuehrer. But my parents were religious Christians, and as religious people they disagreed with the Fuehrer's statement that *"Es muss heraus aus unserem Blut, dieser Fluch vom Berg Sinai! Dieses Gift, mit dem Juden und Christen die freien und wunderbaren Instinkte der Menschen verdorben und beschmutzt ... haben."* 'It must be gotten out of our blood, this curse from Har Sinai! We must rid ourselves of this poison by which Jews and Christians have made filthy and dirty those free and wonderful instincts of the human being ...." Hitler, *yemach shemo*, believed that religion was a curse that destroys man's positive, primal instincts (*Hashem yerachem*). He literally waged a war against G-d.

Therefore, we had to hide our religious observance. We secretly gathered to pray in private homes. As a matter of fact, in the final year of the war, a family friend who was one of the heads of our local Nazi party told my parents that he had seen our family's name on a list of people slated to be deported to Auschwitz for our "sin" of practicing Christianity. (Gentiles interned in Auschwitz received much better treatment than the Jewish prisoners.). The war came to an end before that occurred. So, as you can see, I grew up with a very strong belief in the Almighty and in the truth of the Bible.

It was tremendous luck — or, as I realize now, *hashgachah pratis* — that my father was not drafted into the *Wehrmacht* (the home defense). He was the only German worker in a local screw factory, and screws were necessary for the war effort. (All the other workers were prisoners from other countries. No, they were not Jews; Jewish prisoners were reserved for more difficult and dangerous work.) Whenever my father was called up to serve, the head of the factory told the draft officials that if my father was taken away he would have no choice but to close the factory. My father felt that G-d was protecting him.

We had a picture of Hitler, *yemach shemo*, hanging on the wall above our dining-room table. When I asked my mother about it, she explained that, by law, we were required to have his picture prominently displayed. There was a very real fear that Nazi officials would check that this law was obeyed. Of course, there was a huge picture of him hanging in our classroom.

At the start of each school day, we were required to hold up our hands in the Nazi salute while singing a song about our love for the Motherland and for our beloved Fuehrer. Although it was difficult to hold up our arms for so long, we had no choice. The teacher slapped us across the face if she found that we were using our other hand to support our raised arm. After all, we were Germans, and Germans must be strong!

Were you aware of what was happening to the Jews?

Not many Jews lived in our town. The only Jew I remember was our family doctor. He fled to South Africa.

When my parents' friends came to visit, they would huddle together to speak secretly. One evening, hiding behind the closed door, I heard my mother's friend talking. Her son, who had been drafted into the S.S. because of his Aryan features and pure German blood, had just come home for his first furlough. He said to his mother, "Mama, you can't imagine what we are forced to do in Poland." He said that, as a religious person, he did not know how he could possibly go back. On the day before he was to rejoin his unit in Poland, he shot himself.

My mother worked in the town of Kassel. She told me that one day they drove all the Jews through the town. People lined the streets, throwing eggs at them and shouting hate-filled words. My mother stood there, weeping and feeling guilty that she was a member of the crowd. What astonished her most was that these were otherwise nice, normal people.

One night, when my parents thought I was asleep, I stood behind the door in the dark and listened to them talk about the concentration camps and the mass slaughter of Jews. It was forbidden to speak openly about it, but everyone knew. After the war, when people said they knew nothing about what happened, I did not believe them. My parents told me to pray each day that under no circumstances must our country win this war. And that I must never talk about this. I never did.

How did you come to Judaism?

First I became a Catholic. I felt there was something missing in my religion and decided to go back to the source, which I erroneously thought was Catholicism. And so, in my early twenties, I became a Catholic — and a very devout one at that!

During this time, I traveled to England to learn English. While working in England, I received a letter from a professor for whom I had once worked. He was recruiting young people for a program entitled *Aktion Sühznezeichen* — Operation Reconciliation. The program sent students to work for six to twelve months in foreign countries where the Germans had left their mark of destruction. They had already rebuilt an orphanage in Norway, planted trees in Holland, and built a water carrier in Crete. The professor wanted me to join a group that was traveling to Israel to work on a kibbutz. But I wasn't interested. No milking cows for me! I had other plans — to make a pilgrimage to Rome, center of the Catholic faith.

In Rome, I found a job working as a translator in the Papal Oriental Institute. One day, the head of the Institute asked me, "What do you want to do with your life? Marry the Emperor of China?" It suddenly dawned on me that I had no plans for the future. I was just floating through life, without any direction.

I left the Institute and found a secluded spot where I could spend some time in private meditation. I asked G-d to let me know what I should be doing with my life, to direct me onto a path that I could follow. I spent several hours in solitude, pouring my heart out to the Almighty. When I entered the students' dining room to eat lunch, I immediately noticed that I had received an express letter from Germany. I had no doubt that the answer to my prayers was in that envelope!

The letter was from the same professor who had tried to convince me to work on a kibbutz. He wanted me to join a group of German students who were presently in Holland, training for a six-month stint on a kibbutz. Knowing my precarious financial situation, he had even included a train ticket. So I traveled to Holland to join the German students there.

Although we wanted to help the Jews build their land, the Israelis were not at all interested in our assistance. After half a year of searching for a kibbutz willing to let us work for them, Kibbutz Urim, a secular kibbutz founded by Americans and located in the northern Negev, agreed to take us.

I loved the kibbutz. Since I spoke English, I was able to relate to the people there. Being devout, I also tried to convert them to Catholicism. But the kibbutzniks just laughed at my efforts, and asked me how I could believe in a god that has caused so much blood — especially Jewish blood — to be spilled. Their rebuttals were better than my arguments aimed at converting them. As a result of these discussions, I realized that I really didn't understand what I believed in. I decided that when I returned home, to Germany, I would learn more about my religion.

Back in Germany, I enrolled in a Catholic seminary. It was a three-year program leading to a teaching degree in Catholicism. It was there, in the Catholic seminary, that the first seeds of doubt were planted. I realized that many of the things that I had always believed in stood on very shaky legs. I couldn't live a lie. I wanted to return to Israel. I'd felt so at home there.

So after graduating the seminary, I returned to Israel. I changed my name from Christel to Michal and enrolled in an academic *ulpan* in Nazareth-Illit.

At first, the *ulpan* refused to accept me because I wasn't Jewish. It was only when the Catholic archbishop, an Arab, wrote a beautiful letter of recommendation, saying that he would personally appreciate any assistance extended to me, that I was able to enroll. But I wasn't the only non-Jew. There were two priests and a nun enrolled in other classes.

While attending the *ulpan*, I lived in a church complex in nearby Nazareth. In exchange for doing various chores, I was provided with a small room and three meals a day. I didn't need much money. I purchased a motorcycle, which saved me the expense of bus fares. With room, board, and transportation basically taken care of, I was able to live on almost nothing.

After graduating from the *ulpan*, I started looking for a job in social work. The director of the *ulpan*, Yosef, had a friend who was responsible for all the social workers in Northern Israel and who had, in the past, helped him find positions for his students. He offered to drive me to her home in Kiryat Tivon and introduce me to her.

It was a beautiful, sunny day. The director began to introduce me to his friend, but when she realized that I was a German, she refused to have anything to do with me. She wouldn't even let me into her house! I can understand her. Originally from Germany, she had fled the country in 1932, just before Hitler's rise to power. Some of her family had perished in the Holocaust. Since I wasn't invited inside, I waited on the porch while Yosef went inside to speak her.

Although the woman didn't allow me into her house, she was very polite and sent out her adult son, Eli, to keep me company. We started talking. It felt as if we had always known each other. Eli eventually became my husband.

Michal's story brings tears to my eyes. It's really a tragedy. Today, Michal is totally religious. But her children — her Jewish husband's descendants — are not Jewish.

We all know that intermarriage is a serious problem. What many of us don't realize is that the Jews in Israel are not immune. Many of the secular Jews there know almost nothing of their heritage. A friend of mine — the lone Chareidi woman attending a weekly women's group run by her HMO for women coping with a medical condition — told me that several times when she's given the Jewish outlook on topics under discussion, the other women look at her in amazement and make comments such as, "I never knew that Judaism addresses these issues!"

When a Jew marries out, he is turning his back on everything that is holy — usually because he has no idea what he is leaving behind.

We wanted a Jewish wedding, but of course that was impossible since I wasn't Jewish. I wanted to convert, but I had no idea what that meant. Eli and his family weren't at all observant. I loved Israel and the Jewish people, and I was marrying a Jewish man. I thought that was enough to be accepted by the *beis din* as a sincere convert. After all, what else was there to being Jewish?

Before going to the *beis din*, someone told me that when the *dayanim* asked me if I switch lights on and off on Shabbos, I should lie and say that I didn't. So when the *dayanim* asked me that question, I automatically replied, "No." A second later, I told the truth and said, "I mean, yes." Then they asked me several questions about the Bible, which, of course, I was able to answer. After all, I had spent the past three years studying the Bible in seminary. I explained to them that I had been a Catholic, but that now I wanted to convert.

The *dayanim* asked me what I knew about the mitzvos. I told them that I knew nothing. So they opened a file for my case and told me that they would be in touch with me sometime in the future. I was very far from being ready to convert. I realized that Judaism was the source, but I had no concept of what Judaism entails.

Since I wasn't Jewish, Eli and I could not marry in Israel. (In Israel there is no such thing as a civil marriage. All marriages are registered in the rabbinate. Couples who cannot marry there travel to Cyprus for a civil ceremony.) We did the same. After our wedding, my husband studied in Germany to become a glass engineer, after which we moved back and forth between Germany and Israel.

In 1968, while living in Germany, I converted to Judaism, but the conversion was later found not to be kosher since I did not accept the six hundred and thirteen mitzvos. My mitzvah observance consisted of lighting Shabbos candles and refraining from turning lights on and off on the Shabbos. On Friday night, my husband prayed and we sang Shabbos songs, but we didn't do anything else. We thought that what we were doing was considered "keeping Shabbos."

Everything changed in 2004, when we were vacationing in Italy. Eli was out in the ocean, windsurfing. He loved windsurfing and spent hours on his surfboard. He used to tell me that there, in the water, he felt very connected to Israel. After all, the Mediterranean joins Europe to Eretz Yisrael. Meanwhile, as he surfed, I sat on the beach watching him. The children playing, the seagulls, the pounding of the waves; it was all so relaxing and beautiful.

I waved to Eli, and he waved back. Then I walked out through the waves to him, to ask him how to use my camera — and found him stretched out on his surfboard, dead.

I arranged to have Eli's body transported from Italy to Germany. I wanted him to be buried in the Christian cemetery that was within walking distance of my home. *[A clear indication of just how far Michal was from true observance, even as she thought she'd converted!]* I don't own a car, and I wanted to be able to visit the grave easily. Eli's family was upset that I was planning to bury him in a Christian cemetery. They pressured me to inter him in the nearest Jewish cemetery, which was almost an hour's drive from my home. But I refused. I wanted him near me.

Meanwhile, the company that was transporting the coffin from Italy to Germany lost the body! They were unable to find it for six days. The entire time, I kept insisting that Eli be buried in the Christian cemetery, while the family and the rabbi kept pressing me to inter him in a Jewish cemetery. Finally, on the sixth day, the rabbi begged me, "Please, surrender your desires to be near him for the sake of the peace of his soul." I agreed. Half an hour later, the body was found at the border! His coffin had gotten mixed up with another coffin. The company that transferred the body later told me that in their decades of transporting corpses, such a thing had never happened. *Baruch Hashem*, my husband was *zocheh* to a proper burial.

After Eli died, I continued studying about Judaism. I took an online course about keeping kosher and learned many new mitzvos. After five months or so of studying online at aish.com, I traveled to Israel for a few days to speak to a rabbi personally.

I showed my conversion papers to one of the rabbis at Aish HaTorah, a renowned *kiruv* yeshivah. He asked me if he could show them to a senior rabbi. I agreed. I was positive that everything was fine. After all, I kept kosher and Shabbos, and felt very, very Jewish! But I was told that the documents were worthless. I had never really converted. I was not Jewish!

I was shocked! I couldn't believe that my original conversion was meaningless. But then, I hadn't accepted the yoke of mitzvah observance; I hadn't fully tied myself to the Jewish people. I was totally confused. I talked to G-d all day long and shed many tears, until I finally came to the realization that I couldn't live a lie. I must undergo a proper conversion.

In March 2007, at the age of 72, I went to the *beis din* in Jerusalem to convert. I related my life history and was told to return the following day for an examination. The next day, the *dayanim* asked me many questions about Jewish philosophy and halachah. I must have done well, because I was told to return again the following day.

The next day, the *dayanim* again asked a lot of questions — about Shabbos, prayer, and my feelings toward Christianity. They came to the conclusion that not only was I knowledgeable about Judaism, but I also loved it. They told me to stand up and declare that I would observe all the six hundred and thirteen mitzvos, and that I accepted the written Torah as well as the Oral Law. Then I recited *"Shema Yisrael."* Out loud.

The following day, I immersed in the *mikvah*. I was Jewish! Upon leaving the *mikvah*, I could not stop weeping. One of the women who accompanied me there hugged me and told me not to worry. A lot of new converts have such an emotional reaction.

I feel so honored to be a Jew. Like all Jews throughout the world, when I open my eyes in the morning I say, *"Modeh Ani,"* and when I go to sleep I recite *Krias Shema al Hamittah*. I keep a kosher home, am *shomer Shabbos* and say *Tehillim* every day.

After such a long journey, I feel I have attained inner peace. Throughout it all, G-d showed me His love, and opened the door to *teshuvah*. G-d wanted me to be alone, to confront myself and my budding Jewish soul. He carried me to Jerusalem and arranged my conversion. What a special gift He has given me. I am so glad to be home ... forever.

RECONNECTING

"Shlomo asked Rav Moshe for a *berachah* for us to have children, which he gave us. It took twenty years for that *berachah* to be fulfilled. Throughout that entire time, I never once gave up hope."

Channie Dickman

One of the most wonderful aspects of interviewing is the opportunity it gives me to reconnect with my friends and get to know aspects of their lives that I never knew about before. Channie and I go way, way back — to 1971, when we were roommates at BJJ. In those pre-Rebbetzin David days, the BJJ dorm was located in an old Arab building on Rechov Nili in Katamon. Channie and I shared a room with three other girls. Our friendship picked up again many years later, when she and her family moved to Eretz Yisrael. Interviewing Channie provided me with an opportunity to learn more about the years of her life when we were not in contact. What a wonderful gift!

I'm a second-generation Detroiter, and before that, my ancestors on both sides came from Lithuania. Growing up, I was definitely very aware of my Jewishness, but that was about the extent of it. One time, a woman showed up at our front door and offered to teach my siblings and me stories from the Old Testament. My mother took her up on it. All was well until we finished *Devarim* and she started teaching us the New Testament. That's when my mother told her to leave — and the four of us found ourselves enrolled in a Hebrew School.

When I was twelve years old, a wonderful religious family moved into the other half of our two-family house. They would invite my older brother for Shabbos meals. The beautiful Shabbos atmosphere had an impact on him to such an extent that within two months he was *shomer mitzvos*. He started wearing a *kippah* to public school. The kids there used to make fun of him for wearing a "beanie cap." They would tease him and pull it off his head and throw it around. But despite all these challenges, my brother continued wearing his *kippah*.

One Friday night, my brother returned home from the Shabbos meal and noticed that my mother had turned off the light in his room. He was very upset and said, "Mommy, I asked you not to turn off the light in my bedroom." Then he caught himself and added, "But now that it's off, please, please, please don't turn it back on." I thought he was totally nuts. Later on, when I noticed him fumbling in the dark, searching for something, I turned the light on for him. He got really upset and screamed, "You shouldn't have done that. But now that you did it, please, whatever you do, don't turn it back off again!" I was positive that he had completely lost his mind!

My mother complained to my grandmother that my brother refused to eat her food. My grandmother wisely answered, "Evelyn, you grew up in a kosher home. You know how to keep kosher. Don't force your son to prepare his own food. *Kasher* the kitchen for him." My mother *kashered* the kitchen.

I was absolutely miserable in public school. Most of the kids there teased me relentlessly. So when a *frum* neighbor asked me, "How do you like school?" I told her that I hated it. She continued, "Would you like to go to a Jewish school where you'll have lots of friends and learn about Judaism?" Of course, I was thrilled at the idea. That's how my sister and I ended up in Bais Yaakov Detroit.

With some outside help and a lot of perseverance, my Hebrew skills slowly improved until, by the end of the year, I was among the top girls in my class. Although my brother was learning in Telshe, Chicago, and my younger sister and I were learning in a Bais Yaakov, our parents remained non-religious. My sister and I were invited out for Shabbos meals. Very often I'd sleep at a friend's house, so that after the *kedushah* of the Shabbos *seudah* I wouldn't have to return home to the sounds of television. During *bein hazmanim*, when my brother was home from yeshivah, the three of us would shmooze until two or three in the morning, cracking jokes as we supported each other in our commitment to *Yiddishkeit*.

After graduating Detroit Bais Yaakov high school, I came to Israel to study at Machon Sarah Schenirer — known today as BJJ. To tell the truth, I really didn't even consider coming to Israel until my high school principal, Rabbi Goldstein, told all the girls in our class that every *frum* girl should attend seminary in Eretz Yisrael. He said that it was an experience that would change our lives.

Although I thought the dorm was a bit dingy, I was absolutely shocked at the bed — a thin foam mattress placed directly on a wooden board. But I guess I should have been happy there were no bedbugs! My first night I was so uncomfortable that I barely slept a wink.

But Hashem wanted me to realize how lucky I was to have that thin foam mattress! The following morning, I went with two other Detroiters to visit a friend in Beer Sheva. We missed the last bus back to Yerushalayim and ended up spending the night bedded down on the hard stone floor of their living room. By morning, every bone in my body ached and I was in agony. After that, the mattress at the dorm seemed like the height of luxury!

The truth is that it's hard for me to remember much about my sem year because that was the year my father passed away. He was *niftar* at the beginning of the year, on erev Succos. He was underneath a car, fixing the brakes, when the car lurched forward and crushed him.

My father's *levayah* was on Chol HaMoed Succos, which meant that the *shivah* didn't start until after Simchas Torah. Rabbi Goldstein instructed my mother not to inform me of my father's *petirah* until after Succos. That Shemini Atzeres and Succos I stayed in Geulah, at the home of a close friend from Detroit. On *motza'ei*

Simchas Torah, my friend, who was aware of the situation, asked me to please stay for the night. The following morning a *chashuvah* rebbetzin who was visiting from Detroit broke the news to me. I am forever grateful for the gentle way she told me of my father's death. I sat *shivah* in my friend's house.

Shivah was an extremely trying time. When my friends came to be *menachem* me, I didn't want them to feel uncomfortable so I talked with them about all sorts of silly things, except the one thing that I should have spoken about — my father. Before returning to the dorm, one of the *madrichot* warned me that I shouldn't talk about my loss with the other girls, since it might upset them to the extent that it could ruin their entire year. So, instead of talking about my feelings and making peace with them, I bottled everything up tightly inside me. That entire year, I half-expected to receive a letter from home stating that my father was alive and well, and that the story about him being killed in an accident had been nothing more than a bad joke. It wasn't until after I was married for seven years and visited my father's grave for the very first time (!) that I actually accepted the fact that he was no longer alive.

Anyone who's ever spent time in a girls' dorm knows that it can become quite *freilach,* with all the singing and dancing that goes on there. But I was an *avel*, and couldn't participate in any of the parties or spontaneous midnight kumsitzes. Although I did reasonably well scholastically, I missed out on the entire experience of that year in Israel.

Instead of returning to the United States that summer, another Detroiter and I decided to go to Neve Yerushalayim. Although today the idea of transferring from BJJ to Neve Yerushalayim sounds ludicrous, in those days it there were very few options if one wished to stay and learn for a second year.

Before starting Neve, I asked the school's director, Rabbi Revson, if there was a place for a girl like me in his school. He replied that there was definitely room for me to grow there, and then continued, "Having you here will give the new *baalos teshuvah* an opportunity to see how a *frum* girl behaves." I was accepted on a full scholarship.

Going to Neve gave me a chance to remain in Eretz Yisrael and continue learning. The teachers were fantastic, and the girls wonderful. They were so enthusiastic about mitzvah observance. Since I had been *frum* for all of four years, they expected me to have all the answers and were constantly questioning me about my actions. That in itself forced me to grow.

I met my husband right after Chanukah. Shlomo was learning in Netzach Yisrael.

We left Eretz Yisrael to get married in Detroit, planning to return to Israel immediately after the wedding. But once we were in the United States, reality set in. We didn't have a penny to our names! How could we possibly establish ourselves in Israel?

That's how we ended up living in Flatbush. Shlomo went to *Kollel* while I worked as an assistant bookkeeper at MTJ *[Mesivtha Tifereth Jerusalem — a prominent New York yeshivah]*. Less than a year after our wedding, Shlomo asked me to arrange for us to speak with MTJ's Rosh Yeshivah, Rav Moshe Feinstein. Shlomo asked Rav Moshe for a *berachah* for us to have children, which he gave us.

It took twenty years for that *berachah* to be fulfilled. Throughout that entire time, I never once gave up hope. Once, a relative told me, "Face it. You might never have any children." But I was absolutely positive that we ***would*** have children. The only question was, when?

During those twenty years, I met a lot of other couples facing the same challenge. Many were totally obsessed with it; that's all they could think about. But we took it one year — actually, one day — at a time. Hashem had *rachmanus* on me: I never dreamed that we would end up having to wait so long to become parents, but, *baruch Hashem,* our wonderful daughter, Sarala, was well worth the wait!

There were times, of course, when reality hit us hard. An uncle once said something to me about having a child, and then, in a desperate, strangulated voice added, "With Hashem's help, may you be blessed with a child." These words were said with such intensity that it suddenly dawned on me that, while I was having a great time living my life, I didn't realize how quickly the years were flying by.

Most of my friends were sensitive to my situation. On the odd occasion when I'd find myself at a wedding or other *simchah* with a group of women talking about such fascinating subjects as the pros and cons of diaper changing, I'd slip away to join another group.

Shortly after our twentieth wedding anniversary, Rav Michel

Twerski blessed us with *hatzlachah* in our endeavors to become a family. Less than a year later, our little Sarala was born. We named her after both my grandmother and Sara *Imeinu*.

People often ask me about the challenges of being an older parent, but I really don't feel that it's much of a challenge. Both Shlomo and I are very young at heart! When Sarala was a baby, I looked ten years younger than my chronological age, and Shlomo still had no grey hair. Once, when I took Sarala with me to have my *sheitel* done, the *sheitel macher* smiled brightly at her and said, 'Hi cutie pie! You're supposed to be twenty years older!' Another time I said to her, "Sarala, are you going to listen to your old mommy?" She retorted, "You're not an old mommy! You're a new mommy!"

We made *aliyah* in 2002, when Sarala was eight years old. I tell people that we originally planned to return to Israel immediately after our wedding; it just took us twenty-nine years to get here.

Why did we decide to move to Israel? After the events of 9/11, we realized that America was not the safe place we'd thought it was. One evening, on the way to a wedding, my husband suggested, "Instead of investing so much money in buying an overpriced house, let's move to Israel." I was shocked! It had been fifteen years since we'd last discussed *aliyah*.

We were on the first *Nefesh b'Nefesh* flight to Israel. They made a big party for us at the Ben Gurion airport. Binyamin Netanyahu delivered a speech. But it was the middle of July, and the huge hangar where the ceremony took place was not air-conditioned! Afterward we ended up waiting for hours to get our papers processed before proceeding to my nephew's home in Jerusalem.

Although I had spent seven months preparing for our *aliyah* — attending *aliyah* workshops, doing research, packing up our house, purchasing things to take with us — I was not excited about the move. My heart was not in it. But in the taxi, driving up to Jerusalem, I felt overwhelmed with excitement as I realized that I was finally coming HOME.

Today, the Dickmans are an integral part of the frum Ramat Beit Shemesh community and active in helping other olim adapt to their new home. Their emunah peshutah and simchas hachayim are inspirational to all who know them.

THE CHAREIDI TAXI DRIVER

"It occurred to me that if *I* became a taxi driver, I would be able to help women, help my husband, and do what I really enjoy — driving!"

Revital Levi

A Chareidi woman taxi driver — what a contradiction in terms! At least that's what I thought, until I met Revital Levi.

The doorbell rang at exactly one o'clock. "Hmm ..." I thought, "just on time. At least she's prompt." I opened the door to find a tall, slender woman dressed in a pale-blue suit with a matching hat standing there.

"Before I forget," she began, "I promised your mother-in-law that I'd give you my recipe for milchig bourekas."

Two weeks before the interview, my husband had arranged for Revital to drive my mother-in-law to Ranaana. The two women had spent the entire two-and-a-half hours on the road exchanging baking tips. I later found out that before her marriage, Revital had been a professional pastry chef at the King David Hotel.

I was born and raised in Alon Shvut, a modern Orthodox community. As long as I can remember, my family was involved in the tourist industry. My father operated a hotel. Before that, he was a tour guide. So it was just natural that, given my love of baking, after graduating high school I attended Hadassah's School of Culinary Arts to learn to become a pastry chef. Upon finishing the course, I got a job at the prestigious King David Hotel.

But all that changed when I met my future husband. He felt that it was not suitable for an Orthodox woman to work in such a secular environment. So after our marriage I left the King David Hotel to become a full-time housewife and, within a year, a mother. *Baruch Hashem*, we had seven boys within seven years.

Meanwhile, to support our growing family, my husband worked long hours driving a cab. We called him a Shabbat Abba because the only time the kids saw him was on Shabbat. When my youngest, twin boys, were four years old, I felt that I had to do something tangible to ease my husband's burden.

On the religious radio stations, I often heard women ask the rabbis questions regarding *yichud* with male taxi drivers, which, by the way, is often problematic. It occurred to me that if *I* became a taxi driver, I would be able to help these women, help my husband, and do what I really enjoy — driving!

I consulted several leading rabbis — from both the Ashkenazi and Sefardi communities — before starting the lengthy process of attaining a permit to drive a cab. Although some of these rabbis frown on having women drive, they all welcomed the idea of a religious female taxi driver, since I would be providing a much-needed service.

To become a taxi driver I had to take a battery of medical and psychological exams, driving tests, and theory tests. I was tested on all the rules and regulations necessary to become a bus driver — which, by the way, is something I would like to do in the future.

What about your children? Who takes care of them while you're driving the taxi?

My husband and I share a taxi, so one of us is always at home with the children. I am often hired to meet girls or women at the airport. Many of the flights arrive in the middle of the night or early morning when the children are asleep, so that's not a problem. But now that I'm working, my husband helps out a lot with the housework and spends much more time with the children.

At first, my children were very embarrassed. Driving a cab is not exactly the typical *frum* woman's job! Now, however, when people ask my children what I do, they reply, "She's a taxi driver." And then they add, "But she only drives women."

By the way, there are a few other women taxi drivers in Jerusalem, including one Arab driver. She wears a snood so people often think she's *Chareidi* — until they see her pick up male passengers.

When I first started working, a woman hired me to meet her niece at the airport. She was very organized, and had even prepared a sign with her niece's name on it for me to wave in the reception hall. When the flight landed at three o'clock in the morning, I was there, holding my sign and waiting for the girl to come out of customs. I saw a religious teenaged girl, looking around as if she was expecting someone to be waiting for her. I walked over to ask her if she was the girl I was there to pick up. I mentioned the girl's name and, to double check, showed her the sign and asked her if she was that person. Both times, she responded in the affirmative. But later, as we approached Jerusalem, I asked her something about her aunt in Ramat Shlomo. She said, "What aunt in Ramat Shlomo? I'm going to Kiryat Sefer. Aren't you taking me to Kiryat Sefer?"

I was flabbergasted! But, at this point, I had no choice. I had to drive her to her destination; I couldn't leave a young girl stranded in the middle of the night. On my way to Kiryat Sefer, I called my client's aunt to explain the mix-up. She was furious; she thought I had done it on purpose to get another fare. After I dropped the second girl off in Kiryat Sefer, I drove back to the airport to pick up my intended fare. But just as I got there, the aunt phoned to let me know that her niece had already arrived safely in Jerusalem.

Although the girl's aunt apologized for being angry with me, she never called me again. But ninety percent of my customers *do* call again. They enjoy driving with me. We talk about cooking, child care, and other feminine topics. We share recipes — and then, of course, the next time I drive them somewhere, they tell me how the recipes came out.

Although most of my trips are to the airport, I have driven women anywhere from Arad in the south to Maalot in the north. Last summer, I chauffeured two *chareidi* performers around the country. They were presenting a play on parent-child communications. They even got me involved: I operated the production's audio track.

Women often ask me to take them to meet Rebbetzin Kanievsky. It's difficult to get an appointment with the Rebbetzin, so I just show up without one. *Baruch Hashem*, my clients always manage to get in. The first time I took a group of women to visit Rebbetzin Kanievsky, I told them that if we could not get in to see the Rebbetzin they would not have to pay me for my time. Meanwhile, I told my son that I'd pay him five *shekels* if we succeed in getting in, and asked him to recite *Tehillim* for our *hatzlachah*. *Baruch Hashem,* we were *matzliach*! When I asked the Rebbetzin for a *berachah*, she *bentched* me that I will have lots of *maaser* money to give to *tzedakah*.

My customers view me as their friend. I receive invitations to attend their *simchos*. Last year I exchanged *shalach manos* with all my customers. This year there are too many, *baruch Hashem*!

Have you encountered problems with tzenius?

I originally planned on driving only women, but several *rabbanim* requested that I drive couples as well. In principle, I will never take a man who is not accompanied by a woman. One time, however, I found myself in an extremely awkward situation. An elderly couple with a grown son in a wheelchair flagged me down. I assumed that the three of them needed a cab. But the husband and wife lifted their son out of the wheelchair, placed him on the seat next to me, closed the door, and told me that someone would be meeting their son at his destination. That is when I realized that the son was traveling by himself.

I wondered what I should do. I didn't want to be driving alone with a man, especially if he was sitting in the front seat. On the other hand, it would have been callous to ask the parents to lift their son out of my cab. So I took the fare. That was the only time that I did such a thing, but it would have been a disaster to have done otherwise.

What is the secret of your success?

Tefillah! I tell my children that if they want an allowance, they should *daven* for my success. They recite *Tehillim* for me. Each week, I give my children an allowance comprised of one percent of my earnings. Believe me, they pray from the bottom of their hearts that I make a lot of money!

In addition, both my husband and I are positive that our success is dependent on three factors: *tzedakah*, *tzenius*, and *shalom*. *Tzedakah* — we are careful to give *maaser*. *Tzenius* — we prevent *pritzus* by my driving women. And *shalom* — we work together as a couple to support our family.

What are your plans for the future?

Five years from now, I hope to be very, very busy driving my taxi. I would like to have enough work to be able to support my family so that my husband can sit and learn.

I am always amazed at the unique niches we create for ourselves, at our ability to discover our strengths and talents and then channel them for the betterment of our families. Mother, pastry chef, taxi driver — and who knows? — perhaps one day a bus driver .... Such diverse talents, yet all channeled toward the same goal: creating a Yiddishe home, a true mikdash me'at.

POSTSCRIPT: *After writing up this interview, I emailed a copy to my mother-in-law. She wrote back: "Did you know that she gave me a package of yummy home-baked pastries to take on the plane with me? Actually, I saved them until I got home, and enjoyed them so much."*

SIMPLICITY IS GREATNESS

"A large part of the school's success was a result of Rebbetzin Kaplan's *berachah*. There's really no logical explanation for how a young kid from America went on to become principal of an Israeli school."

Chedva (a pseudonym)

Chedva and I go back many, many years. When I was a newlywed living in a tiny yeshivah community located on a Moshav in the Negev, she was the Rebbetzin, the woman we turned to for guidance and advice. She taught me how to make challos, kasher a chicken, make gefilte fish. In my eyes, she was an older married woman; but in reality she was really a young "vibelah": Her oldest was just seven.

Today, although we've become contemporaries, I still turn to Chedva for guidance and advice. She has the unique ability to come up with the most amazingly perceptive comments while somehow making you feel that it's really your idea, not hers. Whenever I describe Chedva to anyone I say that she's always there when you need her, and never there when you don't. That's because between giving shiurim, being involved in her children's and grandchildren's lives, and being available for her mother around the clock, her schedule is extremely full. As we were talking, I realized that after finishing our interview, she would leave the house to run errands, then drive to Beit Shemesh for a school consultation, and then on to the Negev for a graduation and a visit with her children! But as we spoke, I never felt rushed. It was as if she had all the time in the world for me. She was one hundred percent, totally, there for me.

I grew up in New York. Although I studied in Rebbetzin Kaplan's seminary, I really went through the rainbow. For elementary school, it was public school in the morning, Talmud Torah in the afternoon. I went to a local girls' yeshivah high school, but our class was very special. Many of the girls from that class are well known rebbetzins today. Several of us continued on to Rebbetzin Kaplan's Bais Yaakov seminary. Upon graduation, Rebbetzin Kaplan asked three of us to teach there. So I ended up becoming a teacher in Bais Yaakov High School!

Rebbetzin Kaplan was amazing. As a new teacher, I made quite a few mistakes. I thought that I knew it all .... When we're young we think we know it all, and as we get older we somehow become less knowledgeable! She was very careful in how she corrected me. In addition to teaching classes, I tutored a student from a non-religious home. The girl probably had a learning disability, but in those days we didn't know the meaning of the word. I once put a lot of effort into helping her prepare for an exam, but she got a dreadful mark and I was disappointed. I must have used a cliché, like, 'If you would just try a bit harder ...,' because later Rebbetzin Kaplan called me into her office. She filled me in a bit on the girl's background and then said something like, 'You are such a good teacher that this girl thinks the world of you! Because she thinks so much of you, you can't imagine what those words did to her. She was devastated." In her beautiful, soft-spoken way, Rebbetzin Kaplan corrected and guided me while making me feel that I was doing a great job!

When I informed Rebbetzin Kaplan that my husband and I would be moving to Eretz Yisrael and that I would not be able to continue teaching in Bais Yaakov High School, she asked me where in Israel I was moving. I told her, "The Negev."

"You're moving to the Negev?" she asked. "There's no Bais Yaakov there. So you'll start one!"

Although it took a while for her *berachah* to materialize, it was eventually fulfilled.

You've had such rich teaching career — Bais Yaakov principal, seminary principal, AND school supervisor, in addition to teaching all the different grades. Could you give us some practical advice, whether teaching our own children or someone else's?

The first thing is *siyata d'Shemaya* — and that holds true in every endeavor. During my teaching years, whenever I said, *"Atta chonen l'adam daas* — You graciously endow man with knowledge" — in *Shemoneh Esrei*, I would add a special *tefillah* asking Hashem to put the right words into my mouth, so that I would say the right thing in the right way at the right time to reach each of my students properly, with love and respect.

I once participated in a five-year *chinuch* workshop. Every week, I traveled from the Negev to Jerusalem for the program. All the women in the course were accomplished educators — principals, seminary teachers, and well-known rebbetzins. We all looked forward to our weekly meeting. The most important thing I learned from this course was that when a person talks things over, he crystallizes his own ideas. Then he can form a wise plan of action and make appropriate decisions. Active listening is one of the most important tools we can use to help people around us grow and develop.

It's also important for kids — for anyone, for that matter — to feel that you enjoy being with them, that you like them, because when you like someone, that person will automatically like you back. That's the power of *ayin tovah*, a good eye, seeing the good in others.

One experience that stands out in my life happened when I was a principal. One day, out of the blue, a mother phoned to thank me and to tell me how much her daughter loves school. She said that I have such a nice relationship with the girls. What happened? The girls had been decorating their classroom after hours, and I asked if there was anything I could do to help. The girls answered, "No, thank you. We can manage." My response: "I know you can manage, but I just love being with you, doing things with you!"

What was it like moving to Eretz Yisrael forty-three years ago?

We moved to Eretz Yisrael in the summer of '65. That was just before a *shemittah* year, which means that this year is our seventh *shemittah*! That was the year I learned to eat rice. I almost never ate it before that, but the potatoes were all wormy, and there wasn't much else available.

We were a few yeshivah families living in a small moshav in the Negev. The moshav relied on the *heter mechirah,* but we didn't, of course. My husband was learning in Yeshivat Hanegev in Netivot, which had just opened. We purchased all our food from the yeshivah. There wasn't a lot of variety, but we were a young couple and we didn't need much. I remember getting canned meat! Can you imagine, canned meat?

Three years later, we moved together with a new yeshivah — which, by the way, is today considered one of the best in Israel — to a different moshav. The moshav was founded by Hungarians who came there straight from the DP camps. Later on, in the fifties, a group of Moroccan families also settled there.

The North Africans were really *korbanos* of Zionism. The State ripped the children away from *Yiddishkeit*, and the parents weren't knowledgeable enough to stand up for their rights. The regional counsel was Mapai — which later became the Labor Party — and very anti-religious. When the North Africans arrived in Eretz Yisrael, the country was very, very poor — food was still rationed — and they were put under a lot of pressure to work on Shabbos and enroll their children in non-religious schools.

The Hungarians had arrived earlier, right after the war. While the women remained in the *maabarot* the men were sent to the moshav to construct the houses with their own two hands! To give you an idea of how desolate the area was, one of the women wrote a letter to her husband, giving the address as "in the wilderness." The letter reached its destination!

The Hungarians couldn't get over how "extravagant" we were. They thought I was nuts for watering my grass; what a waste of water. The yeshivah *bachurim* dormed in deserted houses (many of the original Hungarian immigrants had moved away to Bnei Brak or Yerushalayim). There were no street lights, so the streets were pitch-dark (which was not so unusual in those days). Since the boys learned until late at night, they kept a light on outside their dorms to be able to find their way home at night. This angered some of the moshavniks to no end. What a terrible waste! So they broke the bulbs to save electricity!

Many of the moshav families raised chickens, and some had cows. One time, when my sister (today a well-known *macheneches*) and her husband came to us for Shabbos, she was chased by a cow that had gotten loose.

You started the Bais Yaakov there?

First of all, a little background. When we arrived at the moshav in 1968, there was a Poalei Agudah elementary school on the moshav, with 57 boys and girls in eight grades. After sixth grade, most of the Hungarian immigrant families sent their children to Bnei Brak for school, while the Moroccan families sent their kids to the government religious school on another moshav.

The *cheder* was the first *chareidi* school to open on the moshav. It was really very small, just two boys learning privately with my husband.

When the boys were five, we decided to send them to the *cheder* in Netivot for first grade. But first they had to be tested by a psychologist to see if they were ready. The psychologist tested them on reading readiness — but they were already learning *Chumash*! The kids thought the psychologist was nuts! Then he asked the children, "Where do we buy bread?" They answered, "At the yeshivah," which, of course, from the psychologist's perspective was the wrong answer. But since the local store sold bread with a *hechsher* that we didn't rely on, we really did purchase our bread at the yeshivah.

After one year in Netivot, the two boys returned to learning privately in our house. Eventually a few other boys joined them. We purchased a globe and they taught themselves geography. Arithmetic was taught on trips to the local grocery store. They learned the entire *Chumash Bereishis* by heart — believe it or not, they were able to quote any *pasuk,* verbatim! Afterwards we took a boy from the yeshivah to learn *Mishnayos* with them. He then continued on to Gemara, then *Rishonim* and *Acharonim*. He even taught the boys to write a summary of everything they learned. The boys were really a part of the yeshivah, yet they were just young children. It was a very unique learning experience, and it worked. It was the beginning of the moshav's excellent *cheder*.

We started the Bais Yaakov when my oldest daughter was in second grade. At first, the "school" was in my house. It had five grades, one through six, but without a fifth. There were seven girls in the first and second grades, and five girls in the third, fourth, and sixth grades.

I taught the higher grades. They learned in a classroom converted from a shack in our backyard that had once been used to raise baby chicks. Another woman taught first and second grade in my living room. The girls sat around the dining room table. One day, the table just collapsed, which the kids thought was really fun. Boy, did they have a blast that day! We even had an end-of-year outing, using the Peugeot station wagon of one of the mothers. It was all very official; the yeshivah paid us our salary, and continued to pay it for three years until we were recognized by Chinuch Atzmai and received government funding. The classes were held in different homes until eventually we moved into a school building. Then I even had an official title: school principal!

I think a large part of the school's success was a result of Rebbetzin Kaplan's *berachah*. There's really no logical explanation for how a young kid from America went on to become principal of an Israeli school.

It was a tremendous *zechus* to be part of building a *makom Torah* in Eretz Yisrael. In the beginning, the yeshivah boys would come to us every other week for tea and cake after the meal. On Rosh Hashanah and Yom Kippur, the *ezras nashim* was full of playpens and babies. We ate the Purim *seudah* together with the yeshivah. Although today the Moshav is just an hour-and-a-half bus ride from Jerusalem, in those days it took hours to get there, and of course only a few families had their own phone, so we were really isolated.

It was an amazing time — an incredible experience. Hashem really led me; there's no logical explanation. If you had told me when I was newly married what my life would eventually look like, I wouldn't even have known what you were talking about. I wouldn't be able to fathom it. If someone had told me that today I'd have so many children, grandchildren, *kein ayan hara* — well, in those days I considered six to be a huge family!

The moshav was much more than a place to live; it was a family. Most of the families who lived there were poor. We never even dreamed of meat. I raised vegetables and picked fruit from our trees to supplement our income. Every Friday, the vegetable man, who sold fruits and vegetables from a horse-drawn wagon, would bring me all the fruit that he had not managed to sell before Shabbos. A friend would come over and together we'd sort the fruits: the good fruit to the yeshivah, the rotten fruit to the trash, and anything in between we'd use to make fruit soup, jam, cakes, you name it. Our families ate a lot of fruit soup. It was really delicious!

We almost never bought clothes. I loved to sew, and made new clothes for my family using old clothes that we got in packages. I once made a beautiful jacket from a full corduroy skirt that someone sent me. But life was very different then. We never felt that anything was missing. Actually, we were the rich Americans— we received packages from abroad!

When I told one of my daughters about this interview, she said, "When we were children, whenever you mentioned Chedva, you always told us that she's an 'isha l'dugmah' — an example of the type of woman we should try to emulate." As I write these words, I try to define for myself what it is that I wanted my children — and myself — to emulate. It's pashtus, simplicity. Sometimes life is not easy. There will be times when we'll look back and ask ourselves, "How did I ever have the emotional strength to do what I did?" But that's our strength as Jewish women — doing what we have to do without fanfare, with a simplicity that's really greatness.

FROM KIPPAH TO TICHEL

"Our home was submerged under twelve feet of water for over three weeks. But it wasn't just water — it was water mixed with chemicals from all the cars and factories that were also flooded. Everything was ruined ..."

Yael Aldrich

A few years ago my sister Sheila, who was then living in Chapel Hill, North Carolina, phoned me and said, "Debbie, my best friend's son and wife are coming to Israel for the year, to learn in a yeshivah. Please take care of them."

At first, I was a bit wary. Sheila is not religious, and the last time we had received this type of request (from another family member), the person turned out to be non-Jewish. My sister assured me that her friend's son and his wife were definitely Orthodox and that they were coming to Israel to study in an Orthodox yeshivah program for the year.

So I dutifully took down their number and phoned to invite them for Shabbos. When I explained to Yael Aldrich that my sister was her mother-in-law's best friend, she listened politely, and then respectfully said that it wasn't a good week for them. Two weeks later, I tried again, and again she politely declined my invitation.

"One more time, and that's it," I thought. "Obviously these people are not interested in spending Shabbos with the Shapiros!"

The third time I called, Yael carefully asked, "Uh, what exactly do you mean by Shabbos?"

I was a bit confused. After all, I had been told that these people were frum, but how frum could she be if she didn't know what I meant by Shabbos?

So I politely answered, "Well, if you come for Shabbos we'll expect you to arrive before I light the Shabbos candles" — I explained what that was — "and then you'll have to stick around until after Havdalah" — and I explained what that was. "But don't worry," I added, "you'll have your bedroom and we'll provide you with everything you need, except pajamas!" I wondered what in the world had I gotten myelf into ....

"Can I phone you back in a few minutes with our answer?" Yael asked. I agreed, and silently hoped that the answer would be no. But it wasn't.

I found out years later that the Aldriches assumed that since my sister is Daniel's mother's best friend, and since Daniel's mother is not religious, obviously our family was also not religious.

Friday afternoon, the Aldriches boarded the #16 bus that would take them from Beit Hakerem to Ramot Polin. When they alighted from the bus and saw the little boys riding their bicycles, peyos flying in the wind, Daniel looked at his wife and commented wryly, "This looks like it might be religious neighborhood."

A few minutes later they knocked on our door and my husband, already wearing his shtreimel and beketcheh, opened it. "Come on in," he welcomed them into the living room. "I'll call my wife."

We later learned that they had brought enough food for the entire Shabbos in their suitcase. They assumed that even though we weren't very religious (sic), they'd find something kosher to eat at the meal (probably challah and jarred gefilte fish), and then, while we relaxed, probably in front of the T.V., they planned to go to their bedroom and enjoy a real Shabbos seudah. They were pleasantly surprised to find that they could actually eat in our house!

That was the beginning of a wonderful relationship. We felt a bit like family; after all, Daniel was my sister's best friend's son. We had the privilege of hosting the Aldriches for many Shabbosim.

But it was only thanks to this interview that I learned about Yael and Daniel's incredible journey to Torah-true Judaism.

Our family moved to Winston-Salem, North Carolina when I was five years old, after my father retired from the military. I attended boarding school for eleventh and twelfth grade. That's where I met Daniel, my future husband. At the time, neither of us was connected to anything Jewish.

After high school, I attended college in Staunton, Virginia. Right across the street from the college was a Reform temple — actually, it was a historical landmark because it had been built before the Revolutionary War! I noticed Jewish activities happening there; for example, during Succos there was a real *succah*. One day I wandered in, curious, and started talking with the rabbi. I was interested enough to begin taking classes and attending services, which, by the way, took place every other week because the synagogue shared the rabbi with another community.

For my second year of college, I transferred to the University of North Carolina, Chapel Hill, which was close to my family and was also the university where Daniel was studying. I became involved in the Hillel there. Although Daniel wasn't interested at all, I used to drag him to their events. Eventually I became head of Hillel. I was leading Friday-night services and cooking Friday-night dinners for sixty to eighty students each week.

Although I was much more knowledgeable than the average Reform Jew, I wanted to learn more about Judaism. The Reform rabbi taught a class on kashrus that inspired me to slowly start keeping kosher. At first, I stopped eating *tereifah* meat and fish, then I stopped eating milk and meat together. Later, I became a vegetarian. By the end of the year I had stopped eating in restaurants and was basically eating only kosher.

I wanted to become more traditional, but since I was the only one who could lead the Reform services at Hillel, I continued attending Friday-night services there. Shabbos morning, however, I attended services in the Conservative temple that was located in the next town. I even studied the Conservative "halachah" book, which states that it's okay to drive to shul on Shabbos (sic) but not anyplace else. So although I drove to the synagogue on Shabbos morning, I was careful to drive directly there, and of course I never listened to the radio during the ride! Then I would return to my dorm room and spend the rest of the day relaxing, enjoying my Shabbos.

That year, I also changed my major from biology to religious studies. I was seriously considering becoming a Conservative rabbi. By then, I was wearing a *kippah* full time (!), occasionally put on *tefillin*, and had made my own *tallis*, which I wore each Shabbos. I didn't know about *tzitzis*, so I didn't wear them.

As I listen to Yael describe what she looked like as a college student, I can almost see her smiling over the international telephone wires. It's difficult for me to even imagine this eishes chayil wearing a kippah!

At the community's Lag B'Omer picnic, I met Rabbi Avraham Peretz Friedman, *shlita*, Torah U'mesorah's *kiruv* activist at Duke University. He would eventually become my rabbi.

My first impression of the Friedman family was of a mother with a bunch of young kids plus what I thought was a teenage boy of around sixteen. Imagine my surprise when I discovered that the "teenage boy" was the rabbi!

I was really impressed at their *mentchlichkeit*. They were so sweet, so friendly, and so, so normal! She is a lawyer; he has an engineering degree from Columbia.

The Friedmans were the only people eating kosher at the picnic. Their son, who was around seven at the time, asked his parents if he could buy some popcorn at the popcorn stand. His parents told him to first check to make sure it was kosher, which it wasn't — and the boy accepted that without argument! He didn't cry. He didn't have a fit. He simply didn't eat it. I was amazed, really amazed. I had never seen such a young child with such incredible will power. That made a very big impression on me.

I asked Friedmans where they went to shul. They told me that they *davened* in an Orthodox *minyan* that was held in the basement of the Conservative synagogue — the same Conservative synagogue where I attended services each Shabbos morning. The following Shabbos, I drove to the Conservative synagogue as usual (wearing my *kippah* and *tallis*, of course). Halfway through the service, I suddenly remembered that there was another service going on in the basement. I went downstairs to check it out.

It was lovely. After the services, Rabbi Friedman invited me to his house for lunch. During the year and a half that I had been attending services at the Conservative synagogue, no one had ever invited me for Shabbos lunch. I was amazed at what I saw at the Friedmans. A real Shabbos, the way it's supposed to be! Eventually I started spending all my Shabbosim with the Friedmans.

> *We tend to think that, to succeed in kiruv, we need to know all the answers. But for many, if not most, baalei teshuvah, it was the warmth and simchah of a Yiddishe home that prodded them to begin their journey. Creating a warm and joyous home is an investment with eternal dividends. As for knowing all the answers — well, who said we have to know everything?*

By this time, Daniel and I were officially engaged. I decided that I would become either a Conservative rabbi or *frum*. Daniel asked me what being *frum* entails. I asked the rabbi. He explained to me that it would involve observing three basic mitzvos: Kashrus, Shabbos, and the laws of family purity. Daniel's reaction was, 'Okay. I'll do those three things. But I won't *daven* three times a day, and I won't wear a yarmulke!' So that was it. We were going to be Orthodox!

Ours was the first Orthodox wedding in Chapel Hill in who-knows-how-long. We had to scrounge around for ten Jewish men, and only three were *shomer Shabbos*. Most of our guests weren't even Jewish.

The previous year, SEED had sent a group of *bachurim* from Ner Yisrael to Chapel Hill. We became very friendly with them, and they had told us that when we married, we should come up to Baltimore for a *sheva berachos*. So the day after our wedding, we piled into the van with the Friedman clan, and Rabbi Friedman drove five hours to Baltimore. That's when I was introduced to Uncle Moishy and the Mitzvah Men!

The *bachurim* of Ner Yisrael, true to their word, made a grand *sheva berachos* for us. They invited tons of people; it was like a real Yiddishe wedding, with a huge *seudah*, dancing, everything. The waitresses were Bais Yaakov girls. The only thing missing was our parents. We also received some beautiful presents, including my *leichter*, which were later destroyed by Hurricane Katrina.

> *As Yael describes that beautiful sheva berachos, I can hear the emotion in her voice. She was so moved by the community's chesed. Mah tovu ohalecha Yaakov ....*

After our marriage, we moved to Berkeley, California. I worked as program director of Chabad, while Daniel went to graduate school. Every Shabbos we ate at the Chabad house.

There was one man whom I can only describe as "wild eyed" because of his animated enthusiasm. He kept on inviting us to come to his house for Shabbos lunch. We kept on putting him off. Finally, after several weeks, we felt that we had no choice and joined his family for the Shabbos day meal.

That's how we became friendly with Dr. Daniel Gordon and his wonderful wife, Dr. Beth Marcus. At the time they had two children; today they have a lot more and are living in Baltimore. We went to them almost every Shabbos. After graduating from Harvard Medical School, Dr. Gordon had spent a year learning in Yeshivas Darchei Noam. His wife learned in Shearim, a well-known seminary in Yerushalayim.

They encouraged us to grow as much as possible, which included coming to daily *minyan*. Daniel really didn't want to get up at six-thirty in the morning to *daven*. I told him that if he went, I'd go with him. So every morning there were a dozen or so men davening on one side of the *mechitzah*, and me on the other! *[By now, she was wearing a tichel, not a kippah!]*

After a while we felt confident enough to make our own Shabbos meals. Dozens of Jewish students used to congregate in our house every week. We even managed to make a *shidduch* between two of the singles! That Pesach, we had forty guests for our first Seder, thirty-two for our second — and this was the first time we were making Pesach! By this point, Daniel was really excited about *Yiddishkeit*. He even prepared a weekly *dvar Torah*, usually straight off the Darchei Noam website. The meals were beautiful, with lots of discussions and singing.

The following year, the Gordons, who had learned in Darchei Noam, and Rabbi Friedmen who had taught there, convinced us to go to Israel to learn in yeshivah. So after Daniel received his Masters from Berkeley, we packed our belongings and moved to Israel for the year.

> *That was when I first met Daniel and Yael. Hearing her story, I am surprised at how new they were to Yiddishkeit when they came to us. They had seemed so completely at ease in their Torah observance.*
>
> *How did you change that year?*

How could we not change? We were immersed in Torah! Up until that point, I had read tons of English *sefarim*, but in sem I learned to understand Torah from the inside. I was taught how to crack the code that is Rashi, Ibn Ezra; how to understand *Chumash* and the *Nevi'im* from the perspective of the greatest minds of all time. In addition, we had amazing role models. We knew that we wanted to be religious — and we *were* religious — but we still hadn't decided what type of religious Jews we wanted to become. During that year, my husband went from learning the *alef-beis* to being able to learn a Gemara on his own! Thanks to the tools he acquired that year, he was able to continue his learning, and just this year received his *semichah* in Yerushalayim.

We also made lots of new friends that year, like you guys. *[She means my family]*. Meeting you was a huge turning point for us. Both you and your husband are very different from any of the people we had met before. *[This is great for my ego ... I think. Let's see where she's taking this ....]* We had never met people so "into" their *chassidus*, living such a different lifestyle. *[Hey! And I thought we we were so normal.]* Getting to know you was a beautiful experience. *[Ahh ... now I feel better.]*

From Israel we went to Boston, where Daniel studied in Harvard for his Ph.D. Every night he learned in our shul's *beis medrash* with Rabbi Dovid Moskovitz, *shlita*, and Rabbi Shmuel Ochs, *shlita*. Meanwhile, I got involved in Aish HaTorah and organized their Boston Partners in Torah program. Every Wednesday night there were between twenty to thirty *chevrusas* going. I also had a *chevrusah*. So, as you can see, we were very active in the community.

Six years ago, we traveled to Japan for the first time as Daniel worked on his first academic book project. We lived in Tokyo. There were about five *frum* families: two of them Chabadnik, two Israeli, and us. We had a lot of guests, and many of the Jewish people who came to Tokyo on business ended up spending Shabbos with us.

After our year in Japan, we returned to Boston, where I got very involved in *kiruv* programs, including *Me'or Maimonides* for local college students. Then my husband was offered an excellent position as professor of Political Science at Tulane University in New Orleans. We decided to move there.

> *The summer before Daniel and Yael moved to New Orleans, they visited Israel and spent a Shabbos with us. By then, they were a family. Their oldest, Gavriel Tzvi, was already two. I remember sitting around the living-room table, listening to Daniel and Yael talk about their future plans. Yael was gung-ho on moving to Israel, to a new yeshivah community just outside of Jerusalem. Daniel wasn't as excited. He had several reasons why it wasn't appropriate, among them professional considerations. But the one that stuck out in my mind because of its irony was the safety factor. "A lot of people argue that it is safer to live in the United States," he explained. A mentch tracht un d'Abeishter lacht .... Instead of moving to Israel, they moved to New Orleans.*

The New Orleans Jewish community was very small. There were two Chabad shuls, a tiny Chabad school, the Orthodox synagogue where we *davened* (this was later swamped during the flood and all the *sifrei Torah* ruined), a small synagogue in the French Quarter, three kosher restaurants, and a grocery store. Other than us and the rabbi of the synagogue and his family, most of the families were older. There were dreams of creating a *makom Torah*. The rabbi hoped to bring in *kollel* families and there were plans to construct an *eiruv*. But these plans have yet to materialize.

The Thursday before Hurricane Katrina, we said goodbye to the Ner Yisrael yeshivah boys whom we had hosted for their two-week stay in New Orleans as part of Torah Umesorah's SEED program. The following Shabbos, in addition to several walk-in guests, we hosted a *frum* military doctor stationed in Mississippi. After Shabbos the doctor phoned the base and was told to return immediately. All military personnel were needed to secure the base for hurricane mode.

The doctor told us that the storm would be a big one. Then one of our Shabbos guests phoned to tell us to evacuate. Although she had lived in New Orleans for seventeen years, and over the years evacuation had often been recommended, this was the first time it was mandatory. When she told us that there would be no water or electricity for three days, we were convinced!

We thought we were leaving for just a few days, so we packed a bag with only three days' worth of clothing, plus our Shabbos outfits, a few toys, my crock pot with Shabbos leftovers, and my *kesubah*. All the houses in New Orleans, including ours, are built on stilts to keep them above flood level. Ours was built four feet above the ground. We assumed that the worst — and even this was unimaginable — that could happen would be a flooding of six feet of water. So we removed anything that we thought could get ruined from the bottom shelves and placed them either on the table or on higher shelves. In the end, however, our house was flooded with twelve feet of water, and everything was ruined.

We left at four o'clock Sunday morning, and promptly found ourselves stuck in a colossal traffic jam. It took us about two hours to travel one-and-a-half miles! But it was impossible to return to the city. All the lanes were outbound, and police with guns were standing along the side of the road, telling people that they could not go back.

We crawled along until we finally arrived in Houston. When we weren't listening to Uncle Moishy, we were listening to the emergency radio channel. At first, it didn't sound different from any other hurricane. It was bad, but certainly not terrible. Later on, when we heard reports that the levee had broken, we knew we were in big trouble. That *erev Shabbos* we'd ridden our bikes over the levee to buy ice cream at the kosher ice cream store! It was less than a mile from our house.

Our home was submerged under twelve feet of water for over three weeks. But it wasn't just water — it was water mixed with chemicals from all the cars and factories that were also flooded. Everything was ruined, except for one little ceramic wall hanging that my mother-in-law had purchased in Israel. Candlesticks, *sefarim*, dishes — there was nothing left.

When we first realized the extent of the damage, we were absolutely dumbfounded. The hurricane occurred at the end of August, and we had moved to New Orleans at the start of the summer. Our lives were just beginning to return to normal. We had just purchased new furniture for the house. We had started having guests again, and had even hosted the SEED *bachurim*. School had been scheduled to begin the day after we left the city. Everything had been so normal — and then, almost instantaneously, our lives were turned upside down! We had no idea if Daniel's university would open again, or if he even had a job.

We stayed at a hotel full of evacuees. Everyone was in a state of shock. People had worked their entire life for their beautiful homes, and now — poof! — everything was gone. But for us, it was different. We had just moved to New Orleans. Daniel had just finished his Ph.D. at Harvard and this was his first job. We really hadn't put down roots yet.

After the initial shock, we felt a tremendous sense of freedom. We weren't sure if Daniel had a job; we had no home or belongings anymore. Everything — the entire world — was now open to us. We considered learning in Israel or returning to Boston; we were free birds!

My mother-in-law phoned to let us know that Daniel's uncle, who lived in Houston, was out of town and that we could stay in his house. We arrived there and started to decompress. Daniel took the boys swimming in his uncle's private pool. Meanwhile, the phone calls started rolling in. Everyone called: the OU, Agudath Israel, you name it! It was so strange. They were all so concerned for our welfare, yet we were having a good time at the pool, trying our utmost to be normal.

Everyone vied for the privilege of helping us. Jewish communities throughout the country — Denver, Boston, Scranton — offered free housing and tuition for a long as we needed it. "Just come," they said. "We'll take care of you."

One night when we were eating out at one of Houston's kosher restaurants, one of the other patrons asked us where we were from. We told him that we had come from New Orleans. When we went to pay our bill, we discovered that he had covered it for us!

On Shabbos, we stayed in the *frum* area of town and *davened* in the United Orthodox Synagogue. At the end of the services, there was an announcement warmly welcoming us to Houston and mentioning that we had come from New Orleans.

After the services, a man in his fifties came over to us and wished us a *"Gut Shabbos*." He then asked, "You lost a lot in the hurricane?"

"Yes," we answered. "We lost a lot."

He responded, "You lost a lot, but you didn't lose everything. I lost my wife last year, and I lost everything. You still have each other." He was not being mean; he was just reminding us how lucky we really were. Nothing had really happened. We had lost ***things***, but we were still together as a family.

After Shabbos, the rabbi told us that some members of the congregation had invited us to their homes Sunday morning. I remember pulling up in front of the first home we went to and being completely shocked. They were, to put it mildly, very, very far from being poor. The man of the house opened up a closet the size of my living room and told us to take whatever we wanted. It was all very, very expensive stuff. Someone took my kids to the children's room and started piling beautiful clothes into brand-new backpacks, outfitting them from head to toe! Then they gave us money, and offered to settle us in Houston. This repeated itself in every home that we went to! But by that point, we had already decided to return to Boston.

Everyone was wonderful and sweet. Many non-Jews helped us, too. Daniel's mentor and main professor in Harvard asked him to return to Harvard. She arranged for Harvard to pay him a salary until Tulane University figured out if it was reopening. (In the end, though, we didn't take the money; Tulane actually paid its professors even though they were not on campus working.) She offered to set him up with his own office, buy him a computer — basically, put him back on his feet professionally.

So we returned to Boston. On the drive from Houston to Boston, we stopped in Atlanta for gas and tried to pay with our credit card. But because we had already started processing our change of address at the post office (something we did right away, since all letters sent to New Orleans were basically trashed) and we didn't yet know our new postal code, the credit card was not accepted.

We went into the office to pay cash. The woman ahead of us in line had won $200 with a scratch-off lottery ticket and had come to the office to redeem the ticket. She overheard us discussing the credit card mix-up, understood that we were from New Orleans, and handed us her winning ticket. Although we told her that we really didn't need it, she insisted that we take it!

Someone in the Boston *frum* community gave us use of a fully-furnished basement apartment in the *frum* neighborhood — complete with *sefarim* and toys for the children. It was amazing. Our friends there know my tastes and set up the apartment accordingly! We really saw how Katrina brought out the good in people.

Late Friday night, just two weeks after we had moved into the basement apartment, our oldest son ran into our bedroom yelling, "The floor's wet." It was true! The floor really was sopping wet! It had been raining hard for several days in a row, and our apartment was flooding. Even though it was the middle of the night, we banged on our neighbor's door, and *shlepped* most of our belongings up to their house.

We wondered what Hashem wanted from us. *Perek Shirah* compares the Torah to water, so perhaps this was a divine message to put more Torah into our lives? But first, on a practical note, we had to move into a drier flat. One of the *rabbanim* in Boston offered us his attic apartment. We remained there for six months, until Tulane University reopened and we returned to New Orleans.

How had the community changed?

Well, to begin with, our synagogue didn't exist anymore. It had been completely underwater for three weeks and everything was ruined. One of the kosher restaurants had closed for lack of business. Everyone was very depressed. Everything was lost, and most people in the community felt there was no future there.

For six months, we lived in a Chabad *kehillah* near the university. I worked evenings for the community, while my husband taught Political Science at Tulane University and *Yiddishkeit* in the local Chabad house. We also had tons of guests, mainly university students.

At the end of the year, Daniel received a fellowship to return to

Harvard to work on a manuscript for his first academic book. So we uprooted ourselves — again — and returned to Boston, to the same attic apartment that we had lived in before moving to New Orleans.

We returned to Japan in July 2007, and will be leaving in just a few weeks, at the end of July 2008. Daniel spent this year in Japan working on his second book, about how different communities respond to natural disasters.

Why did he choose that topic?

Because of Hurricane Katrina. This book focuses on three natural disasters: Hurricane Katrina, the Indian Ocean tsunami of 2005, and the Kobe earthquake in 1995. He examines how different communities responded to natural disasters, and how that response either accelerated the community's recovery or prevented it from happening.

While Daniel spent the day writing, I was busy cooking — everything in Japan is made from scratch — cleaning and home schooling our three children. And of course, we have loads and loads of guests, of all kinds.

You homeschooled your three children?

Yes I did! Before leaving Boston I spoke with the principal and teachers at of our children's school, Torah Academy. They gave me lots of ideas, books, and supplementary material. Although I do most of the teaching, my husband teaches one morning and one afternoon a week. I like to keep the classes structured, so when I am teaching, I really don't do anything else. I even give my oldest, a first-grader, real tests. He scores close to a hundred each time!

Although I'm happy to be leaving Tokyo, I am also sad. We've influenced a number of people. One of our regular guests recently told my husband, "You're my rabbi." Although he has a long way to go, he has started keeping some mitzvos. Another one of our "regulars" is leaving to yeshivah in Elul. I feel privileged to have lived in Tokyo and to have had the opportunity to help so many *Yidden*.

Where are you headed now?

West Lafayette, Indiana. Although there are close to one thousand Jewish students at the university there, there is only a very small Orthodox Jewish community. We want to make a difference in people's lives, to do *kiruv*.

Every week, I read in the paper how this or that rabbi or *gadol* says that every Jew must do his part for *kiruv*. We have lots of experience, especially with college students, and we enjoy working with people who want to learn about *Yiddishkeit*. And, unlike the average *frum* person, we are able to live outside of a Torah center. We are comfortable homeschooling our children and living in a place where there are few of the amenities that most *frum* people need to survive. We asked a *she'eilah* and our *rabbanim* gave us their blessings.

Where do you see yourself ten years from now?

I don't really know. I would like to live in a normal, *frum* community with normal, *frum* people. But I have a feeling that we will continue traveling. I can't imagine that life will ever be boring!

LIFE IN A WHEELCHAIR — LOOKING UP

"The weaker I became physically, the stronger my *emunah* became. When a person is well, he says, 'Hashem runs the world!' But when a person is, G-d forbid, sick, he *knows* it!"

Mrs. Tova Silverstein

Tova Silverstein was born in Belgium nearly seventy years ago. After the Second World War, her family immigrated to New York, where she was privileged to study in Bais Yaakov of Williamsburg under the legendary Rebbetzin Vichna Kaplan. Tova and Rabbi Shraga Silverstein married in 1958 and moved to Eretz Yisrael in 1970.

I met Tova close to a year ago, when I went to purchase some medicine in a pharmacy located in the same building as a facility for the elderly. In the garden in front of the building, I noticed an acquaintance of mine sitting next to the fish pond and speaking with a woman in a wheelchair.

I walked over to say hello, and was immediately won over by Tova's warm, welcoming smile. The moment Tova looked me directly in the eyes and said, "Well, what brings you to this part of town?" I realized that although the woman sitting across from me was physically incapacitated, her brain was very much alive! Half an hour later, I had to tear myself away from one of the most intellectually stimulating conversations that I'd had in a long time.

Since then, I look forward to Shabbos afternoons. That's when I walk fifteen minutes or so to the nearby Ramat Eshkol neighborhood to visit Tova. But it's never just Tova. There's always a group of other women there who, like myself, enjoy Tova's sharp wit and clear Torah perspective on the world.

Tova is paralyzed from the waist down. Before she became ill, she and a friend owned a hat store in the center of Jerusalem. Tova was a professional designer. She loved working with her hands and gave short mini-courses to women on how to create things in the home. A few years ago, following fairly routine surgery, Tova developed an infection of the spinal cord.

For a full year, I lay in bed, almost completely paralyzed. I was in agony, and the pain was aggravated by even the tiniest movement. Everything appeared hopeless. Even the doctors were pessimistic. They were positive that I'd remain that way forever. But thank G-d, I didn't.

How did you cope? It must have been so difficult? [I feel slightly foolish asking the obvious.]

When a person is in such desperate straits, a lot of silliness falls by the wayside. Being sick really tests one's *emunah*. I had to focus on what's important. The weaker I became physically, the stronger my *emunah* became. When a person is well, he says, "Hashem runs the world!" But when a person is, G-d forbid, sick, he *knows* it!

People waver in their *emunah* when things go wrong. But a Jew's *emunah* is constant, NO MATTER WHAT happens to him! When it's good, Hashem runs the world; and when it appears to be bad, Hashem is also running the world. When I was in severe pain, I *davened* constantly for relief, but although the pain did not go away, I continued to have *emunah*.

We cannot understand everything. If, for example, Einstein would explain his theory of relativity to me, I'm not arrogant enough to think that I'd understand it. So how could I possibly fathom Hashem's ways? *Emunah* is the basis of everything. As Jews, we believe that Hashem rules the world, that there is none besides Him. We say, *"Ein k'Elokeinu*. It is only after we affirm our *emunah*, and say, *"Ein k'Elokeinu,"* that we can ask questions. Only then can we say, *"Mi k'Elokeinu?"* But the basis of everything is *emunah — Ein k'Elokeinu*.

It was Tova's emunah that enabled her to cope with constant, agonizing pain. "Your words are giving me chizuk," I tell her. "They're special."

Emes is always special.

A person brings himself with him into his sick bed; into his old age. That's why it's so important to develop yourself, to grow, to work on yourself.

When a person is ill, G-d forbid, or facing any other major test, it's as if he's being put under a microscope that magnifies whatever is already there. But, of course, it cannot show something that does not exist. The way we react to a *nisayon* defines who we are.

Hashem tests us with both "good" and "bad" things. Having great wealth is also a type of *nisayon*; a person who has cultivated the *middos* of generosity and empathy will use his wealth properly, while a person who is cruel and selfish will hoard it and become a miser.

I've been sick for two years. I was completely paralyzed for close to twelve months, totally unable to move. Today, I can move my upper body. I am not in pain. I can knit, read, do things, talk, think. I have so much to be grateful for.

I can't help but smile. Those words are so typically Tova: "I have so much to be grateful for." I ask Tova how she survived that first year of constant pain and almost total paralysis.

How did I cope? First of all, I learned not to move, because even the tiniest movement caused me agony. And, of course, I *davened* for the strength to survive the pain. People were marvelous. I had nonstop visitors. They helped the time go by. Many of the people spoke about their own problems. I learned that many people with two healthy legs are miserable — much less happy than I was!

Before I got sick, I had always appreciated such things as my good health, my family, etc. After becoming sick, I was doubly appreciative. We take so many things for granted. We have to remind ourselves to stop and say thank-you for what we had, as well as what we have. I had over sixty years of good health. How many people do you know who can claim such a blessing? Many of my contemporaries are no longer alive, so why shouldn't I be grateful?

> *But didn't you ever want to give up? Didn't you ever feel that you couldn't take the pain any longer? I can't imagine lying immobile, in constant pain, for an entire year.*

When things got really rough, I asked several people if *ye'ush* is considered *kefirah*. I was told that it is not. But although *ye'ush* is not *kefirah*, I didn't want to get to that stage. Our lives are limited, and our understanding is also limited. Hashem gives us life, and Hashem can take that life away from us. Our lives are never really "ours." Once we understand that, we realize that we can't ask, "How can Hashem take it away from me?" It was never mine to begin with. It's His, and it has always been His. I didn't create myself; He did. That's the basis of *emunah*.

Very often I found myself giving *chizuk* to the people who came to visit me. They were broken; they were questioning — and I was giving the answers! I was lying in bed, completely immobile, in tremendous pain, and being *mechazek* my visitors! No one wants to be sick, but if you've been fortunate enough to have a strong Jewish background, you go to that background for comfort when the going gets rough. Words that until then had been just words, suddenly became real. My *emunah* prevented me from giving in to despair.

Of course, I mourned my loss. For example, I loved walking through the streets of Jerusalem and exploring the courtyards behind the *shuk*. I lost that, and I'm sad that I don't have it anymore. But at the same time, I am grateful that I once had it — and, of course, I will always have the memories.

All men fear death, but for too many people the fear of death prevents them from living! Yes, I still get frustrated with my physical limitations, but I avoid anything that will cause me to become depressed. Maybe that's denial, but focusing on that which I *can* do rather than what I cannot do enables me to live.

When tragedy strikes, we must give ourselves permission to mourn our losses, but then we must get on with life. I went through all the stages — the anger, the mourning — but at one point I realized, "Enough! I must continue. I must live!" A person needs to give himself permission to cry, to feel the pain, but he should not get stuck in that pain; that's depression. A person must move on, go forward, and continue moving toward life.

Tova is presently writing a book about the past three years in her life, entitled "... and I Am Thankful." She allowed me to read the first two sentences: "My name is Tova. I almost died."

Why do I mention my name in the first sentence of the book? I once read a fascinating autobiography of a woman, but there was something that bothered me about the book. It took a while until I realized what it was. The woman never used her own name! She was either a mother or a grandmother or a businesswoman, or whatever — but she was never herself. Being an *ezer k'negdo* doesn't mean that one's essence vanishes! Our foremothers were very real people. They had names and strong personalities. They didn't disappear once they were married.

What are your goals for the future?

I want to live as long as Hashem lets me, and be a reasonably happy person. I have a lot to be thankful for. Period! I'm almost seventy, I have a husband; I have children, grandchildren, and great-grandchildren. What more could I ask for? A castle in Spain? I was given what every human being *davens* for, and I am aware that I was given it. Too many people are brain dead — they might be breathing, but they are not using their mental capacities. They are not thinking! We must be aware of all the kindnesses that Hashem does for us. Next time you say a *berachah*, listen to what you are saying!

Baruch Hashem, now I am able to do things with my hands. I make baby hats and baby blankets. I enjoy designing them. The desire to do something is also a gift.

Since I've moved here, to this facility, I've met so many wonderful people, forged so many new friendships. Hashem has been very good to me.

As I left, I was overwhelmed by a sense of gratitude. Among the many things I have to be grateful for, I am extremely thankful to have been introduced to a person who has so fully integrated emunah and bitachon into her life.

IT WON'T HOLD ME BACK

"'Your children deserve to grow up in a real home; a home where their mother does all the things she did when she was married.' At that moment, I realized that my children and I were a family, and that together we could, and would, create a warm and loving home."

Chavie (a pseudonym)

I've known Chavie for years. We sat together on miniature chairs at our children's preschool parties. We bumped into each other at the local pediatrician. Every once in a while, we enjoyed a bus ride together. She always seemed so — well — typical would probably be the best way to describe her. Then I heard her story.

Baruch Hashem, today I am very happily married — we're about to celebrate our twenty-sixth wedding anniversary. But thirty years ago, I wasn't. I was a young divorcee trying to raise three small children alone. It wasn't easy.

Tell us how you got from there to here.

I married in the early seventies. My husband learned in *kollel*. I was a Bais Yaakov graduate. On paper it sounds so run-of-the-mill, yet we were far from the mainstream. We came from unusual backgrounds. We were both *baalei teshuvah* who had somehow made it in the system, but never really fit in. We had absolutely no idea how to go about creating a warm, Yiddishe home.

My husband was never satisfied with himself or with life in general. Wherever we lived or whatever he was doing, he always felt that if he would only be somewhere else, or doing something else, he'd find that illusory pot of gold at the end of the rainbow. But, of course, it was always just out of reach. So we were constantly moving. In the five years of our marriage, we lived in fourteen different houses in five different cities and two continents. I dreamed of the day I would stay in an apartment long enough to sew curtains!

Our *Yiddishkeit*, too, was constantly fluctuating. My husband was trying the various hats on for size, but nothing seemed to fit. I tried to be a good wife and go along with the constant change; after all, I didn't want to rock the boat. But at the same time I was flooded with guilt. This was not where my Bais Yaakov education was supposed to be taking me! I found myself sucked into a lifestyle that went against my beliefs. Television became a permanent addition to our living room. It wasn't long before *Sesame Street* and *Leave It to Beaver* were part of our daily schedule.

Although my life was in constant upheaval, I felt secure in my marriage. Money was more than just tight, and we were always looking to new horizons, but I thought of our family unit as an anchor of stability. This was my husband; these were my children, and even if we didn't always see eye to eye, we loved each other and were building a family together. At least that's what I thought.

Then, one Shabbos, as I was setting the table for the *seudah*, my husband walked in the door and announced, "I can't continue living a lie. I'm getting in the car and driving to work." The homemade *challos* were warming on the Shabbos urn, and the house smelled — well, the best description would be "*Shabbosdik*" — and my world as I knew it had just crumbled. I can't say that I was completely shocked. For several weeks I had been having a recurrent nightmare in which my husband did exactly what he did that Shabbos afternoon. I would wake up furious, and then be upset at myself for letting a silly dream have such an impact my emotions. So I'd put on a smile and pretend that everything in my life was just hunky-dory.

But I wasn't the only one pretending. "Don't think this is a spontaneous decision," he continued. "I haven't been keeping kosher for the last month or so." It suddenly dawned on me that my nightmares had been a reflection of something real, something that I couldn't put my finger on but that I had sensed with my womanly intuition. I felt soiled and taken advantage of. Aren't marriages supposed to be based on mutual trust and honesty?

What a horrifying scenario. What did you do?

I begged my husband, "Please, have *rachmanus* on the children. Let me take them to a neighbor. I don't want them to see their father be *mechalal Shabbos*." I grabbed my three precious little ones and ran out of the house. The next time my children saw their father was twenty-five years later, when they were married and had children of their own.

My friends were not as surprised as I was. They had noticed things and chose to remain silent. They didn't want to be accused of trying to destroy a family.

That Shabbos passed in a blur of tears and anger. Somehow, I returned home, made *Kiddush* and ate the Shabbos *seudah*. Instead of *zemiros*, we sang children's songs from the Mitzvah Tree album.

I was living in a small town in the Midwest, and there was a *gadol* visiting from New York. On *Motza'ei Shabbos*, the *gadol* instructed me that if and when my husband called, I was to ask him if he would be willing to give me a *get*. That evening, when he phoned, I asked the crucial question. His answer: "I don't believe in those things anymore. I don't want to be a hypocrite."

I have the uncanny ability to remain calm, cool and collected in the most excruciating situations; it's the little things, like milk spilling into the vegetable bin, that break me. I realized that I'd have to play a game, and began showering my husband with compliments. "You're such a devoted father. You always put the children's needs first. I can really understand where you're coming from, but I'm not there and I don't want to go there. Give me a kosher Jewish *get* so that I'll have the *menuchas hanefesh* I need to raise the children properly." I touched something deep within him — his love for his children — and he promised to cooperate.

How long did it take for you to actually receive the get?

I phoned the rav with the good news (isn't it amazing how our definition of "good" can change so drastically?). Half an hour later, he called to tell me that an *av beis din* would be coming from New York on Monday morning to convene a *beis din*. "We were in contact with Rav Moshe Feinstein," he explained. "He said to make sure that you get your divorce immediately, before your husband has a chance to change his mind. And then we'll whisk you out of here so that the children won't have to deal with a non-religious father."

I was flabbergasted. Everything was happening so quickly. But I felt calm. Rav Moshe was involved. I was in good hands.

The Rav instructed me to contact my husband and ask him to please come to the shul on Monday morning to give me the divorce. He added, "*Daven* that he will not go back on his promise." *Baruch Hashem*, he didn't. (Note: Although a *get* is usually given only after a civil divorce has been finalized, in this case the *rabbanim* were worried that my husband would disappear and I'd be left an *agunah*. Therefore, the *get* was given months before the civil divorce was finalized.)

Monday morning, I walked into the shul as a married woman and left as a divorcee. I couldn't believe how dramatically my life had changed. Yes, there had been signs, and yes, there had been problems, but I had always assumed that we would manage to get over those humps and continue building our family together.

My memory of the following few days are a fog of contrasting emotions. I careened between relief that I was not an *agunah* and grief that my dream of a loving, happy marriage had burst.

What carried you through that difficult time?

The *rav* kept telling me that I was lucky to have been able to get out of the marriage so quickly. On an intellectual level I understood, but emotionally, I was a wreck.

Tuesday evening, a member of the community showed up at my front door with a two huge bags of groceries. I was surprised. But I was absolutely flabbergasted when, crammed in among the chicken, dairy, canned goods, and pasta were several bags of flour and yeast. "Why in the world would I want to bake now?" I asked the woman who had brought the order.

"You bake challah every week," she countered. "Why should you stop now? Your children deserve to grow up in a real home; a home where their mother does all the things she did when she was married."

At that moment, I realized that my children and I were a family, and that together we could, and would, create a warm and loving home.

Wednesday afternoon I returned home from spending the afternoon with the children at the playground, and found a note taped to the front door. "Call the Rav immediately," it read.

The Rav informed me that I would be leaving to Israel the following morning.

"But the baby doesn't have an American passport," I pointed out. "She won't be able to leave the country without one."

"Don't worry," he responded. "You'll receive the passport in New York. Oh, and by the way, someone will be coming to pick you up in a few minutes to drive you to the photographer to take the baby's passport photos." I felt overwhelmed. How could I have managed without this wonderful community's support?

I spent that evening packing my belongings and phoning members of the community to say goodbye. I phoned a friend in Israel and explained the situation. "Just come," she said. "People here will help you."

All I remember from the flight to Newark was that my six-month-old baby screamed much of the time, my two-year-old kept on complaining that his stomach hurt, and my "big" almost-four-year-old boy talked incessantly.

We arrived in Newark at three o'clock Thursday afternoon. My flight to Israel was leaving at nine o'clock the same evening. I'd be arriving in Israel early Friday morning.

Two young men were waiting for us at the terminal. "We're the rabbi's sons," they told me. "There's a car waiting outside. We'll have to hurry if we want to make it to the passport office before it closes at five." We had less than two hours to get from Newark to Manhattan.

"But what about my suitcases?" I asked.

"There's no time to take them. We'll pick them up when we come back tonight to put you on the flight to Israel."

I didn't even try to protest.

We raced out of the terminal to a waiting car. Somehow, we managed to get to Manhattan by a quarter to five. The plan was for me to leave my two older children in the car with the driver and one of the Rav's sons, while the other son accompanied me and the baby to the passport office. But just as I was about to jump out of the car, my two-year-old, looking slightly gray, moaned, "Ima, Ima! I ..." and then proceeded to throw up all over my skirt.

After rushing to the ladies' rest room, where I used paper towels and water to clean myself as best I could, we skidded into the passport office with a few minutes to spare. The passport was ready. They just had to attach the baby's picture and wait for me to fill out the forms. The rav's son later explained to me that a well-known *askan* had worked hard to expedite the process.

We had lived in Israel for the first four years of our marriage. The previous year, my husband had decided that he would never be happy living there, so we moved to a small town on the East Coast, and then a few months later to a different small town in the Midwest. Imagine my astonishment when, upon boarding the plane, the two men sitting in the seats ahead of me were rabbis at my husband's yeshivah in Israel, who knew both of us well. After a short explanation, they grasped the situation and immediately offered to assist me with the children. They held my six-month-old throughout the flight, freeing my arms so that I could take care of the other two children.

The two men sat and learned throughout the flight. (Oh, how long since I'd heard the sweet sound of *limud* Torah ...!) When it was time to show the movie, the stewardess requested that they turn off their light so as not to disturb the other passengers. At that exact moment, we heard a pop. It was the projector light. Now that it was impossible to show the movie, the men were able to continue learning!

I found myself sobbing as the plane touched down in Israel. I was home! Home! I had no place to live and perhaps twenty dollars in my pocket, but I had my family and I knew that together we would create something beautiful.

Amazing. What happened next? What was your first step in starting your new life?

A close friend was waiting at the airport to greet me. "The *mashgiach's* family is expecting you to stay with them until you get settled," she said.

I was jet-lagged, exhausted, and smelled of vomit, yet I felt like dancing. I was free. No more nightmares. I had changed trains in mid-journey and had chosen life.

At the same time, I was petrified.

When my taxi pulled up in front of the *mashgiach's* home, the entire family rushed out to greet me. The *mashgiach's* wife gave me a big hug and then said something that I'll never forget. "Chavie, use this time to grow. Being divorced is a life circumstance — a challenge. It doesn't define you as a person. Many renowned people have been divorced. I'm sure that they never wanted to be there. No ones does. Yet, when they found themselves in that difficult situation, they didn't allow it to hold them back. Don't allow it to hold *you* back!"

Thanks to her, I never defined myself as a divorcee. Instead, I was a *frum, ehrlicher* woman, creating a strong, healthy family despite the hardships of being single. Those years molded me and gave me the emotional strength that I eventually needed to remarry and build a new family.

THE ISRAELI EXPERIENCE

"Today, the girls spend their breaks gabbing on their cell phones with girls from other schools, or speaking with their parents in America — believe it or not, they talk to their parents at least once a day — and then come crying to me that they haven't succeeded in making friends at school! If only they would get off the phone and start living their lives!"

Aviva Haymann

When I mentioned to Rabbi Michoel Green of Bnot Torah that I'd like an inside look at American seminaries in Israel, he suggested that I interview Mrs. Aviva Haymann, one of the school's three mechanchot. From the few brief conversations we had before we met, I could tell that this was going to be one interview I would enjoy. Aviva is a very energetic, positive person, with clear-cut ideas and a keen understanding of today's young people. It was a pleasure to meet her, and I feel privileged to share her story with my readers.

I was born in 1973 and grew up in San Jose, California, in what is today known as Silicon Valley because of the large number of high-tech companies there. My parents are *baalei teshuvah*. They became *frum* after getting involved with the Hillel House at the University of Washington in Seattle. They are what are commonly known as "modern Orthodox." But in a community such as San Jose, far from the centers of mainstream Orthodoxy, it took real commitment for my family to keep what they did. On Yom Kippur night, for example, at least a dozen people would camp out in sleeping bags in my parents' living room so that they wouldn't have to drive to shul on the holiest day of the year. Kosher food was not readily available, so my Mom made everything from scratch.

My parents never had the opportunity to attend a yeshivah or seminary. But they had tremendous *nachas* when any of us children surpassed them in our knowledge or level of observance. They did not feel threatened by it in any way.

There was no Jewish high school in San Jose. When I was eleven years old, we moved to Long Island, New York so that I wouldn't have to leave home for high school. When we landed in New York, my father took us straight from the airport to a kosher ice-cream parlor. I still remember my sense of wonder at the variety of ice creams available — and what was even more amazing, they were all kosher!"

In Long Island, I attended HANC [acronym for Hebrew Academy of Nassau Country], a modern, co-ed day school. At the time it didn't even dawn on me that learning together with boys was problematic. I was the *frummest* kid in the class. At age thirteen I stopped wearing pants. And then, once I was wearing dresses all the time, I realized that it would be ridiculous for me to swim in a mixed swimming pool.

Just to give you an idea of how little I understood, when I was in twelfth grade I had an interview for one of the American seminaries in Israel. The rabbis interviewing me said, "I understand that you go to a co-ed school." I answered, "Yes," and thought to myself, *So what?* Then he said, "If you were to see one of the boys from school on the street, would you speak to him?" I answered, "Sure." After all, wouldn't it be rude not to? I couldn't understand what he was trying to get at. The rabbi continued, "But if he were to invite you out to pizza, would you go?" I never, ever went out for pizza — it just wasn't me, so I answered, "I guess not." I thought the whole conversation was completely ludicrous. When I told one of the *rebbeim* in school about it, he laughed and said, "Aviva, just go to Israel. Then you'll understand."

I went to Israel just a few days after my seventeenth birthday to attend Bnot Torah, commonly known as Sharfman's. It was 1990, the year of the Gulf War.

> *That was a very intense year. What was it like being in Israel during the War?*

About half the girls went home, including me. The truth is that I really didn't panic; all the *Gedolim* said not to worry, that nothing would happen. But my mother was nervous, so I returned to the States for her sake. I came back to Israel a few weeks later, when it was obvious to everyone that Hashem Himself was guarding us from harm. But the Scuds were still falling.

The return trip to Israel was quite an adventure. On the tarmac, before boarding the El Al plane that would take me from Rome to Eretz Yisrael, I had to remove every single item from my suitcase and declare that it was mine. In Eretz Yisrael, we were handed gas masks as we alighted from the plane!

That year in Bnot Torah completely changed my life. By the end of that first year, I realized that I really didn't know anything — which is why I returned the following year to attend the second-year program. After finishing that year, I remained in Israel as a *madrichah* while attending Touro College in Jerusalem. I eventually earned my BS in mathematics.

Being a *madrichah* was a full-time job. In the morning, I tutored girls. In the evening, I had to be in the dorm for them. Whenever we had an in-Shabbos, the *madrichot* prepared all the food. In those days, every seven girls had their own apartment with a fully- stocked kitchen, which they learned how to use. The girls were responsible for preparing all their own meals. There were even basic cooking classes and a class on how to make challah. Today, however, things are different. In the secular world, the universities are vying for students; one university even offers a Jacuzzi in every dorm room. This has impacted on our world as well: Religious girls expect more *gashmiyus*. They want accomplishment without effort.

Before I came to Israel, I thought the entire country was a desert, with camels roaming freely on the streets. Although Israel was certainly not a desert, it was much simpler than it is today. We were totally into the experience of being here, whereas today the girls still have one foot in America. They are constantly on the cell phone talking to their parents or to their friends in other schools. My father would call once a month, at a preset time. The rest of the time we kept in contact through letters. Because we were on our own, we learned to be independent. Since we couldn't talk easily (no phones!) to our friends in other seminaries, we learned to become close with the girls in our school.

Today, the girls spend their breaks gabbing on their cell phones with girls from other schools, or speaking with their parents in America — believe it or not, they talk to their parents at least once a day — and then come crying to me that they haven't succeeded in making friends at school! If only they would get off the phone and start living their lives

How did you meet your husband?

Through a *shadchan*. I had been a *madrichah* at Sharfman's for six years, and of course I was very interested in getting married. Someone told me about a *shadchan* who makes *shidduchim* for the boys in the Mir. My interview with him lasted all of five minutes. He asked me if I want to live in Eretz Yisrael, and I answered yes. He asked how old I was, and I told him I was twenty-five. Finally, he asked if I am looking to marry someone who wanted to remain in learning, which I did. He wished me *hatzlachah*, and that was that. I viewed that interview as a real waste of time!

A week later, the *shadchan* phoned to tell me that he had just discovered that the fellow sitting behind him in the Mir, whom he had assumed was married, was not, and suggested that I meet him. I was positive that the suggestion was completely out of the ball park. After all, the *shadchan* barely knew me. But, *baruch Hashem,* it wasn't ....

Daniel and I were married in Eretz Yisrael. Once I was married I could no longer be a *madrichah*, so I became a *mechanechet*. I've been involved with Sharfman's for the last eighteen years — first as a student, then a *madrichah*, and now as a *mechanechet*. My husband continued learning in the Mir.

Which girls go to Bnot Torah?

We're a *frum* school that caters to modern girls as well as to Bais Yaakov girls who have had a difficult time with the system. We're dealing with precious Jewish *neshamos*. It's a real balancing act to provide structure and discipline without breaking the girls. On a humorous note, Rabbi Sharfman often reminds the staff that we must give the girls a bit of rope — but not enough for them to hang themselves. The entire staff spends hours relating to the girls on a one-to-one basis. That means really listening to what they say, so that we can properly address their needs. When I speak with the girls, I spend most of my time listening. It's only after I have heard them out fully that I give my input — usually in a few short minutes, because I know that only after really listening to what they have to say and showing the girls that I really care, will they be willing to hear what I have to say.

What are some of the major issues that the school has to deal with?

Girls today struggle with things that my generation never had to deal with, especially the influence of the media. Girls are brainwashed that they must be thin — or else. They are petrified of looking fat. Today's lack of *penimiyus* and emphasis on the external is the complete antithesis of *tzenius*!

Tzenius is a tough issue. Once we realize where the girls are coming from, it's easier to focus on the positive. I tell the other teachers, "While you look at the girl and see that her skirt is short and too tight, the girl views herself as a *tzadekes* for wearing a skirt at all!" These girls really do not understand that they are not dressing properly.

Let's say, for example, that a girl comes to class wearing a short skirt. If I scold her, she won't listen to me. Instead, I smile and quietly tell her to go back to the dorm to change her skirt. Usually she'll listen. Rebbetzin Spetner, an expert educator, once told us that the word "*tzenius*" should only be used in a positive context. Instead of criticizing a girl's skirt ("That's not *tzenius*") if she is improperly dressed, when she *is* dressed properly, we should say something to the effect of, "That dress is so beautiful — so *tzeniusdik*."

As with everything, the girls are much more willing to accept what we tell them about *tzenius* if they feel that we are saying it because we truly care for them — which we do. Because we really care about the girls, we help them find practical solutions to problems with *tzenius*, and then assist them in implementing them. I've even been asked by girls who want my feedback to go clothes shopping with them.

What is the key to getting the girls to want to change?

Really, truly caring for them. The girls should never feel that we're trying to missionize them, that we're trying to a score a hit. It's only when they know that we genuinely care about their welfare and want them to live happier, more fulfilled lives that they become more open to listening to what we have to say.

"A few years ago, one of our students — a girl from a *frum* background — insisted during her entire first year at Bnot Torah on wearing a black necklace with a silver skull and crossbones. I cannot tell you how many faculty members told Rabbi Sharfman how pained they were that he was allowing her to continue wearing such a thing. Rabbi Sharfman's answer was, "The necklace is not the problem. Reach the girl, and the necklace will disappear." The girl spent that entire year trying to define herself. She was really struggling and looking for *emes*. When she returned the following year for the second-year program, she was without the necklace. Today she's married to a *talmid chacham* and building a true Torah home.

But every girl is a story. Every girl who comes to seminary in Israel changes and grows. It's a year that leaves its stamp on the girls for generations — because, in many ways, it defines the type of home that they will eventually build.

JEWISH ROYALTY

"When we first came to Eretz Yisrael, my husband asked someone if it's possible to purchase an apartment for five thousand dollars. The man answered, 'Yes. On Har Hamenuchos' (Jerusalem's main cemetery). So that is exactly what we did. Although we never had much materially, we always had what we needed. I have no doubt that my husband has a beautiful apartment in *Olam HaEmes*."

Rebbetzin Poultorak

I first met Rebbetzin Poultorak about ten years ago, when she and her husband, the former rav and dayan of Lyon, moved to Ramot Polin. I often ran into her at the local grocery store or while waiting at the bus stop. Filled with energy and love of life, I assumed she was, at the most, in her late fifties — until she made a remark about something that had occurred, "just after the war."

I was born in July 1935, in Mulhouse, a city in Eastern France, not far from the Swiss and German borders. I was five years old when the Second World War broke out, and the oldest of three children (eventually, we were five). When the Germans invaded France, my father was serving in the French Army. My mother grabbed her three children and, together with my maternal grandparents, joined the thousands of others fleeing the Nazis. While we were on the run, my mother gave birth to her fourth child.

We found refuge in Montfaucon, a small village in the middle of unoccupied France, together with thirty other Jewish families. Now that there were four children in our family, my father was discharged from the army and allowed to rejoin us.

The French peasants were very nice to us. We were "their Jews" and they protected us. They never told the French officials about the Jewish families who were living in their village.

> *After conquering France, the Nazis divided the country into two zones, an "Occupied" zone and a "Free" zone. The German Wehrmacht occupied the northern, "Occupied" zone. The southern, "Free" zone was under the control of the Vichy regime — a puppet government. The Vichy regime collaborated with the Germans in rounding up Jews and sending them to Eastern Europe, where the majority were murdered in the concentration camps.*

We were privileged to have brought a *sefer Torah* with us to Montfaucon. In some *kehillos* in Eastern France, it was the custom that the person who purchased *Chasan Torah* had the privilege of keeping one of the shul's Torah scrolls in his house until the following Simchas Torah. My grandfather was *Chasan Torah* on the Simchas Torah prior to the invasion of France. Therefore, he had a *Sefer Torah* in his house. Before leaving the city, he asked the shul's *Rav* what he should do with the *Sefer Torah*. The *Rav* instructed him to take it with him when he fled the Germans, and then to return it to the community when the war was over. My grandfather was eventually able to fulfill both of the *Rav's* instructions.

I have wonderful memories of our life in Montfaucon. My father worked as a traveling salesman, selling fabric to the farmers in the surrounding villages. My mother stayed at home and took care of the family. Although food was rationed, we had plenty to eat: lots of milk, butter, and eggs. Before Pesach my parents would make the dangerous trip to Lyon, which was in occupied France, to purchase meat and matzos for the holiday.

One year, my mother traveled by train with a live goose to bring it to Lyon to be slaughtered. The train was crowded with German soldiers. The goose made such a racket that my mother was petrified she would end up being the one *shechted*, rather than the goose.

We attended the village school, together with the other children in the village. I don't remember anyone ever making fun of us or making anti-Semitic comments. Sometimes we'd go out into the fields to help the farmers tend their cows. It was an idyllic existence, an island of safety in the surrounding inferno.

I'm sure my parents were aware of what was going on around us. Five of my uncles were deported to Auschwitz; two survived and three were killed. But we, as children, never felt threatened. Our home was a happy home; there was no sadness, just normalcy.

Actually, there were several other villages that also protected Jewish families. One of the most famous was a village not far from Montfaucon called Chambon-sur-Lignon.

> *The 5000 residents of Chambon-sur-Lignon risked their lives to save 5000 Jews, mainly children. They hid the children in homes, on farms, and in public institutions, and when the Nazis came searching for Jews, they hid them in the countryside. They also obtained forged ID and ration cards for the Jews hiding in their village, and helped many of them cross the border into Switzerland. Some of the residents were arrested by the Gestapo for their role in saving Jews, and at least one was murdered. In 1989, French producer Pierre Sauvage produced an award-winning documentary film, entitled* Weapons of the Spirit, *about the Jews of Chambon. Sauvage was born in Chambon. At the age of eighteen, he learned that he was Jewish and that during the Holocaust his parents had found refuge in Chambon.*

After the War was over we moved to Lyon, where many survivors had come together to create a Jewish community. Although we attended public school, we also attended Talmud Torah twice a week, as well as Sunday school and Shabbos afternoon get-togethers. Since we didn't attend school on Shabbos, every *Motza'ei Shabbos* my sister and I would go to our schoolmates' homes to copy class notes and get our homework assignments. We felt completely accepted and never sensed any anti-Semitism.

But although the community was wonderful, my father was unable to make a living there. When I was sixteen, he was offered a job in Colmar, a city in Eastern France not far from Mulhouse, the city where we'd lived before the war. I was extremely upset about the move. I had many good friends in Lyon and didn't want to start my life all over again. So I told my parents that instead of going to Colmar with them, I would be attending the seminary in Gateshead, England. My parents weren't enthusiastic, but they accepted my decision.

When I first came to Gateshead in 1951, the seminary was only six years old. In those days, the town was a coal center, and physically, it was horrible. There were coal mines all around the city and the pollution was terrible. Everything was sooty and black. White clothes quickly became grey. If you touched anything, your fingers would turn black from dust.

But I loved it. No, I didn't love the city — I loved the school. The *ruach*, the friends, it was all so special! In those days, the whole concept of seminary, of girls learning Torah, was a novel, almost revolutionary one. There were only six girls in our class, and thirty girls in the entire seminary. We felt that we were doing something new and exciting.

There was no dorm, so we roomed with families. There were anywhere from two to eight girls to a room. An older, unmarried woman, Miss Agulnik, cooked our meals. Meals were simple; Britain was still reeling from the war and food was at a premium. In the winter, we froze. There were small heaters with coin slots; one coin would provide a half-hour of heat. But none of us had much money to operate the heaters. My husband, *ztz'l*, learned in Gateshead Yeshivah. He remembered breaking the ice in the *negel vasser* cup to be able to wash in the morning!

But although the physical conditions were far from luxurious, the learning was tremendous. We had incredible teachers: Mr. Cohn, Rabbi Mordechai Miller, Rabbi Dov Sternbuch, and, for a short while, Rabbi Dessler. Rabbi Moshe Schwab taught us *mussar*. I had never studied Torah before. A whole new world opened up for me.

After graduating from Gateshead Seminary, I spent a year in Paris teaching Jewish children. In the morning I taught in a Jewish day school, and in the afternoons I taught small boys in an after-school Talmud Torah. Life in Paris was extremely expensive, so even with the two jobs I was just barely managing to make ends meet — and I really didn't have too many expenses, as I was living with my aunt and uncle! But teachers never earn a lot of money.

I met my husband while living in Paris. A relative of his made the *shidduch*. He was learning in Gateshead Yeshivah from 1949-1955, and it was during this period that we married. He was exactly what I was looking for: a *ben* Torah with good *middos* and lots of ambition.

My husband, Rav Yaakov Poultorak, was born in France in 1930. His father was from Poland and his mother from Germany. He spent a portion of the war in Paris, together with his parents, and part of the time hidden by peasants in a small village in Brittany.

My husband was fifteen years old when the war ended. He left the village and moved back to Paris to be with his family. He became involved in a Jewish youth group. Like the other young people in his group, he volunteered at a shelter that housed many of the indigent survivors streaming into Paris. He remembered that one of the things he did was to spray the survivors with insecticide, to rid them of lice.

My husband attended a technical college, where he majored in chemistry. He was brilliant, and everyone predicted that he would become a very successful scientist. But at age nineteen he left everything to learn Torah in the Gateshead Yeshivah. He was one of the first French boys to learn there.

My husband's education in chemistry eventually came in handy. While still a *bachur* in Gateshead, he opened the first *shaatnez* laboratory in England. After we were married, this became one of our main sources of income. Later, when he was a *Rav* in Lyon, he applied his knowledge of chemistry to *kashrus* supervision. He eventually became a world-renowned expert in the field of *kashrus*.

We became engaged in 1954. My husband traveled from Gateshead to Paris to meet me, and then remained in Paris to visit with his parents. But he was so bored that he asked a religious doctor to teach him how to become a *mohel*. Even then, he was preparing himself for his future role as *Rav* and leader of a *kehillah*. In that role, he would eventually circumcise many babies — as well as children and adults!

We were married in 1955. Our wedding was in Mulhouse, the city where I was born. It was a very simple wedding. I borrowed a dress from a friend. Our wedding *seudah* was held in someone's living room. There were about forty-five guests. *Sheva berachos* were family affairs. Everything was simple — and simply perfect!

As newlyweds, we moved to Gateshead, where my husband learned full-time in yeshivah. He spent his entire day immersed in his learning, preparing himself to become the *gadol* that he eventually became. In addition, he worked in the *shaatnez* laboratory a few hours a week. I worked as a mother's helper, assisting mothers who had recently given birth. I cleaned house, bathed the older children, and did the laundry.

We lived on the bottom floor of a three-story house. Another couple lived on the second floor, and an older girl lived in the attic. The bathroom and kitchen were shared by all three tenants. We all got along very well.

One year later, in 1956, my husband received his rabbinical ordination from Rabbi Lopian and Rabbi Gurwicz. Soon after that, Rabbi Waltner, a Hungarian *Rav* learning in the Gateshead *kollel*, was asked to start a yeshivah in Tangiers, Morocco. He took a few young couples with him, including my husband and me. My husband was offered the position of principal of the Jewish elementary school there. He was twenty-six at the time.

There's an interesting story about how the yeshivah started. The previous year, one of the members of the Tangiers community asked Rabbi Waltner, "If I construct a building for a yeshivah, will you come to Tangiers to be the Rosh Yeshivah?" Rabbi Waltner thought the man was just kidding around, and laughingly answered, "Yes, of course." Exactly one year later, he received a telegram informing him that the construction was complete and the community was waiting for him to open the yeshivah!

I loved Tangiers! It was such a beautiful community; such a lovely place. It was during our first year there that we became a family. When the baby was old enough to stay with a babysitter, I taught in my husband's school.

But after just one-and-a-half years, my husband was drafted into the French army. This was during the Algerian War. Thank G-d, he was not sent to the front. He was stationed in Strasbourg — which has a large Jewish community — for eighteen months. He was even able to arrange an evening *chavrusa*. While he was in the army, I stayed with my parents in Colmar. *Baruch Hashem*, my husband was able to join us every Shabbos.

My husband completed his military service in 1959. The Tangiers' Jewish community asked him to return there to open a yeshivah high school. He accepted, on the condition that *limudei kodesh* be taught by *avreichim* from the *kollel*. We lived in Tangiers for five years, until 1964.

Tangier's Jewish community was very special. But one thing that really stands out in my mind was the unity that existed among the different Jewish *kehillos* that lived there. Tangiers was an international city. Many different types of Jews lived there: Hungarian refugees, French Ashkenazim, Sefardim, and Moroccan Jews. Everyone felt an integral part of the community.

All the yeshivah families were, like my husband and me, young. We were all there without our parents and extended family to help us, so we became like one big *mishpachah*. Everyone helped everyone else. There was a wonderful sense of excitement; we were creating something new. We were building a *makom Torah* where none had existed before.

But all that came to a close in 1964, when the community disintegrated. Everyone left. We returned to France, where my husband joined the Strasbourg *Kollel*.

We remained in Strasbourg for four years. During this time, my husband learned practical rabbinics from Rabbi Horowitz, who later became a *dayan* in the *beis din* of the *Eidah HaChareidis* in Jerusalem.

In 1969, my husband accepted the position of *Rav* of the Ashkenazi *kehillah* in Nice. We remained there for three years, until 1972, when he was asked to be *Rav* of the Ashkenazi *kehillah* of Lyon and principal of the Jewish girls' high school there.

In Lyon, my husband was very busy teaching, issuing halachic rulings, and leading the community. When we first moved there, we had eight small children. By the time we left we had ten, so I was very busy raising my family. In addition, I taught in both the girls' high school and the Talmud Torah. I also taught *kallahs* and was in charge of the *mikveh*. But I had lots of help. My first four children were girls, which made life much easier!

Rebbetzin Poultorak really does not like speaking about herself. She's thrilled to talk about her late husband's accomplishments and the wonderful communities they lived in, but she shrugs off her own achievements, explaining, "We just did what we had to do." The Poultorak household was an extremely busy one, with many guests, including numerous baalei teshuvah and potential gerim. The house was teeming with people coming to ask shailos, to ask the rav or rebbetzin for advice, or just to experience the warmth of a true Yiddishe home. Amidst all this activity, Rebbetzin Poultorak calmly took care of her family, ran her household, and worked with the community. She was the backbone, the pillar of strength and stability that allowed her husband to accomplish all that he did.

We had a lot of satisfaction from our work, but we never made a lot of money. But, then again, we were never looking for material things. We always lived simply, dressed simply. Even today I go to the local *gemach* to get much of my wardrobe. The main thing is that is the clothing be modest and *mentchlich*.

Whenever I meet Rebbetzin Poutorak, she is tastefully — but never ostentatiously — dressed. It's obvious that she is aware of her exalted position as a bas melech, and clothes herself appropriately.

I was always particular to wear clothes that my husband liked, even if I didn't especially care for them. Whenever I purchased a dress or a *sheitel*, I made sure to first tell the shopkeeper that I was buying it on the condition that I could return it if my husband didn't like it. After all, how often do I look at myself? But a woman's husband sees her all the time, so he's the one she should try to please.

As Rebbetzin Poultorak says these words, her pride in being a Jewish woman is obvious. There is no hint of apology. She knows who she is, and is proud of it.

During the years we lived in Lyon, my husband organized Lyon's United Kashrus, which supervised the butcher shops. Before we came, the many kosher butcher shops were without any supervision. My husband created a unified supervision with one standard that all the butchers were required to keep. He never took bribes. On more than one occasion, the butchers were so furious with his uncompromising stance that they threatened him with murder. But he never moved even an iota from the halachah.

My husband headed a *kashrus* agency that supervised many different products throughout Europe. He only gave his *hechsher* if he, personally, had visited the factory to ascertain that it was in keeping with his strict, uncompromising standards of *kashrus*.

My husband was also active in increasing *taharah*. He constructed nine *mikvehs* in Lyon and the surrounding areas. As *Av Beis Din*, he also arranged *gittin* and converted *gerim*.

I often accompanied the female *gerim* to the *mikvah* to complete their conversion. Many became like family to us, and we are still in contact with some of them. After we moved to Israel, my husband continued to head a *Beis Din* that converted French-speaking *gerim*.

When our youngest daughter refused to attend the non-religious Jewish school in Lyon, we moved to the Aix-Les-Bains, where there was a flourishing *Chareidi* community. My husband, however, as *rav* and *manhig*, remained in Lyon to lead the community. Every Shabbos, either my husband would travel to Aix-Les-Bains or I would travel to Lyon. When our youngest was fifteen and left France to attend Manchester Seminary, I returned to Lyon.

Ten years ago, when my husband was sixty-seven and I was sixty-two, my husband retired from the rabbinate. With a new *Rav* to lead the community, he didn't feel it was right for him to remain there. So we moved to Israel.

We came with just five thousand dollars. My husband hoped to be able to buy an apartment with that amount! *Baruch Hashem,* Kollel Polin offered to rent us an apartment.

> *The Rebbetzin's apartment is tiny. The front door opens directly into one long, fairly narrow room, which is the combined living room and dining room. The kitchen is a tiny, windowless alcove off the main room. In addition, there is a small bedroom and a small bathroom with a mini-bathtub, plus a medium-sized porch for the succah. One wall of the living room is covered with floor-to-ceiling bookshelves. On*

the opposite wall is a desk and more bookshelves. There is a small dining-room table in the center.

Even before we settled into our new home, my husband became involved with the French-speaking community. In the last decade or so, a lot of French speakers have immigrated to Israel, but before we arrived there was no organization to help them integrate into Israeli life. So my husband established an organization called "Cerfi." Cerfi assisted French-speaking immigrants with things such as finding the right schools for their children and then getting their children into those schools, deciding which neighborhood is most appropriate and finding a suitable apartment. My husband was in touch with a lot of different *rabbanim* and *askanim* who were available to advise and offer assistance to the immigrants.

In addition, my husband taught in a French seminary. *Sefer Yeshayahu* and the *Sfas Emes* were his specialties. My husband did all this without pay. He just wanted to help people and to spread Torah.

Of course, my husband also continued to *pasken shailos*, both for the French community living here in Israel and for those living abroad. We received a lot of phone calls from abroad, including quite a few from English speakers. A year before he passed away, he found the schedule a bit too rigorous. By nine o'clock at night he was exhausted, so we unplugged the phone. But the rest of the day he was constantly busy, answering *shailos* and giving *eitzos*. In addition to the constant phone calls, people came to our home to discuss personal issues with my husband. Many couples came for help with *shalom bayis* issues.

Wasn't that a bit awkward? After all, the apartment is very small. Didn't they feel uncomfortable talking with you around?

I wasn't around. When people came to discuss personal matters with my husband, I would either go into the bedroom and read something, or take a walk.

That must have been so difficult for you!

No. Why should it be? I could always do things around the house later. And I enjoy taking walks.

I am flabbergasted. I could not even imagine leaving my house several times a day (she couldn't even work in the kitchen, since it is nothing more than a small alcove off the living room) or locking myself into the bedroom (she couldn't even go out to use the bathroom, as that, too, is off the living room) to give total strangers a sense of privacy! And then, if I were to do something like that, I would view it as the ultimate self-sacrifice. Yet Rebbetzin Poultorak thinks nothing of it. After all, she enjoys walking. And who doesn't like relaxing in bed with a book?

My husband passed away a year-and-a-half ago, on *Rosh Chodesh Av*, 2007. It's been a very rough year-and-a-half for a lot of people. So many people relied on him for so many things. I also miss him terribly.

Today, I work for two-and-a-half hours each morning, helping my daughter with her babysitting service. It's hard physical work, with a lot of bending down and picking up the little ones. But I love it. It gives me a reason to get up in the morning.

I'm seventy-three. My husband worked until his last day, and I hope to do the same. When we first came to Eretz Yisrael, my husband asked someone if it's possible to purchase an apartment for five thousand dollars. The man answered, "Yes. On Har Hamenuchos" (Jerusalem's main cemetery). So that is exactly what we did. Although we never had much materially, we always had what we needed. I have no doubt that my husband has a beautiful apartment in *Olam HaEmes*.

Rebbetzin Poultorak points to the sefarim that cover the walls of her living room.

See all these *sefarim*? He learned every single one of them. He used them constantly; they weren't decorations. The margins are full of his notes and corrections. Any *sefer* that he didn't use, he gave away.

Before my husband died, he said to me, "I think that I didn't waste my time here." When he wasn't working for the good of the *klal*, he was learning Torah.

Rabbi Poultorak, *ztz"l*, dealt with all kinds of serious *shailos* about *mamzarus, agunot*, and so on, and would regularly consult with the *gedolei hador*, both Ashkenazi and Sefaradi, in Eretz Yisrael, Europe and America. The many *gedolei hador* that he consulted included Rabbi Obadia Yosef, *shlitah*; Rabbi Batzri, *shlitah*; Rabbi Moshe Feinstein, *ztz"l*; Rabbi Padwa, *ztz"l*; Rabbi Moshe Halberstam, *ztz"l*; and the Rebbe of Gur, the Pnei Menachem, *ztz"l*.

Rabbi Poultorak never requested payment for his *kashrus* supervision, for being the *mohel*, for arranging a *get* or for converting a *ger*. He had a monthly salary and was content with that. Any money that he received for these services was immediately donated to *tzedakah*. Many people who need his help feel themselves orophaned today. So many people cried at the *shivah*.

> *I didn't cry at the shivah, but I am crying now. I never knew of the gadol who literally lived next door to me. I could have gained so much, but I didn't.*

A NEW NESHAMAH

"I'd never known that it's possible to become a Jew. I had always assumed that, if you're not lucky enough to be born into it, there's no way to be a part of the Chosen People."

Chava Kolakowski

I read an article about Chava's husband, Rabbi Yitzchak Zev Kolakowski, in one of the local religious newspapers. Although his story piqued my curiosity, I was dumbfounded when I read that his rebbetzin was born into a Mormon family. So I phoned Richmond, Virginia, where her husband is rav of a shul, and asked if she would be willing to share her story with my readers. After spending the good part of an hour speaking with her on the phone, I was convinced that this is one woman I will have to meet in person one day.

I was born in Idaho Falls, a "hick town" in Idaho, of course. When I was growing up, the only Jews I knew were some friends of my father's who were totally cut off from anything having to do with their heritage. But they knew that they were Jewish, and would often joke about it. They were the "token Jews" living in our very Anglo-Saxon community.

My family comes from a long line of Mormons. My great-great-grandmother joined the Mormon Church in 1840, when it was first established. She was one of the original settlers who, led by Brigham Young, established Salt Lake City. One of four wives, she was with her family in Illinois when her husband passed away. *Schlepping* her six children, she pulled a handcart with all their belongings all the way back to Salt Lake City.

My father's family originated in Germany and had immigrated to America in the early 1800s, around the same time that my mother's ancestors were making their way to Salt Lake City. They settled in the Wyoming-Idaho area, which is where they've been living ever since.

I was raised in the Mormon Church. Most of the people in my small town and in the small towns around us were Mormons, so it was unusual to know someone ***not*** in the church. It was a very insular, protected community.

Interestingly enough, although my father was a devout Mormon who attended church every Sunday, when I was sixteen years old he did something that was really unheard-of in his circles. He sat me down and said, "Melissa, if you feel that the church is not for you, find something that is." This was very unusual: Mormons don't like questions. Perhaps he himself was dissatisfied with his beliefs. I really don't know and I never had the chance to ask him before he died. But one thing I can say is that I am eternally grateful that he gave me permission to explore and question the religion I'd grown up in. I later learned that he said the same thing to my two siblings as well.

Since I wasn't totally happy with what I had been taught, I started exploring different religions. I tried the different churches — Presbyterian, Catholic, you-name-it, and even looked into Hinduism. In every religion I found something that touched me, yet none of them answered my spiritual yearning.

After graduating high school, I attended Westminster Choir College, a phenomenal music school in Princeton, New Jersey, and worked part-time. I was planning to continue with the same job after graduation, but my company downsized and I was fired. At that point, I had what can only be described as a mini-identity crisis.

I had all this extra time on my hands, and nothing to fill it with. So I started questioning my beliefs again, and wondered where I was headed.

That spring, I traveled to New York to visit a friend of mine who lived in Flatbush. On the subway back to Penn Station, I started thinking about how empty my life was and found myself crying. That's when a lovely *Chassidishe* couple entered the subway car. The woman sat in the empty seat next me. After a few minutes, she turned to me in a very dignified way and quietly asked me why I was crying. I told her that I had lost my job and didn't know what I was going to do with myself.

She didn't say anything mind-boggling, just, "I'm sorry to hear about that," but her whole demeanor was so special — so unassuming. She was brimming with *chesed*. And although I never saw her again and don't even know her name, she had a tremendous impact on me. I thought to myself, "Here's someone that I would like to emulate." That night, I typed "Orthodox Judaism" into my computer and started reading anything I could get my hands on. It was a quiet obsession.

Some time later I got sick, and ended up spending several months in the hospital. Somehow or other, my roommate and I started talking about Jews. In passing, she mentioned that Sammy Davis Junior, a black entertainer who was very famous in the sixties, had converted to Judaism (through a Reform conversion). I was shocked. I'd never known that it's possible to become a Jew. I had always assumed that, if you're not lucky enough to be born into it, there's no way to be a part of the Chosen People.

As soon as I was discharged from the hospital, I made an appointment to speak with Rabbi Elazer Teitz, the *rav* of Elizabeth New Jersey, where I was living. Interestingly, although my apartment was about a mile away from the shul, it was within the confines of the *eruv* and there were many *frum* families living in my neighborhood.

I told Rabbi Teitz that I wanted to convert to Judaism. Of course, he tried to dissuade me. He gave me lots of reasons why I shouldn't, and told me that as a non-Jew, all I was required to do was keep the *sheva mitzvos bnei Noach*.

But that wasn't enough for me. I still wanted to convert; to be part of the *am hanivchar*. Rabbi Teitz sighed and responded, "Well, if you really want to be a Jew, the first thing you need to do is begin dressing like one." On the spot, he taught me the basic *halachos* of *tzenius*. That afternoon I returned home and threw away all my pants. From then on I tried to dress according to the guidelines that he had given me.

But I still had a lot to learn, and I had no idea where to learn it. In desperation, I posted an ad in a community bulletin stating that I was looking for someone to teach me about Torah and mitzvos. The man who answered the advertisement had studied in Ohr Sameyach in Israel and was now studying at the Landers Institute in New York, working toward his *semichah* and a degree in psychology. He sent me an email suggesting a few books for me to read. I continued to email him with questions, and he would answer them to the best of his ability.

When the Bialer Rebbe of Bnei Brak came to New York, the Rebbetzin needed a ride from Williamsburg to Great Neck, New Jersey. My mentor was very close with the rebbe and sent me an email asking if I'd be willing to drive the Rebbetzin. Of course I was thrilled at the opportunity to have some private time alone with such a special individual.

During the drive, the Rebbetzin urged me to speak with her husband. So when we arrived in Great Neck, she sat down to help me write a *tzetel* and asked me for my Hebrew name. When I told her that I wasn't Jewish, she became even more adamant that I speak to her husband, and even pushed me up to the head of the line.

When I told the Rebbe that I was a candidate for conversion, he was very discouraging. He spoke a lot about the six million *kedoshim*, and that by aligning myself with the Jewish people, I would also become the target of anti-Semitism. I responded that, although I was not yet Jewish, I felt the pain of *Am Yisrael* and was willing to accept the consequences.

The Bialer Rebbe arranged for me to meet with *Rav* Peretz Steinberg of Queens, the head of a *beis din* that dealt with *geirus*. Rabbi Steinberg urged me to study with a local rabbi, but the local rabbi in Elizabeth was much too busy to learn with me. It was a Catch-22 situation.

Meanwhile, I continued to write to my mentor. He suggested different books, but none of them could take the place of a teacher. Then, when I wrote that I would soon be traveling to upstate New York, he suggested that I stop to *daven* at the *kever* of the Satmar Rebbe, *ztz"l*.

And so, while driving north, I stopped off in Monroe to *daven* at the rebbe's *kever*. It was a foggy day, and I had no idea what I was doing there. I felt lost and confused. What do people ***do*** at the *kever* of a *tzaddik*? I quietly asked Hashem to guide me; to show me what I should be doing with my life.

Although until then I'd wanted to be Jewish, as I left the *beis hachaim* it became a burning, overwhelming desire. I MUST be Jewish! I couldn't remain a *goy* any longer. I also knew that my *neshamah* was somehow connected to *Chassidus*, and that I wanted to lead a Chassidic lifestyle.

Meanwhile, I continued *davening* in the local shul and eating my Shabbos *seudos* with different families. Then I saw a newspaper article mention that a Chassidic Center had just opened up in the neighboring town of Westfield, New Jersey. On Shavuos, I drove there to attend a *shiur*. (Don't forget, I still wasn't Jewish, so it was actually prohibited for me to keep Shabbos!) At the end of the *shiur* the rabbi, Rabbi Block, came over to speak with me. I told him that I was a candidate for conversion and that I was looking for a teacher. He suggested that I study with his rebbetzin.

That was the beginning of a wonderful relationship — and one that literally revolutionized my life! Every Wednesday evening I would join Rebbetzin Block for supper, followed by learning *halachos*. At the same time, I attended many classes at the Chabad House and spent most *Shabbosos* there. Rebbetzin Block and I developed a very close relationship, and even today I still consider her my mentor and ask her advice on many different subjects.

Eventually, Rabbi Block told me that he thought I was ready for conversion and that he was going to inform the *Av Beis Din*. A few days later, the secretary of the *beis din* called me to arrange a time for an interview. I was told that they'd test me on my knowledge of *halachos*. I was very nervous that I would not pass the test. Instead, they asked me about my family. A few months later, the *beis din* called again to inform me I had an appointment at the *mikveh* for the following morning. This was it! I was about to become Jewish!

At the *mikveh*, the *rabbanim* asked me lots of questions, this time testing my knowledge of halachah. They wanted to be absolutely sure that I understood what I was getting myself into. I remember praying that Hashem help me answer the questions correctly. I was so nervous that I was literally shaking!

I obviously passed, because they told me to get ready for the *tevilah*. Just before my immersion, the *rabbanim* asked me if I was positive I really wanted to convert. "Once you immerse in the *mikveh*," they warned me, "there's no going back."

As I was leaving the *mikveh*, the *rabbanim* wished me a huge "Mazel Tov!" I felt that something within me had changed, that I had different essence — which was true. I left the mikvah with a new *neshamah* — a *heilige Yiddishe neshamah*. I was very aware of that *neshamah* — after all, it was brand new! — I wish that I had the same tremendous feeling of awareness — and awe — today that I had then.

As a convert, I was able to choose my own Jewish name. I chose Chava — *em kol chai* — because that was the name the Bialer Rebbe from Bnei Brak had told me to use. He said that it expressed my essence.

Everyone loves a *shidduch* story, so here's mine .... Although Hashem really made our *shidduch*, it was the Bialer Rebbe who orchestrated it. My husband, Rabbi Yitzchak Zev (Joseph) Kolakowski, is the yeshivah *bachur* who answered my advertisement for a teacher, and who referred me to different books and teachers. After the Bialer Rebbe met me for the first time, he told my future husband that, once I was Jewish, I'd be a good *shidduch* for him. My husband was a bit surprised, but he trusted the Rebbe.

After I converted, the Rebbe told my husband to wait forty days before meeting me. And so, as a newborn Jewish woman of forty days, I started seeing my future husband. It wasn't long before we were engaged.

Shortly after our wedding, my husband and I moved to Richmond, Virginia, where my husband became rabbi of the Young Israel. Now, two-and-a-half years later, he's opened a *kiruv* organization called *Nachalei Emunah*.

It was not easy to be thrust into the position of rebbetzin when I was so new to both *Yiddishkeit* and marriage! Because of my position, people often came to me for advice. Due to my inexperience I made a lot of mistakes. But I had excellent mentors: Rebbetzin Block, the Chabad Rebbetzin with whom I'd studied prior to my conversion, and Rebbetzin Steinberg, wife of the *Av Beis Din* who converted me.

I'm often called in to speak with young people who are veering from the *derech*. I tell them that for two-and-a-half years I fought for something — my Jewishness — that they received on a silver platter. "You can't just give up on something that I worked so hard for," I point out to them. Coming from me, this is easier for them to accept.

What about your birth family? Do they accept the changes you've made in your life?

Hashem blessed me with a wonderful, supportive family. They're extremely respectful of my lifestyle. They even bought a special set of kosher pots and pans for when I visit, and they never phone on Shabbos or Yom Tov.

It's funny ... When I was a kid growing up in Idaho, all the women prepared special pastries for the winter holiday. I wanted to be original and do something different, so I made — hamentaschen! Today, my mom often reminds me of that and laughs, saying she should have known that I'd become a Jew!

PLANTING SEEDS IN SAN FRANCISCO

"The intermarriage rate here is 80%! If I were to dwell on that and really feel the spiritual holocaust that is taking place here, I would be so upset that I would never be able to accomplish anything. Instead, we concentrate on the many individuals who, with Hashem's help, we have influenced."

Isabel Lipner

I first met Rabbi and Mrs. Lipner in 1969, just a few weeks after they moved to San Francisco, California. She was a mature married woman with four small children; I was just fifteen, a teenager struggling to define my identity. I remember my excitement at meeting Orthodox Jews who were so deeply committed to Torah life. I was mesmerized as I listened to Rabbi Lipner share his dream of establishing a Jewish school in ultra-liberal San Francisco. He hoped to create a new generation of committed Jews who would revolutionize the community and build a vibrant Orthodox kehillah.

The dream never materialized. San Francisco has remained, well, San Francisco. Behind the scenes, however, there exists a continual qui-

et revolution. Individuals (no, not the masses, but each individual Jew is a world unto itself) have turned their lives around to become Torah observant, ehrlicher Yidden. There are hundreds, if not thousands, of former San Francisco residents whose lives have been impacted by Rabbi and Mrs. Lipner's dream. Ironically, most would never even consider living in San Francisco!

Why did you and Rabbi Lipner decide to move to San Francisco?

In 1969, Rabbi Schneur Kotler, *zt"l,* and the heads of Torah Umesorah prevailed upon my husband to start a Day School in San Francisco. Two Lakewood *bachurim* accompanied us. They literally went door to door, trying to find "guinea pigs" for their experiment. The school started with 53 students, from nursery to third grade.

When we first came to San Francisco, we were both very young and very idealistic. I was only twenty-five. We had four children, aged four, three, two, and a newborn.

Moving to San Francisco was a real culture shock. Here, for example, someone offering me a ride would not think twice about stopping off at the local Safeway to buy (non-kosher) meat for supper. That would never happen on the East Coast. Even if the people are not *frum*, they are sensitive to the fact that I would find their eating non-kosher meat offensive.

The intermarriage rate here is 80%! If I were to dwell on that and really feel the spiritual holocaust that is taking place here, I would be so upset that I would never be able to accomplish anything. Instead, we concentrate on the many individuals who, with Hashem's help, we have influenced.

In some cities, the Reform and Conservative make accommodations for the *frum*, but here many of the liberals simply do not tolerate Orthodoxy. When we first moved to San Francisco, the liberal establishment told us pointblank that in San Francisco our type of Orthodoxy is not tolerated, and that we would be out of here in less than six months. It's thirty-nine years later, and we're still here. On a personal level, however, we've encountered many Reform and Conservative Jews who have been very supportive of our work, and without their financial assistance we could never have survived.

Can you tell us about some of the individuals whose lives you have impacted?

One day, we received a phone call from a boy who, to protect his identity, we'll call Igor. Igor had been thrown out of public school and asked to be accepted into our school. A kid has to do something really bad to be thrown out of public school, so we weren't excited at the prospect of accepting him into the Hebrew Academy.

My husband met with Igor and was touched by his honesty. Igor was completely upfront and listed all the things that he had done wrong. We accepted him into our school on probation. Over the course of the following year, his behavior was so bad that we really should have thrown him out dozens of times! But we couldn't. There was something about him that was special.

Throughout that entire year, Igor never wanted to *daven*. But at a school Shabbaton that was held prior to graduation, my husband noticed him voluntarily joining in the *davening*. After graduation he traveled to Israel on a secular Army program and found his way to Aish, where he remained for three years. Today, he's learning in a regular yeshivah and is an incredible *masmid* and an *iluy atzum*. He completely turned himself around, from being an aggressive kid who drove his teachers mad (the teachers would tell my husband, "It's either him or me") to one of the most refined people I've ever met. That's the power of *limud Torah*! He even succeeded in being *m'karev* his mother. She wears a *sheitel*, phones my husband with her *shailos,* and is one of our regular Shabbos guests.

Another boy — let's call him Dima — was planning to become a professional hockey player. He attended a special school for athletes on a full scholarship. When, at the end of eleventh grade, his scholarship was terminated due to financial difficulties, he transferred to the Hebrew Academy.

When Dima first came to the Hebrew Academy, he didn't know a thing about *Yiddishkeit*. Three months later, he and his younger brother were ready to have a *bris milah*. After graduation, he attended Ohr Sameyach's summer program. He returned to San Francisco before Rosh Hashanah and spoke with my husband about his future. He wanted to become *shomer Shabbos*, but realized that that would be the end of his dream of becoming a professional hockey player — and his parents had sacrificed so much for him to be able to fulfill that dream.

My husband listened to his dilemma and said, "Dima, I'm positive that you'll make the correct decision. I just want you to know that, no matter what you decide, I'll always be your friend."

On Yom Kippur night, right before *Kol Nidrei*, Dima came over to my husband and said, "I did it. I told my parents. I won't be a hockey player." That evening, my husband's *derashah* was about *mesirus nefesh* — and Dima. Today, Dima is attending college and learning in a yeshivah.

I don't know where these special *neshamos* come from, how they are capable of turning their lives around and making such a total change in one short year. I am really in awe of them

Sometimes we don't see changes until years later. Our job is to *plant the* seed *and hope that, with Hashem's help, it will grow.* Baruch Hashem, over the years we've had many wonderful surprises — students who were totally irreligious at graduation and today are *shomrei* Torah and mitzvos.

In addition to our work at the school, simply by residing in San Francisco we impact the community. We've invited Jewish neighbors, acquaintances, and even workmen to join us for Shabbos or Yom Tov (I tell those who do not live within walking distance of our home that they will be incarcerated for twenty-five hours!). These invitations are often the beginning of a close relationship. Many of our former *"bnei bayis"* now have large, *frum* families of their own.

If it wasn't for these success stories, we would have thrown in the towel ages ago. This is what keeps us going. Speaking to you, I condense the stories into a few short sentences. But in real life, it's not simple. It's two steps forward, one backward. It was a real struggle for these people to turn their lives around.

What was it like raising children in such an environment?

It wasn't as difficult as one would think. When we moved to San Francisco in the sixties, there were a few *frum* families still living there. In addition, the kids who were not *frum* were wholesome. We also sent our children to camp on the East Coast to meet other "Martians"! For high school, the boys went to Ner Yisrael in Baltimore and the girls to Bais Yaakov in either Baltimore or Denver.

People in San Francisco stare at us because we look so different. I always get a kick when people with green hair and multiple earrings gawk at US!

Looking back on the last thirty-nine years in San Francisco, are there things you would have done differently?

I became good friends with one of the Jewish secretaries at our school. I really liked her, and the feeling was mutual. She had been dating a non-Jewish man for seven years and was upset that there was still no talk of marriage. The fact that he was not Jewish did not even bother her. "If I wanted to live your lifestyle, I'd have to marry a Jewish guy. But since I don't, there's no reason to marry a Jew," she explained. Her mother wanted her to break it up — not just because the boy wasn't Jewish, but because it had been going on for so long without any prospect of marriage — and asked for my advice. I suggested that we arrange for the girl to "win" a free trip to Israel (paid for by her mother, of course) to study in a yeshivah environment. But I was afraid to send her to Neve. I thought it would be too much of a culture shock. Instead, I sent her to a very modern yeshivah. It was a disaster. The school was lacking warmth, and although I made it very clear that the girl had no Jewish background, they assumed that she knew much more than she actually did. She hated the yeshivah, returned to San Francisco earlier than planned, and eventually married her non-Jewish boyfriend.

But, as we all know, things happen for a reason. And in order to survive here, I need to focus on the successes. We've had lots of *peiros*, lots of *nachas*.

How can we best share Torah with the not-yet-religious Jew?

Don't be judgmental! Don't look at people as a "project." Reach out with honest love and caring.

We are *zocheh* to *siyata d'Shemaya* if our *kiruv* is *l'shem Shomayim*. Doing it for the sake of Heaven is the key. All the experts say never argue — but once, I found myself arguing over *hashkafah* with a not-yet-religious lawyer. After he left, my husband told me that I had ruined it, that the fellow would never come back. But he did — because he enjoyed the intellectual stimulation of our arguments!

Hashem directed me to argue, even though it was the wrong thing to do, because that was exactly what I *needed* to do!"

What are your plans for the future?

There is no word in *lashon kodesh* for retirement; it's not a Jewish concept. I hope to continue teaching kindergarten until I stop enjoying it. Then I'll find something else.

As Jewish women, we are given the exalted task of creating a mikdash me'at, a miniature Bais HaMikdash. With our special intution, we can create that mikdash me'at in Lakewood or Yerushalayim — or even San Francisco.

QUEEN FOR ETERNITY

"I tell people to buy a kitchen timer and set it for fifteen minutes. At the end of the fifteen minutes, stop — and continue the following day, again for just fifteen minutes. You'd be surprised at how much a person can accomplish in just a quarter of an hour!"

Queene Parnes

Every Shabbos afternoon a group of women — some still raising families, others great-grandmothers — congregate at Tova's, a wonderful woman, paralyzed from the waist down, who hosts us graciously from her wheelchair. Like women everywhere, we schmooze about everything from the best way to make an omelet to existential questions about Jewish identity. The first time I met Queene (pronounced Queenie) Parnes was at this Shabbos afternoon get-together.

Tova introduced Queene to me as an efficiency expert. That sounded intriguing, especially for people like me, who push off indefinitely the inevitable mundane aspects of life, such as filling out forms or organizing photo albums. My interest was piqued.

My real name is Malka. But it wasn't a good idea to use such a Jewish-sounding name in public school. Many of the girls translated their names into English. My sister, Fraidie, was called "Joy," and my friend Bracha, "Grace." My father suggested that I add the "e" at the end of my name so that no one would mix me up with the Queen of England! My grandfather would always call me the "Queen frum England."

After moving to Israel in 1971, Yaakov (Jack) and Queene Parnes went into the industrial sewing-machine business. Yaakov set up the factories, while Queene took care of the paperwork.

How did you learn to be so efficient?

It comes naturally; it's just a part of me. After graduating high school, I worked for my uncle's import-export firm. I organized their entire filing and inventory system. Later, I became an executive secretary for a major Jewish organization. I organized all the papers — there were a lot of them — and created a filing system.

My children even made sure to be sick efficiently: two came down with mumps at the same time, two of them got chicken-pox at the same time, and two of them had their tonsils out at the same time!

When Yaakov Parnes passed away in 1981, Queene opened her own business as efficiency consultant.

What exactly does an efficiency consultant do?

For years I described my job as saving people from drowning in paper! I go into private homes and organize the papers in a tailor-made filing system. Sometimes I just end up throwing useless papers into the "circular bin." But I have often discovered very valuables papers, such as bonds, life-insurance policies, etc., that the people I worked for never knew existed!

I enjoy working myself quickly out of a job, and tailor each family's system to its individual needs. One client, for example, asked me to organize five or six huge boxes of financial papers. I sorted them out by creating separate files for each institution. The people were thrilled; finally, they could keep tabs on their money. Last year

I had an emergency call from a woman whose husband is a pack rat. A flood caused by a broken pipe had destroyed many of their important papers and made others barely legible. I managed to salvage quite a few documents, found copies of others, and made a simple-to-use filing system — making sure that everything was kept in water-resistant, metal filing cabinets!

Could you give us some efficiency tips?

Stay on top of the paperwork! I tell people to buy a kitchen timer and set it for fifteen minutes. At the end of the fifteen minutes, stop — and continue the following day, again for just fifteen minutes. You'd be surprised at how much a person can accomplish in just a quarter of an hour! Yet fifteen minutes is not an overwhelming amount of time.

I also suggest that all papers be kept in one place, either a table or a desk, so that you won't have to race through the house searching for your telephone bill. Once a week, clear the table or desk of all the papers. (No, don't dump them into a drawer. Put them away!).

Even with everything computerized, financial papers such as bank statements, tax returns, and tax receipts should be kept for seven years. Things like grocery bills and credit card receipts (if paid up) can be thrown away. Very important papers such as the deed to your house or apartment, or a life-insurance policy, should be kept forever. You can throw your old car insurance policy out ***if*** you renew in annually and don't have a claim on it.

The most basic part of being organized is having a place for everything and keeping everything in its place. My purse, for example, has lots of different pockets. I am particular to keep the same things in each pocket so that I always know where they are. I know people who don't. Every time their cell phone rings or they need the key to their front door, they need to search their entire purse until they find it!

The fewer possessions one has, the easier it is to stay on top of them. My daughter-in-law calls me a minimalist. But getting rid of things is not always easy. I have one sister who's has been trying to do it for the last twenty years, without success. She recently gave away four of her six (!) salad bowls — but the following Shabbos she was presented with a new one!

It sounds so simple but, as we all know, it's the discipline of a lifetime. Queene grew up in a much simpler world, before the "Me" generation; a world where self-restraint and discipline were considered a virtue.

What was it like growing up in Montreal over half a century ago?

When I got married in 1950, there were about 60,000 Jews living in Montreal. Only a small minority were Orthodox. My mother was very active in the Orthodox community; she belonged to almost every committee.

Everyone knew everyone else. We were all interconnected — one huge family. Since there were no *yeshivos* or day schools, people hired private teachers — Reverend Greenblatt for the boys, and his eldest daughter for the girls — to come to the house and teach the children. My parents hired Reverend Greenblatt's daughter to teach my sister and me. She eventually married my uncle.

Although people did not have a lot of money, the standard of living was comparatively high. We lived in a tenement, but the inside was beautiful!

The main problem was a lack of religious education. Although many members of the community remained religious, and some became even more religious, a large percentage drifted away from observance.

For many years, there was no *shomer-Shabbos* bakery. My mother headed a committee that collected money to open a kosher bakery and find a religious Jew to operate it. It was a double mitzvah; the community needed a bakery, and the Jew needed the *parnassah.*

Queene, you grew up during the Great Depression. What was that like?

Interestingly enough, my father's business actually improved during the Depression. He dealt in gold and antiques, and people were selling these things to survive. So we were relatively well off. But when the war broke out and the economy boomed, people stopped selling their belongings and our financial situation plummeted. We ended up having to sell many of our own belongings to get by.

As a child, I was an introvert. My mother pushed me to be more sociable. At the time I resented it, but today I am grateful. I loved singing and acting and in high school I took voice lessons and learned music. Believe it or not, I am still using these talents today. I belong to a group of women who are all over seventy. Every year or so, we put on a performance for the ladies in the neighborhood. Once a year I organize and host a baby shower to benefit *Nefesh Echad b'Yisrael*, an organization that helps women with high-risk pregnancies. Because I keep my living room uncluttered with extra furniture, I can seat fifty women.

How did I meet my husband? In the Catskills! The first time we met, I was impressed that he realized that Winnipeg and Montreal were completely different cities. Whenever I told an American that I was from Montreal, they would automatically ask if I knew someone in either Winnipeg or Vancouver, because they assumed that all Canadians knew each other. But, as it turned out I really did know (or at least know of) Yaakov's brother-in-law, although he was from Winnipeg and not Montreal. He had made *aliyah* to a religious *kibbutz*, and as secretary of a major Jewish organization I corresponded regularly with him.

On my return to Montreal from my vacation in the Catskills, my father contacted his brother-in-law in Brooklyn to make inquiries about my future husband and his family. He liked what he heard, and invited my future husband to Montreal for Labor Day Weekend.

The other side, of course, was making its own inquiries. They contacted Rav Unger, the Karshover Dayan, in Montreal. Rav Unger phoned my father and said that he would like to meet with us, explaining that Mr. Parnes had asked his opinion on the *shidduch*. Since I also came along (after all, I was the "star" of the show!) the rebbetzin came in to meet me. When she walked into the room my father stared at her for a few moments and said, "You look exactly like my niece!" It turned out that my father's niece — my cousin — was also *her* cousin... which meant that the brother-in-law my father had contacted to get information about my future husband was the Rebbetzin's first cousin!

As I mentioned before, my mother was on many committees, including the committee to open a *shomer-Shabbos* bakery. Before my wedding, my mother and I went to the bakery to order a wedding cake. The owner asked who I was marrying. When I told him "Parnes from Borough Park," he became very excited. As it turned out, my husband's grandfather, Reb Yosef Yitzchak Parnes, who was *moser nefesh* for *shmiras Shabbos*, gave him $300 to start the business, because he wanted Montreal to have a bakery that was closed on Shabbos.

I left Queene's apartment with a warm, back-home feeling. It was like going back in time, sitting at my parents' round wooden kitchen table, speaking with my mother. There is much we can learn from that generation: the hard-core values that aren't talked about, just lived; the simplicity that is far from being simple; the modest pride in accomplishment. Thanks to their dreams and the hard work they put into actualizing those dreams, thousands upon thousands of young people throughout the world — including Montreal! — are presently learning.

AN OMAHA CHILDHOOD

"My teachers and friends at school were mainly *goyim*. Every single day, before leaving for school in the morning, my mother would remind me, 'Remember you're a Jew. Remember that you're different.'

But the difference was very obvious. The *kedushah* in our home was like the *kedushah* of Yerushalayim."

Esther Macner

Esther Macner (nee Landsman) and I have been friends for close to four decades (gulp!), dating from our year together at Bais Yaakov Yerushalayim. She was (and still is) tiny — and a real go-getter. It wasn't until I had the privilege of interviewing her that I discovered just how incredible she — and her parents, survivors of the Holocaust — really are!

I grew up in Omaha, Nebraska — a real hick town. Most of the religious Jews there were *shochtim*. When my parents first arrived in Omaha, the city had a flourishing religious community. Rav Chaim Ozer Grodzenski's brother was the *Rav*, there were several Orthodox shuls and even a *cheder* where the children were taught Hebrew with a Polish accent. But it had all disappeared by the time I was old enough to go to school.

My first language was Yiddish. That was the language that all the *shochtim's* children spoke among themselves. When I was four, my mother told my older brother to teach me English, so that by the time I'd turn five and start kindergarten, I'd be able to understand the teacher.

My father taught me the *alef-beis*. He said that that was the way it was done in Poland: The women were taught to read at home and by the time they were five years old they could walk into a shul, listen to the *davening*, and know exactly where the *tzibbur* was up to!

When I was three years old, my parents sent me for music lessons. I learned to play both the piano and violin, and was good at both of them. I could play any piece on the violin perfectly, the very first time I tried! Everyone, except my family, assumed I'd become a concert violinist.

When I was thirteen years old, my public-school teacher told me, "Esther, promise me that you'll never, ever, stop playing violin."

I replied, "I can't possibly make such a promise."

The teacher was devastated. "Why not?" he asked. "You have amazing talent!"

"Maybe," I said. "But when I grow up, I'm going to marry and have a large family. Do you think I'll have time to play the violin?"

The teacher gaped at me in shock. This was the last thing he'd been expecting to hear. But I was just echoing the pure, Torah-true *chinuch* that I'd received at home.

You mentioned that your parents were both survivors. Were you aware of that as you were growing up?

Yes. It was very, very — *very* — obvious! At night, my mother would wake up, screaming in terror. It was a scream that one could never forget; it went right under the skin, piercing my heart. I would run to her bed and shake her vigorously to pull her out of her nightmare.

As a result of her experiences during the war, my mother was always nervous that something bad would happen to us. She would be in anguish if we were late coming home. When I had to run errands, I would literally *run*, because I knew that if I took my time I'd be causing her emotional suffering.

> *When Esther was in ninth grade, her parents sent her away from home to attend Bais Yaakov Detroit. It's difficult for any parent to send such a young child away from home, but in Esther's case, it was an act of self-sacrifice that I cannot even begin to fathom. This was before modern instant communication. Letters took days to arrive and long-distance telephone calls were a luxury reserved for emergencies. In many ways, today Israel is much closer to Omaha than Detroit was forty years ago. It's easy to mouth the words that a Torah-true chinuch is our first priority. For Esther's mother, giving her child a Torah education meant overcoming her most deeply-rooted emotions. In a rare display of self-sacrifice, she gave her daughter a gift that will endure for generations to come.*

My father used to say, "Mommy will outlive me." When I asked him, "Daddy, how do you know?" he replied, "Because of all the *chesed* she did in the concentration camps."

After the Nazis cut off the water supply in Stuthof (a concentration camp located near the Baltic Sea. More than 85,000 Jews were murdered there), many women died of thirst. My mother would melt snow and bring the water to the dying women. In order to do this, she had to climb over enormous piles of corpses. Although she had no choice but to step on the dead bodies, she was careful not to step on the faces.

Stuthof was the last camp to be liberated by the Allies. As the front line came closer, the Nazis shoved tens of thousands of inmates, including my mother, onto three boats. The boats drifted in the Baltic Sea for three days while the poor women inside were left without water or food. After one boat was bombed by the Allies and almost all of the inmates drowned, the other two were brought back ashore, and the exhausted women were immediately forced to begin marching. Anyone who couldn't march was shot. They marched for several days, until they were finally liberated. My mother's friend told me that my mother saved her life by using a piece of clothing to literally *shlep* her along during the march.

My father was also a survivor. He balanced my mother's nervous nature with his *simchah* and jokes. For example, when I was four or five, I remember going down to the cellar because of an approaching tornado (which were quite common in Nebraska!). My mother was a nervous wreck, while my father kept on cracking jokes to keep everyone calm. I remember him climbing up the stairs, opening the door to the house and then — to break the tension — very seriously informing us that, as far as he could tell, the house was still standing.

Another early memory: It was thundering and lightning outside, and my father was late coming home from work. My mother was nervously pacing back and forth; the tension was so thick, you could have cut it with a knife. When my father arrived home, he immediately summed up the situation and broke into a big smile. "Esther, come!" he said. "Let's go outside so I can teach you how to make a *berachah* on the thunder!" The tension vanished.

My father was a Gerrer *chassid*. When he was twenty-one, he went to the Imrei Emes, *zt"l*, to ask what he should do for a living. The Imrei Emes instructed him to become a *shochet*. He started learning *shechitah* before the war and completed his studies when he came to America after the war.

My father was one of the first Jews sent to Auschwitz. This was when people thought that Auschwitz was "just" a work camp. Security was not nearly as strict as it eventually became; this was before the inmates were tattooed, and probably before the gas chambers were opened. He quickly realized that Auschwitz was a starvation camp, and that were he to remain there, he would soon die of hunger. Somehow, he and two friends managed to escape during "lunch hour," when security was comparatively lax.

My father and his two friends made their way through the forests to Russia. How did they survive? They would find a clearing in the forest and sit completely still, hardly breathing, while waiting for some animals to appear. Then they would eat whatever the animals ate, while avoiding whatever the animals avoided, assuming — correctly — that if the animals avoided it, it was poisonous.

One time they waited in complete silence for almost an entire day without any animals appearing. Finally, one of my father's friends jumped up and said, "I'll die if I don't eat something!" The other two tried to stop him, but he just grabbed everything in sight and stuffed it into his mouth. He was *niftar* within half an hour.

My father and the other *bachur* buried him, and then continued waiting. Almost immediately, the animals appeared and ate everything — except the types of vegetation that my father's friend had consumed.

My father told me this story when I was ten years old. Despite the many years that had gone by, he still felt guilty that he hadn't been able to stop his friend from eating the poisonous shrubbery.

Getting back to my father's escape from Auschwitz: He made it to Russia, but the situation there was terrible. At that time, people really had no idea what the Germans were up to. My father thought that things were probably better back in Poland. So he returned to Poland, straight into the Germans' hands, and was sent back to Auschwitz. From Auschwitz he was sent to many different "labor" camps. In Majdanek the Nazis placed him in a cattle holder and beat his head with a rifle butt until his skull cracked open and he was left for dead. Miraculously, he survived — but as a result of this injury, for the rest of his life he suffered from terrible headaches. When he was older, this injury caused premature dementia.

My father was in a death march that ended up in the Dachau concentration camp. His group was immediately driven to the gas chamber. My father managed to steal out of the group and hide in a wooded area between the barracks and the gas chamber. He remained there until he slipped into a group of arriving prisoners. A few days later, one of the Nazis recognized him as being from the group that had been sent directly to the gas chamber, and said, "Since you were so smart, I'll allow you to live."

Conditions in Dachau were so horrific that by the time he was liberated, the lower half of his body was completely paralyzed and swollen from lack of food. The Americans hospitalized him and fed him intravenously for three months, until he was finally strong enough to eat baby food. It wasn't until half a year after Liberation that he was able to walk without assistance.

Once, when I was home sick from school, I heard my father's car turn into the driveway in the early afternoon. I was ecstatic! He never, ever, came home before six. My mother, however, became hysterical. "Who knows what happened to him?" she asked over and over again. When my father walked into the house, he was smiling broadly. His thumb was covered with a large white bandage.

My father said, "You have no idea what happened to me today."

My mother, too frightened to even look at his finger, blurted, "Why didn't you go straight to the doctor?"

My father's smile disappeared. "If I allow the doctor to suture the finger, I'll lose feeling in it, and I'll never be able to *shecht* again." (A shochet uses the tips of his finger to check the sharpness of the blade.) "I'll have to take care of it myself."

Since my mother was incapable of even looking at the finger, my father asked me to help him. When he opened the bandage, I saw that the the injury was serious. After he finished bandaging his finger and encasing it in a metal thumb cast, I asked, "Daddy, how did you manage to smile like that when you were in such agony?"

He replied, "Would it have helped to cry? But Esther, *mein kindt*, this is nothing, absolutely nothing, compared to the suffering of even one day in a concentration camp.' When he said those words, I began to understand — a teeny tiny bit — what my parents had been through during the War.

I am always amazed at those survivors who, after losing everything near and dear to them, courageously married and built beautiful Yiddishe homes. They plucked themselves out of the ashes to create what can only be described as eternity. They are true heroes.

The Germans were a highly-respected and sophisticated nation. Who would dream that such high-class people could stoop to such depravity? I attended public school. My teachers and friends at school were mainly *goyim*. Every single day, before leaving for school in the morning, my mother would remind me, "Remember you're a Jew. Remember that you're different."

But the difference was very obvious. The *kedushah* in our home was like the *kedushah* of Yerushalayim. My parents had tremendous *ahavas Yisrael*. They literally loved every single Jew. I grew up knowing that every single Jew is holy. It didn't matter if he was a Litvak or a *Chassid*. There were no differences. We are all members of a holy nation.

It was only when I went to Bais Yaakov Detroit, that I discovered that we are Gerrer *Chassidim*. The other girls asked me if my family was *Chassidishe* or Litvish. I didn't know. On my return home for Chanukah, I asked my father about it. he replied, "A *Yid* is a *Yid*." When I continued to press him, he told me that we were *Chassidish*.

So I returned to Detroit and told my friends. They asked the next obvious question: "So, what type of *Chassidim* are you?" When I returned home for Pesach, I literally drove my father crazy until he told me that we were Gerrer *Chassidim*.

Our home was always open to guests, and strangers were treated like immediate family. All the *meshulachim* who came to Omaha stayed with us. One Friday afternoon, half an hour before Shabbos, just as my father was about to jump into the shower, three *meshulachim* called to tell us that they were stranded in the train station downtown. My father raced out to the car to pick them up, while my mother, sister, and I went down to the basement to make the beds. But that was the type of home we had — every *Yid* was warmly welcome.

My mother never let the *meshulachim* leave without an enormous bag of homemade goodies — she always cooked for an army. One time, a *meshulach* tried to convince my mother that he didn't need the food, but she refused to take no for an answer. The following Shabbos he came back and told us that that week, all his plans had fallen through. Thanks to my mother's thoughtfulness, he had food to eat.

When I was a little girl I remember accompanying my mother on Succos to visit non-religious survivors. She'd bring a *lulav* and *esrog* and ask me to help them make the *berachah*. Of course, they were all very impressed that such a young child knew how to "*bentch*" *lulav* and *esrog*! Then, as they reminisced about life before and during the war, I'd sit and listen while my mother empathized. She was *mekarev* many people this way.

My mother loves people and people love her. She sent many young people to yeshivos and Bais Yaakovs, and they went on to build beautiful Jewish homes.

My father would wake up every morning at three o'clock to learn before *davening*. Then he'd go straight to work, and return home at around six o'clock in the evening — if we were lucky! Between learning with us children, his community involvements, and helping out at home, his evenings were extremely full. Sundays were devoted to driving the *meshulachim* around and helping them collect money. He refused to accept payment for this.

During the summer, my father would always quote the words of Akavia ben Mehalalel in *Pirkei Avos*: "Reflect on three things, and you will not come within the grip of sin: Know from whence you came, whither you go, and before Whom you are destined to give a future account and reckoning." He even put the words to music. At my father's funeral, when the *Chevrah Kadisha* recited this Mishnah in front of the Gerrer *beis medrash*, my sister and I caught each other's eye. We both felt as if it were our father speaking to us.

I learned the meaning of *simchah* from my father. He would take my hand and say, "Come on, Esther! Let's snatch a mitzvah!" That was his greatest joy — grabbing yet another mitzvah!

Our family only ate from my father's *shechitah*. Sometimes the entire family would travel to a nearby farm to slaughter half-a-year's worth of chickens at one go. Before *shechting* each chicken, my father would gently pet it and speak to it, to be sure it was completely calm ....

My father had *semichah*, but none of us knew about it until after he was *niftar*. Our rebbe, the Gerrer Rebbe, is very particular that no exaggerations be written on a tombstone, since doing so causes the *neshamah* to suffer in the World of Truth. So when the Rebbe gave his approval to the poem that my son wrote to be inscribed on my father's tombstone, in which my father is described as "***Harav hachassid***," I understood that my father must be a an ordained rabbi! It was only years later that I came across the actual documents while going through my father's safety-deposit box. Actually, the Pnei Menachem, *zt"l*, used to call my father the "Omaha Rebbele," so I should have realized it from that.

At the *shivah*, an old family friend who presently resides in Jerusalem told us that he had recently met someone who lives in Omaha. When our friend asked him how he managed to be so religious in such a secular city, he replied, "A *tzaddik* lives there. I get *chizuk* just from looking at that *tzaddik's* face!" That *tzaddik* was my father!

Although he lived in America for close to sixty years, he looked as if he had been plucked straight out of Poland.

You attended public school until ninth grade. It must have been very difficult for you, coming as you do from such a strong Jewish home, to manage in such an environment. How did you get along with the other children?

Although I was the only Jew in my class, I got along well with almost all of my classmates. They respected me for my religious convictions. We had a wonderful time together, but at the same time we all understood that there were limitations to our friendship. I could never be like them, and never wanted to be like them. School was school, and home was home.

When I was in sixth grade, the school opened a cafeteria. All the children who lived more than five blocks away from school — like me! — were required to eat there instead of going home for lunch. I went directly to the principal and told her that I was Jewish (when it comes to *Yiddishkeit*, I was never an introvert), and therefore could not eat the school lunches. She responded, "But there are other Jewish children in our school, and they aren't complaining. Why are you?" I explained that I was religious, and that we only ate kosher food. The following day she announced the creation of a special lunchroom for the children who brought their own food to school — and put me in charge of it!

For ninth grade, my parents sent me to Bais Yaakov Detroit. It was a dream come true. In public school, I'd never had to study for tests. Now, for the first time, I felt that I was finally being asked to use my brain. I was like a sponge, absorbing everything. In Omaha, all my Jewish learning was on Shabbos, when my father taught me *Chumash* with *Onkelos*. But in Detroit, I was studying Torah several hours a day! It was wonderful.

What do you do today?

Baruch Hashem, I have a large *Chassidishe* family, and am very involved in my children's and grandchildren's lives.

In addition, I hold a volunteer position as head of the Jerusalem region's Israeli La Leche League — which includes Beit Shemesh and all the settlements, including Kiryat Sefer. At first, I was the only *Chareidi* woman in the Jerusalem region; today there are many of us. I enjoy working with new mothers and advising our counselors, and hope to continue doing this in the future.

I would like to go back to playing the violin. But being a mother, grandmother, and senior La Leche League counselor are all very time-consuming jobs — and they, of course, are, in that order, my top priorities. Maybe someday, when I have the time ....

AN ARCHEOLOGIST RETURNS

"Our family enjoyed exploring the safari wildernesses. One time, a warthog came right up to us as we were eating our lunch. Another time our car was almost trampled by an elephant!"

Tina

I met Tina and her husband Haskel through a "Help Wanted" ad on Janglo, the Jerusalem Anglo-Saxon newsletter. (Isn't it funny how, in America, we're "Jews", while in Israel, we're "American"?). They were looking for a woman to teach their eight-year-old son Hebrew; I was showing the first signs of carpal-tunnel syndrome and needed to do something other than type all day. It was a good shidduch.

Tina's husband, Haskel, is a professor of archaeology. Tina is presently working on her doctoral thesis in archaeology. They live in Canada, and are presently in Israel on sabbatical.

Although Tina is much more religious than her family, she is still far from being Chareidi. After spending the morning learning about her life and the many challenges she and her husband face in their journey toward full Torah observance, I feel that there is much we can learn from her story. And besides, how could I not write about someone who was almost trampled by an elephant, and spent a summer living in a Zulu hut along with the natives?

I was born and raised in Winnipeg, Manitoba. We were completely isolated from the Jewish community. My parents even sent me to a Catholic school because, scholastically, that was the best school around. It was very confusing. In school I was being taught things that went against everything I'd been taught to believe in, yet I did not know enough about Judaism to be able to refute them properly.

I first got to know my husband on an archeological dig in Serbia. This was right before the Yugoslavian civil wars erupted. As a matter of fact, the day after our group took the train to the site, the train tracks between Belgrade and Zagreb were blown up. We were working on a village that showed early farming and animal domestication (some of the earliest in Europe, in fact) and actually discovered complete dishes and eating utensils. For an archeologist that's a big find — but because of the war that was going on, we weren't able to do anything with it.

Although at the time my husband was far from being religious, he was more connected to the Jewish community than I was. After our marriage we began attending Conservative services, which, for us — coming from absolutely nothing — was a big step. During the summer we traveled to Europe — this time, to Romania, to work on an archeological dig there. I specialize in zooarcheology: analyzing animal bones. One summer I ended up analyzing 40,000 animal bones in Belgrade.

You cannot imagine the amount of information an archeologist can obtain just from analyzing animal bones. By analyzing the bones of a community's animals, we are able to completely reconstruct the socioeconomic patterns of that culture. I can determine, for example, where the elites lived, where the slaves lived, and the types of tools they made. We can even figure out what cuts of meat they ate! When my husband was working on New Amsterdam, in New York, he was able to determine the location of the different ethnic groups based upon the frequencies of pig bones. We can also determine how the animals were slaughtered — which, of course, helps us pinpoint the exact locations of ancient Jewish communities.

But getting back to modern Jewish communities .... While living in a traditional (although not Orthodox) community, I was overwhelmed by the closeness of the community, something that had been very lacking in my childhood where everyone just lived for themselves. When my daughter, Channah, was born, for example, I was deluged with enough cooked food to last two weeks. The more my husband and I learned about our heritage, the more everything made sense and the more involved we became. After Channah's birth, nearly twelve years ago, we started doing Shabbos dinners together, because we wanted to be able to pass our heritage down to the next generation and we realized that we couldn't pass down something that we didn't do ourselves.

Our journey was slow. I loved making Shabbos dinners, and for many years, Friday was totally devoted to preparing for that special day. It's a joy, and I love it; I love making challah with the children and getting the house sparkling clean in honor of the Shabbos Queen. I can't understand why some women complain about all the work that goes into it.

Eventually we wanted more than we could get from a Conservative synagogue. By then we were basically *shomer Shabbos* and eating kosher. So we joined the Orthodox shul. Since we didn't live within walking distance of the shul, we sold our beautiful home and moved into a smaller and plainer one in the center of the Jewish community, right across the street from the shul.

Yiddishkeit made sense. It had a grounding effect on me. The more I learned, the more I loved it and the more involved I became. On another level, however, everything was a struggle. I didn't grow up with that *emunah*; it's not inherent within me, and I am constantly learning. And then there's the issue of being an archeologist. There was, and still is, a constant inner battle between my professional life and my observance of Torah and mitzvos.

> *Rav Dessler writes about the point of bechirah, of free will, and how it constantly fluctuates according to a where a person is standing in life. Putting myself in Tina's shoes, I can imagine how difficult it was for her to reconcile her two lifestyles. Her life revolves around archaeology. As a professor of archaeology, her husband has to do "on site" professional research, usually far from an organized Jewish community. We can only applaud every step, no matter how tiny, towards full mitzvah observance. Becoming frum is a process. We may not achieve perfection, but we strive for growth and change.*

Can you tell us about your work?

I am presently working at Ziyaret Tepe, in ancient Tushan, an Assyrian provincial capital in Turkey. In terms of its importance in the region, the city was immediately below the imperial capital of Ninevah. At the time of the destruction of the northern kingdom of Israel, the exiles were sent to Assyria and various parts of the Assyrian empire, such as ancient Tushan. Every time I dig at Ziyaret Tepe, I look for evidence of the exiles' quarters. Who knows? Perhaps one of our ancestors was among the slaves that were brought there 2000 years ago.

We spent the years 1996-2000 actively digging in South Africa, and were stationed in a little village called Pietermaritzburg. The closest Jewish community was in Durban.

During part of one trip, we were digging up an early Zulu farming community, so we had to live in Zulu huts on Zulu land. Over the centuries, the Zulus have barely changed their lifestyle, so our "home" was very similar to the ones we were digging up at the excavation. Although there was a lot of tribal warfare going on, we weren't frightened. It had nothing to do with us.

Our family enjoyed exploring the safari wildernesses. One time, a warthog came right up to us as we were eating our lunch. Another time our car was almost trampled by an elephant!

We also saw a lot of snakes on our digs. My husband's colleague once noticed a three-meter-long python floating motionless in the river! The python was too frozen to move. Several of the men waded into the water, picked up the python, and placed it on the back of a pickup truck to move it farther downstream; otherwise the Zulus would eat it for supper. But then the python thawed out on the back of the pickup truck and began to attack the men! It was quickly taken out of the camp and let go.

On another occasion, we were exploring a cave that was covered with many different types of animal tracks. One track, however, looked as if it was a huge tire that had been rolled out of the cave and then disappeared at the edge of the cliff outside. My husband's friend, a ranger in one of the safari parks, realized that it was a python track. The python must have swallowed a whole goat before slithering out of the cave. This was frightening, especially since we had no idea how long ago that had happened, and goats are even bigger — and certainly more fierce — than humans!

One time, Haskel and I, together with our oldest daughter, Rachael, visited an excavation in the mountains. Haskel and I climbed down the mountain into the *donga* (a wadi in South Africa) and up the next mountain to get a better view. Suddenly, it started to pour, so we rushed back to the car. But the *donga*, which had been completely dry before, had turned into a rushing river of thigh-high water. Just a few seconds after we climbed back up the mountain to our car, a wall of water about two stories high, carrying whole trees and enormous boulders in it, crashed through the *donga*.

After that, our guide tried to drive us back to civilization. But it was pitch-black outside and many of the roads were washed out or impassable. At one point, our guide stopped the car and said, "Something doesn't seem right. Look at the reflection of our headlights." He got out of the car and discovered that the bridge that was right in front of us had been washed away. I shudder to think what would have happened had we gone even a few more feet.

It took us a long time to return home that evening. At one point, our daughter, Rachael, looked at us in exasperation and asked, "Isn't there a Holiday Inn around here where we can spend the night?"

What unique challenges are you facing today, during your stay in Israel?

As part of our requirements for our fellowship, we live in an area of Jerusalem where there is no Jewish population. Without neighborhood friends to play with, my kids are bored. And then there's the whole issue of Sunday. In Canada, Shabbos was Shabbos, and Sunday was a day to get things done and to spend time with friends. But here, the only day we have is Shabbos, but since we live a distance from the Jewish community, spending time with friends on Shabbos is not really feasible.

After pythons and flash floods, your response sounds delightfully mundane — yet definitely more challenging!

Tina's story of growth and change is still in the process of being written. It is my heartfelt wish that Tina and Haskel merit to be written in the book of true life.

THE HACHNASAS ORCHIM BUSINESS

"Somehow, word got out that people can just pop in to us for a Shabbos meal — which they do, *baruch Hashem*! Our week is squeezed in between one Shabbos and the next. The entire week we are busy preparing for Shabbos."

Sharon Spiro

I met Sharon through Jerusalem Kosher News, a watch-dog organization that keeps people informed of the kashrus situation in Jerusalem. At the end of one alert, there was an open invitation for visitors to Jerusalem to enjoy Shabbos with the author's family, and a link to their website. I was intrigued. When my children were small, I would often read them a story — a Jewish take-off on Dr. Seuss — about a family who had a thousand guests for Shabbos. I'm in awe of people who are able to open up their homes and their hearts (and their pocketbooks!) week after week, to share Shabbos with strangers. So I sent Sharon an email asking if she'd be game for an interview. Luckily for all of us, she was.

I grew up in Washington Heights, New York. My parents were Holocaust survivors; my mother survived the death march, and my father was liberated from Auschwitz. After the war, my father was introduced to my mother's sister. When he saw my mother standing in a food line, he mistook her for her sister and started talking with her. At first, my mother was positive that he was her father — who had been murdered in a concentration camp. I have two photos, one of my maternal grandfather and one of my father, which were both taken when they were the same age. They are almost identical!

My mother, Nellie Ebbe, came from Weissbaden, Germany; my father, Eliyahu Blumner, from Chraznow, Poland. My mother was a *Yekke*, my father a *Chassid*; it was a real "mixed marriage."

I always dreamed of moving to Israel, but it took close to thirty years for that dream to materialize. During those thirty years I graduated high school, went to college, got a master's degree from Wurzweiller School of Social Work, married, and moved to Queens.

My ex-husband and I moved to Israel after our oldest daughter, who had just graduated a one-year Israeli seminary program, told us that she'd be staying in Israel for another year. She explained, "It doesn't make sense for me to return to America to attend Queens College and get a degree in education, when what I really want to do is teach *limudei kodesh*." She ended up getting a teaching degree in *Tanach* from Bar-Ilan University. The other three children were making major changes anyway — one was entering high school, another was ready to go away to yeshivah — so the timing was as perfect as it would ever be. It was really heartbreaking, however, to leave my elderly parents.

We moved to a beautiful two-story house in Hashmonaim, a small community just outside Kiryat Sefer. My ex-husband had a job waiting for him when we arrived. I stayed home for the first six months to help the kids acclimate to their new surroundings. Although I would have preferred to work in my profession — social work — I eventually ended up teaching English. Everything appeared picture-perfect. But it wasn't. Our marriage was on the rocks. We had hoped that, with moving to Israel, our *shalom bayis* would magically improve. But it didn't.

Two years after we moved to Israel, our oldest daughter was getting married — and we were getting divorced. The children and I remained in our home in Hashmonaim. My three older children had been aware of the tension between their parents and were half-expecting us to break up. But it took my youngest son, who was fourteen at the time, by complete surprise. He was devastated.

Shabbos as a single mother was a real challenge. I knew that somehow I would have to create a Shabbos atmosphere all on my own. I remember sitting down with my two younger children and telling them, "Shabbos is really important to me. Now that everything has changed, we have an opportunity to create what Shabbos will be like in our home." We spoke about what we could do to make Shabbos special, how each child should prepare something on the *parashah* and sing together with me. From a day of strain and tension, Shabbos turned into an oasis of tranquility in our very busy existence, a day of holiness that we really look forward to. I'm proud to say that working together as a family, we were able to create an intimate and beautiful Shabbos table.

Could you give me some practical ideas for creating a beautiful Shabbos table?

When the kids were small, we'd usually rush so crazily into Shabbos that by the time we'd sit down to the table we'd be exhausted and tense. To break that stress, I started a new *minhag*. When I *bentched* the children on Friday night, I would also whisper to each of them something that I liked about them and something positive that they did that week, and then they would reciprocate in kind. In addition to creating a real switch in the atmosphere, I learned amazing things about how my children viewed me.

Shabbos afternoon was always game time. Each child was allowed to choose one game, and we'd play it together as a family.

How did you meet your husband, Yechiel?

Yechiel and I were supposed to have gotten married thirty some years ago! When I was in high school, my Mom would often ask me, "Why can't you go out with someone nice?" referring to the tall young man who *davened* in their shul — Yechiel. But I wasn't interested ... at least, not until one Sunday when, as usual, I attended a protest rally for Soviet Jewry. My neighbor offered to drive a few of us kids home, among them Yechiel and myself. The neighbor's car broke down in the middle of Harlem. Although it was scary to be stuck in such a bad neighborhood, I was more afraid of my mother's reaction if I were to arrive home late (this was before cell phones were invented!). Yechiel offered to walk me to the bus stop, and then waited with me until I boarded my bus.

After that, Yechiel and I started dating. We mainly went to Jewish activist things. Eventually we decided to get married. I was seventeen; he was eighteen and a half.

Yechiel's parents really liked me and I felt like a member of his family. But my parents were devastated. Although Yechiel had graduated high school, he was not planning to attend college! Instead, he went straight to work: in a butcher shop, driving a cab, time clock repair. My parents were really worried that without an education we'd end up struggling financially for the rest of our lives. We broke off our engagement.

Yechiel and I had nothing more to do with each other until a few years ago, when I met him as we were walking into a *simchah* hall. He immediately recognized me and came over to say hello, but it took me a few minutes to realize who he was. After all, we hadn't seen each other for over thirty years. Both of us were still married, so I introduced him to my husband and he introduced me to his wife, and then we went our separate ways, assuming we'd never see each other again.

But life is full of interesting twists and turns. Some time later, I got divorced. As a single mother I was working around the clock trying to support my family. Then, after traveling to the States to take care of my critically-ill mother and remaining there till after her funeral, I returned to Israel and discovered that I had cancer.

Surgery, chemo, radiation: I went through the whole thing. Then, in the middle of this nightmare, I received a very nice email signed, "From an old friend." That old friend was Yechiel, who was also single again.

Yechiel and I graduated from emails to speaking on the phone to dating. Believe it or not, we picked up where we had left off more than thirty years earlier! He accompanied me to my remaining chemo and radiation treatments, providing me with the emotional support that I so badly needed.

Yechiel and I were married on 11 Sivan, 2006, almost three years ago.

Could you tell me about your hachnassas orchim business?

Both Yechiel and I dreamed of having an open house. Much to our surprise, we ended up living in Nachlaot, located in the heart of Jerusalem. Hashem directed us to a house that had been bought by an American who decided not to make *aliyah*. She sold it to us at the price that she'd originally paid for it several years before, although the market value was now much, much higher! Hashem sent us such a "*metziah*" so that we would be able to live in the perfect place to have lots of guests!

We love the neighborhood. So many different types of people live here. Yechiel *davens* in a shul about two minutes' walking distance from our house. It's located in one of the several old courtyards inhabited by Yiddish-speaking Yerushalmis. I *daven* in a more modern, Carlebach-style shul.

Somehow, word got out that people can just pop in to us for a Shabbos meal — which they do, *baruch Hashem*! Our week is squeezed in between one Shabbos and the next. The entire week we are busy preparing for Shabbos.

My husband and I each work at two jobs. On a good month, we barely make ends meet. In addition to feeding the locals who would otherwise not have a proper Shabbos meal for one reason or another, we also offer visitors (who would otherwise be paying a fortune for Shabbos dinner at a hotel) what we call the Nachlaot Experience, which is much less expensive than eating at a restaurant and provides much more, in both *ruchniyus* and *gashmius*. The money we earn covers a small amount of what it costs us to provide Shabbos meals for all of our many guests. Although we're far from wealthy, we try to stretch what we have and make our meals really fit for a king!

As Sharon and I speak, the phone rings several times with people calling to say that they would like to come for a Shabbos meal ....

Lots of single people live in Nachlaot. Although they may have an apartment, they don't have a home — so they come to us. And then, of course, there are the truly homeless who join us for meals. A lot of *geirim* and potential *geirim* also live in this neighborhood.

For many, we've become their surrogate family. We've even walked some to the *chuppah*.

I volunteer for Rav Karelitz of Bnei Brak's *beis din*, checking the potential *ger's* references. With my training as a social worker, I am able to assist them in dealing with their family issues. It's not easy for them to leave everything behind.

Once a week, I volunteer in the oncology department at Hadassah Hospital. I basically do whatever needs to be done, from making beds to bringing food to the patients. There are a lot of people out there with no support system, so I end up holding a lot of hands. Because I went through it, I understand what they are going through. They get a lot of *chizuk* from knowing that I was in their shoes and that I am now healthy.

In terms of a real, paying job, I teach conversational English online. I have students in France, Austria, and Italy. I don't hide the fact that I live in Israel, so all kinds of issues come up. It gives us what to talk about!

I am also associate director of Connections Israel, an organization that connects Jewish communities to Israel through *chesed*. My main job is to reach out to communities and individuals with the aim of helping them get involved in helping Israel. In addition, I do a lot of writing and assist in developing educational materials.

My husband is the Israeli correspondent for *Yeshivah World News*. He's also head of Jerusalem Kosher News [http://groups.google.com/group/jerusalemkosher], an organization that reports Kashrus problems in Israel.

The Kashrus situation here is horrendous. Rabbi Landau of Bnei Brak cried at his father's *kever* over the laxity in *kashrus* in, of all places, Bnei Brak. People often assume that if a store is located in an ultra-Orthodox neighborhood, it must be *glatt* kosher, so they don't bother checking the *hechsher*. But not only is it important to make sure there is a *hechsher*, it's also important to make sure that the *hechsher* is reliable. There are several bogus *hechshers* out there. I recently went to a *Chareidi* neighborhood and saw a vendor selling dried fruit right outside a kosher establishment. People erroneously assumed that the vendor was somehow connected to the adjacent store with the *hechsher*. Recently, it was discovered that a very popular fruit shake bar in Geulah had no *hechsher*. They were selling raspberry juice, which has a serious infestation problem.

What are my future plans? Well, I hope to greet the *Mashiach*, very, very soon! And then of course we hope that our family will grow, and that we will be able to host lots and lots of Shabbos guests.

THE CHILD OF MANY MOTHERS

"As a Holocaust survivor, I feel impelled to live my life to the fullest. Those who didn't survive charged those who did to tell the world what happened, so they should never forget! When I speak about the Holocaust, I am doing my part to keep it from being forgotten. We know the truth, and we must teach it to our children and grandchildren."

Rena Quint

When the woman who suggested that I interview Rena Quint mentioned to me that Mrs. Quint had been liberated from Bergen-Belsen as a young child, and that she has no memory of her real family, I knew this was one woman I absolutely must *interview. Here was a woman who had survived the unspeakable. She had been abruptly taken away from her mother and later from her father. In the camps she had seen adopted mother after adopted mother sent to the gas chambers, while she somehow survived — a lone flame among the ashes. Yet, despite the horrors, she, like so many of the previous generation, succeeded in creating a beautiful Jewish home renowned for its chesed and hachnassas orchim, and imbued with simchas hachaim.*

The first ghetto the Germans established was in my hometown of Piotrokow. When they built a wall around the Jewish section, the Jews who already lived there were allowed to stay, so we were allowed to remain in our own home. Jews from surrounding areas were herded into the ghetto and, later on, Jews from nearby cities and towns as well. The ghetto became very, very crowded. Five or six families lived in one apartment, and there was never enough food.

My father worked in a glass factory. The Nazis used all able-bodied men and women as slave labor.

One day, the Nazis entered the ghetto and started rounding up all the Jews who were not working. They came into the houses with guns and screamed for everyone to get out. People were frightened and tried to leave all at once. There was a stampede. Everyone was crying and yelling. We were taken to a very big square. From the square we were marched to the synagogue.

> *Mrs. Quint opens a folder and shows me a picture of an old building. She points out her apartment on the second floor. Turning the pages, she stops at a picture of another building.*

That's what the synagogue looks like now. Today it's used as a library. You can still see the Magen David on it. If you ask the librarian to open a curtain, you can see the indentation where the *Aron Kodesh* used to be. Look, here are the bullet holes ....

In the synagogue, we were crowded into two rooms, the main sanctuary and the *beis medrash*, which was on the floor below. I remember lots of yelling and crying — and shooting. I must have been holding on to my mother. I was about five years old at the time.

I also remember a man standing just outside the shul door. He may have been my uncle; I really don't know. He beckoned to me, calling me by my name, which in those days was Fredgia, and told me to run. I really don't understand why I was willing to run or why my mother was willing to let me go. You're a mother. Would you let your child leave you during a time of danger? Would you let your child just run away like that?

I let go of my mother's hand and ran out of the synagogue. Everyone in that synagogue, including my mother and two brothers, was taken by railway cars to Treblinka, where they were gassed and their bodies burned. The man who told me to run took me back to my father in the ghetto. My father hid me in a cellar.

When my father saw that it was impossible to continue hiding me, he dressed me like a boy. He cut my hair, changed my name from Fredgia to Froyim (Ephraim) and told the Germans that I was ten years old, because ten-year-old boys were considered old enough to be used as slave labor. I'm not tall now, so I couldn't have been tall then — but somehow I got away with it. I worked in the glass factory together with all the men.

I have very few memories of that time. I do remember waking up one morning and discovering that I was covered with pimples. It was probably chicken pox, or German measles, or some other children's disease. At the time, I saw it as the worst thing that could ever happen to me, and was thrilled when the rash disappeared.

I also remember the German Shepherd dogs. If the Germans thought that one of the workers was slacking off in his work, they would sic a vicious dog on him. These types of things one doesn't forget. I also remember the heat of the ovens and the men helping my father cover up for me. But I don't remember much else. After all, I was only five years old at the time.

Eventually — I have no idea how much later — the Germans rounded us up and took us to the train station, together with Jews from the other factories. They loaded us onto cattle cars and we started moving. I have no idea how long we traveled. We had nothing to eat or drink the entire time. With only two pails for our needs, the car stank. People vomited. People died. People walked over each other. There was no air.

When the train finally stopped, the Nazis flung open the doors and threw the dead bodies onto the snow. The rest of us had to jump. There was snow on the ground and we used it to drink and wash our faces. As we were getting adjusted to this new situation, Germans on motorcycles with side cars drove up to where we were standing. Using loudspeakers, they announced that we were being taken to a work camp and that the men should go to one side of the train and the women to the other.

My father realized that the Germans would soon discover my disguise when we'd undress to enter the showers for disinfection. The Germans really didn't care if we were clean or not, but they wanted to confiscate our clothes and make sure we weren't hiding anything on our bodies. It was obvious that I couldn't join my father in the men's camp. My father asked a teacher that he knew if she could keep an eye on me. That woman became my new "mother." I don't remember the teacher's name or what she looked like. When she was murdered, another woman took her place. Over the next few years I had several different "mothers."

That was the last time I saw my father. He gave me some pictures and said that after the war was over he'd meet me in Piotrokow. He didn't live long enough to go back, and I never returned either.

Years later, I did some research and discovered that according to official German records I was in the Piotrokow Ghetto until 1943. From there I was taken to a labor camp and, later on, to Bergen-Belsen.

I remember entering Bergen-Belsen with one of the infamous death marches. Many of the people marching with me had died along the way. We were very cold and sick. I was with a woman — one of my many "mothers" — but I don't have a real memory of her. I was still carrying the pictures that my father had given me. When we went into the showers, one of the guards grabbed my pictures from me and tore them up. For him, it was garbage. For me, it was my last connection with my roots.

It was probably 1944 when I arrived in Bergen-Belsen, but I really don't know for sure. There are no records, absolutely none. Before the war ended, the Germans tried to burn everything, to hide what they had done. When the British arrived, the smell of death and infectious disease was so rampant that they burned the rest of the camp. So I can tell you when I was liberated, but I cannot tell you when I arrived.

When we woke up each morning, we'd pull the dead bodies out of our bunk and dump them outside. There were bodies everywhere. It was perfectly accepted; they were just there. As a child, I didn't know that these were terrible and unusual things. I took it for granted and thought it was normal.

I was in a special section for women and children. One side was for mothers and their children; the other side for orphans. I was always in the side for mothers with their children because there was always someone who "adopted" me as her daughter and took care of me. We were alive because Eichmann was keeping us there to be used as bargaining chips with the Allies.

Most of the mothers and children in my section did not survive. Those who did survive looked like skeletons. The women who adopted me needed someone to love, and I needed someone to love me and take care of me, so we both benefited.

April 15, 1945, the day the British liberated Bergen-Belsen, started out like any other day. I was sitting outside under one of the trees, surrounded by corpses, positive that I'd never get out. No one ever got out of Bergen-Belsen — they just died. When a person was incapable of sitting any longer, he'd simply lie down and die, just like that. But then something happened that had never happened before. Tanks entered the camp. People were running and shouting. The British had arrived!

When the British entered the camp, they found thousands of dead bodies everywhere. No one knew who they were. There was no way to identify them. To prevent the spread of disease, the British bulldozed the bodies into mass graves of 5000 corpses each.

The British tried to give the people who were still alive food, but after starving for so many years many of the inmates were not able to digest real food, and died.

I was ill with typhus. The British brought me to a makeshift hospital, where I lay on a stretcher covered with real sheets! Later on, I was sent with a group of 6000 women and children to Sweden.

The start of a whole new stage in your life. What happened there?

In Sweden, one of the women claimed to be my relative and "adopted" me. She became my new mother. But I was so sick that I was transferred from the DP hospital to a regular Swedish hospital. There, a Christian couple wanted to raise me as their own child, but the hospital personnel explained that since I was Jewish, I belonged in Palestine. I often wonder what would have happened to me had I ended up going with that couple.

I spent one year in Sweden. There I met a woman named Anna.

She had two children: a boy, Sigmund, aged fifteen and a half, and a daughter, Fanny, aged nine and a half — my age. Anna's brother, who had moved to the United States before the war, sent her immigration documents. But while she was preparing to travel to America, her daughter, Fanny, died. Now Anna had an extra immigration document. She asked me if I'd like to go with her to the United States and become her new daughter. She gave me her daughter's name, birthday, and place of birth, and put my picture in her passport. In 1946 I arrived in the United States together with my new mother and brother.

Anna's brother lived in Lindenhurst, Long Island. He and his family took care of us. They were Orthodox. But three months later, while we were vacationing in the Catskills, Anna passed away.

That must have been so painful for you.

I just accepted it. It was something that kept happening to me. I had already lost several "mothers." It was reality. Now that she was gone, I knew that I'd have to find someone else to become close with. I knew that somehow someone would become my new mother.

The first time I ever attended a funeral was when Anna passed away. People stood around her grave and cried. No one explained to me what was happening. They thought I understood. But in Bergen-Belsen, thousands of people had died and were buried in mass graves, yet no one cried. No one mourned their passing. I couldn't understand why everyone was making such a fuss over just one woman. It didn't make sense to me.

After the *shivah,* the family that had brought Anna to the United States decided that they couldn't take responsibility for another child — me. A wonderful family in Brooklyn, the Globes, invited me to their home for Shabbos. At the end of Shabbos they asked me the same question that I had been asked so many times before: Would you like to become our daughter?

Before adopting me, the Globes searched the world to find out if I had any living relatives. They discovered two cousins in Israel. But my cousins were not interested in raising me. They told my parents that life in Israel was very difficult and that I was much better off in America.

This wonderful couple, Jacob and Leah Globe, became my parents. They raised me as their daughter. They succeeded in providing me with a normal childhood. I had toys, a bicycle, a social life; I went to school; I learned to play the piano — everything. I was their only child. They showered me with all their love.

In 1947, my adoptive parents changed my official name from Fanny, the name of the little girl who'd died, to Frances, and finally to Rena. Rena means joy — Freidel in Yiddish. Before the war, my name had been Fredgia, which is the Polish version of Freidel.

My mother lived to be over a hundred years old. My granddaughter remarked that when she arrived in Gan Eden, the first people she encountered must have been my biological parents, who thanked her for raising me like her own daughter. I really had two sets of parents, each of them with their own individual role and merit.

Throughout the years, as I was growing up and later on as I raised a family, I never spoke much about the Holocaust. But in 1981, when my children were older, I attended a survivors' gathering. After that I started doing a lot of research as I began searching for my roots.

Were you successful?

I didn't find anyone who remembered my family. It was as if we had never existed. Then, in 1984, we made *aliyah* and I started volunteering in Yad Vashem. In 1989 I went to Poland with a Yad Vashem group to research my roots. I found my birth certificate and my parents' marriage license. The marriage license provided me with a lot of information: my parents' ages; my mother's maiden name, Nesser; and my grandparents' names. Through these pieces of paper I was able to make a connection with my past. I didn't have any pictures of my biological family and I couldn't remember what they looked like, but now I had their names.

As a Holocaust survivor, I feel impelled to live my life to the fullest. Those who didn't survive charged those who did to tell the world what happened, so they should never forget! When I speak about the Holocaust, I am doing my part to keep it from being forgotten. We know the truth, and we must teach it to our children and grandchildren.

I often accompany groups visiting the camps in Poland as a historian and eyewitness. We usually visit Auschwitz-Birkenau, Treblinka, and Maidanek, the three main camps where Jews were murdered. We also go to Warsaw and Lublin, the site of the famous Yeshivas Chachmei Lublin.

Many of the young people on these tours never realize that these people were killed solely because they were Jewish. I explain to them that my survival was nothing short of a miracle. So many things, all completely out of my control, continually occurred to make sure that I would live. Hitler tried to destroy the Jewish people. When Jews assimilate and intermarry, they are continuing Hitler's job.

Very often, the groups that I lead are mixed, with both religious and non-religious kids. During the Shabbos meals, the religious kids start dancing, and soon the others join in. Within five minutes you can't tell the difference: They're all Jews. They gain a strong sense of Jewish identity. For many of these kids, this is the first step toward discovering and reconnecting with their heritage.

After touring the camps and learning so much about the Holocaust, the kids become extremely sensitive to anti-Semitism. When our groups walk the three kilometers from Auschwitz to Birkenau, we are surrounded by armed security guards who are being paid to protect us. But we are all very aware that sixty-some years ago they were there to shoot us. It's a strange, eerie feeling.

One year, we were traveling on the freeway when there was a bad accident on the opposite lane. Since our group contained doctors and nurses, we stopped to offer medical assistance. The kids were upset. "Why should we stop?" they argued. "Maybe the guy who is injured, or the guy's father, killed Jews during the war." But our people got out, crossed the barrier, and helped the injured driver.

When the doctors and nurses returned to the buses, they explained, "We're doctors. We're Jews. We're human beings. This is what we have to do. If the man dies, of course they will say that the Jews killed him. But if he lives, will they say that Jews saved him? Who knows? But it really doesn't matter. We had to do the correct thing."

We've had our share of anti-Semitic incidents. One time our group of seven buses — that's about 350 people — was on its way to Calsa, where there had been a pogrom after the war, when we received a phone call that about fifty skinheads were waiting for us there. We decided to turn back, though the kids were very upset. They argued that we outnumbered the skinheads and could easily fight them. But that in itself was problematic. The media would focus on the fight rather than the reason we were there to begin with.

When my husband and I visited Treblinka, we were unable to locate the memorial stone for my city, Piotrokow, among the other 17,000 memorial stones there. A few years later, as I led a group of young people to the camps, before arriving in Treblinka I went to each of the buses and asked the kids to look out for Piotrokow's memorial stone. In Treblinka, the weather was absolutely horrible, raining and simply awful. As I was standing at the place where my mother and brothers were murdered, one of the boys in the group — a real hippie with long hair and earrings — raced up to me and said, "Rena! Rena! I found it! I knew I would find it. I ***prayed*** that I would find it!" After he calmed down a bit, he continued, "I come from Argentina. My family knows nothing about being Jewish. No one in my family had anything to do with the Holocaust. But now that I found your stone, I am positive that I am a part of the Jewish people." This boy found his Jewish identity in Treblinka!

On another tour, I was walking in Warsaw on Shabbos morning with a few of the other members of our group, including a very husky he-man kind of Israeli, when some Polish punks surrounded us and began taunting us with all sorts of anti-Semitic remarks. We stood very still and ignored them until eventually they got tired of making fun of us and left. After they were gone, the husky Israeli said, "They called me a Jew. I've never been called a Jew before. I've always been an Israeli. I had to come to Poland to realize that I'm a Jew, not just an Israeli ...."

CHESED 24/7

"I learned that we must be grateful to the poor for giving us the opportunity to emulate Hashem, *Av HaRachamim*. The poor really have an important job in this world — to help those of us who are not poor reach our perfection ..."

Hadassah Yakobovitch

We moved to the Shmuel Hanavi Shikkunim from Ramot, an outlying neighborhood of Northern Jerusalem with a large conginent of English speakers.

Hanging outside the adjacent entrance is a huge sign with the words "Kav HaChesed" printed on it. Every couple of days, huge trucks unload crates of food — chicken and meat, vegetables, and even prepared salads — and bring them into the office located on the ground floor. Every once in a while people crowd around tables piled with brand-new clothes set up inside the entranceway.

One day, my curiosity got the better of me and I decided to see what this Kav HaChesed was all about. Imagine my surprise when I discovered that a former neighbor, Hadassah Yakobovitch, works there! Since then, we keep on bumping into each other, and every time I meet her, she speaks in glowing terms about Kav HaChesed's wonderful work.

I grew up in Jerusalem. My father *[who passed away shortly after this interview]* is a *Rosh Yeshivah*, and *baruch Hashem* I was privileged to marry a *ben Torah* who, today, is also a Rosh Yeshivah. By profession, I'm a teacher. I went into education because I feel a deep need to give of myself to help others. It's something I grew up with; our family was always involved with helping other *Yidden*. That's why today I work at Kav Hachesed. I see it as the fulfillment of an important *shlichus* in this world.

Years ago, I used to work at the *Mo'aitzah Hadatit*, Israel's Religious Council, where, among other things, couples register for marriage. All engaged couples are required to attend one-and-a-half hours of premarital counseling, which includes learning the basic halachos necessary to create a proper Jewish home. My job was to counsel the women. I had ninety minutes to teach them the basic laws and convince them to observe them.

I always gave the women my home phone number and told them to contact me if they have any questions. One of the women — a completely secular young lady — phoned me several months after her wedding and asked if I could review the halachos with her. Of course I took advantage of the opportunity to talk about other mitzvos.

The woman was enthusiastic enough to continue studying with me on a regular basis. Eventually I arranged for several *rabbanim* to kasher her kitchen. Afterward, I presented her with a very expensive set of fine dishes that I just happened to have lying around the house!

> *Huh? How did you just happen to have a brand-new set of dishes waiting to be given away?*

A few weeks before this woman phoned me, a friend of mine told me that she and her husband were selling their wedding presents to cover their debts, and asked if I'd like to purchase a set of dishes. Although I really didn't need them, I couldn't say no. They became the *shaliach* for yet another mitzvah! That was over twenty years ago. Today that "secular" woman's husband is a Biala *Chassid* and the *rav* of a beautiful *kehillah*.

Another time, one of the women I taught — though I have absolutely no recollection of having taught her — sent me a beautiful letter stating that as a result of that one lesson she began to explore her heritage. She ended up at Neve Yerushalayim. Today she and her husband are completely observant.

We used to live in the center of town, about four blocks from the Religious Council, so I was able to juggle my teaching with raising a family. But our move to Ramot made the traveling impossible, and I had to stop.

When the children got older I found a job as vice-principal of a women's seminary. I *loved* working with the young women, many whom were exploring their heritage for the first time. But eventually there were financial cutbacks and I had to leave. That was five years ago. At the time, a friend told me that Kav HaChesed was looking for a public-relations manager. Until then, they had been so busy doing *chesed* that they never put much thought into publicizing what they were doing. But hard reality made them realize that, without publicity, the organization would not be able to continue doing the wonderful things that they do!

Baruch Hashem, I've been working at Kav Hachesed for the last five years. When I first started, Kav HaChesed was part of Radio 10, the Chareidi radio station. Every Friday, people would phone in to the radio with requests for assistance and *for* offers to help — and we simply put the two together. For example, when someone offered to give us vegetables, we advertised on the radio that we needed a volunteer to bring the vegetables to Yerushalayim, and then distributed the vegetables to the poor families that heard about it on the radio station.

Even after the radio station shut down, the *chesed* continued. In those days, Rabbi Marciano, the CEO, worked as a volunteer — in real life he was a *mashgiach* of a yeshivah — but eventually Kav Hachesed took up so much of his time that he began working here full time.

But getting back to me ... when I first came here, no one even thought about public relations. Officially, I was the office manager, making phone calls to tell people to come to the office to pick up their food baskets, obtaining furniture for needy young couples, and thanking our donors. But then, as we developed a stable donor base, we realized that in addition to informal phone calls, thank-you letters had to be sent, articles placed in the newspaper — all the millions of little things that are necessary to keep an organization going.

As I speak with Hadassah, a mildly challenged young man is sitting to my right, filling little bags with candies and other treats to serve as prizes for the children who go from house to house collecting non-perishable goods for the monthly food baskets. It's a shoestring operation: The table where I placed my laptop is wobbling slightly; the chair's upholstery is torn. People are walking in an out and the phones are constantly ringing. There is an all-pervading sense of purpose.

I'm in total awe of Rabbi Marciano, the man behind the organization. You can't even begin to comprehend his level of *ahavas Yisrael*. A couple of months ago we distributed several hundred radiators to poor families, but he refused to take pictures, explaining that by doing so we'd jeopardize our clients' anonymity. Three times a year we make a bar mitzvah for over eighty boys, many who would otherwise never have one. Rabbi Marciano purchases a beautiful pair of *mehadrin tefillin* for each of these children — but, again, he shuns publicity to protect their privacy. He just wants to get things done, quietly and without fanfare.

Can you tell me about some of the people you help?

The first time I saw Mrs. P. come to speak with Rabbi Marciano, I was baffled. She seemed so put together, certainly not the type who would be in need of *tzedakah*. I later learned that her husband is deeply depressed and remains secluded in his room the entire day. Everything, but everything, falls on her shoulders. Since she is such a distinguished woman, none of the many other wonderful *chesed* organizations in Jerusalem are aware of her situation. She's a very private person, but like many of the other people who come here, she felt comfortable opening up to Rabbi Marciano. Every month, we send her a huge basket: chicken, fish, canned goods, vegetables, laundry detergent — you name it. This winter we gave her a radiator, as well as new shoes and coats for all of her children.

The neighborhood *Kupah Shel Tzedakah* gives us a list of families who cannot afford food. Three times a week we send them cooked lunches, plus sandwiches for their children to take to school.

Hadassah, what are your plans for the future?

The truth is, I would love to be out of a job. It would be wonderful if there were no more people in need of the organization's assistance. I learned that we must be grateful to the poor for giving us the opportunity to emulate Hashem, *Av HaRachamim*. The poor really have an important job in this world — to help those of us who are not poor reach our perfection .... Which means that, for the time being, I'll be staying here at Kav HaChesed!

FROM CUBA TO JERUSALEM

"I have no complaints — none whatsoever. If a person wants to complain, he'll always find something to complain about. But that's not what we're supposed to do. We're supposed to look for, and discover, the gifts, while using the challenges as tools for personal growth."

Gladys (Gittel) Yahia

A few weeks ago, while running some errands in central Jerusalem, I bumped into my good friend, Esther. After schmoozing for a few minutes I asked my favorite question, "Would you like to be interviewed?" (I'm always searching for new victims!) Her answer: "No. But you really should interview my mother. She's an amazing woman."

It took several weeks until Esther's mother, Gladys Yahia, and I were able to arrange a free morning to meet. Between taking ulpan classes, going to shiurim, babysitting the great-grandchildren, and organizing family parties, Gladys is (bli ayin hara) one very productive 76-year old.

My parents were from White Russia. They wanted to immigrate to the United States in 1924, but were unable to obtain visas. People suggested that they first travel to Cuba, because from there it would be much easier to get an American visa. But once they got to Cuba, they didn't want to leave. They loved it, and ended up staying for twenty-nine years. Cuba is a beautiful — an absolutely gorgeous — country."

As Gladys recalls the idyllic life in pre-Castro Cuba, her eyes water with emotion.

Cuba is exquisitely beautiful. It's a small island, rich in natural resources. Before Castro came into power, everyone was friendly and warm. We left in 1955, at the very beginning of the revolution. We hated leaving, but we had no choice. Castro was trying to take over and we were in constant fear of his terrorist tactics. Many of the Jews in Cuba were Holocaust survivors. They were petrified of what might happen once Castro gained complete control of the island. *Baruch Hashem* their fears were never realized.

Most of the Jews who lived in Cuba immigrated to the United States. A few went to Israel. But it was very difficult to leave. The night before my father left Cuba, he cried like a baby.

In pre-Castro Cuba, almost all the Jews kept kosher but not everyone kept Shabbos. In Havana, where I grew up, there were two kosher restaurants, several butcher shops and a few bakeries. It was a real community. Today, from what I've heard from the people who managed to get out, there's nothing left.

Castro is not anti-Jewish, but thanks to his social reforms, Cuba turned into an impoverished Third-World country. After the revolution, it became difficult to obtain any food, let alone kosher food. My father-in-law was a very religious man. He didn't flee the country before the revolution and ended up stuck there. It took him several years to get out. He later told us that the government distributed cans of lard as part of their rationing program. Of course he couldn't use it, so he would travel on two buses to reach the house of someone willing to exchange it for vegetable oil. Had he been caught, he would have been shot, or, if he was lucky, imprisoned. That's because exchanging food is considered capitalism, and, in Cuba, capitalism is considered a major offence!

Cuba is a very lush country, with lots of fruits and vegetables. Before the revolution, oranges, for example were so abundant that they cost next to nothing. Today, however, one needs a doctor's prescription to purchase one! If the doctor prescribes the fruit without the "patient" really needing it, the doctor ends up in jail. This is Communism.

What happened to all the fruit? Did it just disappear?

Castro presented them to poor countries in South America, to demonstrate to the Free World the success of his regime.

Castro indoctrinated the children of Cuba to believe that G-d does not exist and that Castro is their savior. At the start of his regime, propaganda specialists would go to the kindergartens and ask the small children, "Do you believe in G-d?" The children, of course, would yell, "Yes." So the propaganda specialist told the children to close their eyes and pray for candies. Afterwards, they would tell them to open their eyes and see if G-d had given them a candy. Then they'd say to the little ones, "Close your eyes again and pray to Castro to give you candies." Meanwhile, they would place a candy on each desk. When the children opened their eyes, the propaganda specialists would point to the candy and say, "See? Castro gives you candy, not G-d. So if you need something, turn to Castro, not to G-d."

Castro also provided all the young children with military uniforms and toy guns, and then taught them to march. They felt so proud to be part of Castro's revolutionary army. This was his way of brainwashing them. Almost all the adults presently living in Cuba were once small children who received candy from Castro and marched in the young revolutionary army. They're completely brainwashed.

The parallel between this and what we see in the Arab countries is chilling. Children there are being indoctrinated with hate, and brainwashed to believe that murder is an ideal to die for.

It took five years for my in-laws to get out of Cuba. The first time they applied for an exit visa, government officials barged into their home and made an inventory of everything — down to the last glass and fork — they owned. They opened every closet and drawer. It was impossible to hide anything. The law was that if, when they receive their exit visa, anything — even the smallest item — was missing, they would not be allowed to leave the country. This was meant to stop them from engaging in capitalism — in other words, from selling their belongings. But in reality, it meant that breaking a glass became a tragedy.

Once Castro came into power, there was almost no contact with my in-laws. All our letters were censored, telephone calls were few and far between, and we had to be careful what we said because there was always someone listening.

On several occasions, my in-laws were notified that they could emigrate, but each time something "happened" that prevented them from leaving the country. What type of things happened? Things like a government official "accidentally" spilling ink all over their exit permit before handing it to them.

They finally left Cuba when we least expected it. One of my husband's cousins invited us to visit them in Florida. The phone rang just as we were walking out of our house to drive to the airport. My husband told me not to take the call; we were running late and he was afraid that we'd miss the plane. As we later found out, the call was from the HIAS, the Hebrew Immigrant Aid Society, informing us that my in-laws had just arrived in the United States.

Gladys becomes openly emotional as she recounts the story of her family's reunion.

When we arrived at my husband's cousin's house in Florida, they told us, "Your parents escaped from Cuba. They're here, with us." I thought they were joking, but they weren't. My in-laws were hiding in the back room. They didn't want to appear without warning because they were afraid of shocking us.

How did they get out? Earlier that day a government official had told them that they could leave — so they left. Just like that! They didn't have a chance to contact us, or even change into better traveling clothes. They left everything behind. Everything! All their family pictures and heirlooms, their clothes, their dishes, everything. The arrived with nothing but the clothes on their back. But they were free, and our family was reunited!

How did you meet your husband?

We met at a Jewish league baseball game. I was seventeen and he was nineteen — two babies. It was 1949, and he had just returned from a two-year stint volunteering in Israel.

Volunteering in Israel? What did he do there?

In 1947, twenty Cuban boys, my husband among them, volunteered to help the Israelis fight the Arabs. He was on board the *Altalena* when it was blown up by the Hagganah.

After the State of Israel was established on May 14, 1948, several military groups continued to be active, in addition to the Hagganah, the main military group that eventually became the Israeli Defense Force. One of the larger subgroups, the Irgun, organized a ship, the Altalena, *to bring weapons and fighters to the newly-formed State. The ship was supposed to arrive in mid-May, but was delayed until mid-June. Meanwhile, on June 1, the Irgun and the IDF signed an agreement stating, among other things, that the Irgun was not to purchase or bring in its own ammunition to fight the Arabs. When the* Altalena *arrived in Israel with weapons for the Irgun, the IDF fired on the ship to prevent the weapons from reaching the Irgun fighters. Several Jewish men lost their lives in the encounter.*

My husband and his cousin were only seventeen years old when they traveled to Israel to fight in the War of Independence. My husband came as part of the Irgun. That's why he was on the *Altalena* when it was bombed by the Hagganah. One of his closest friends, who was sitting right next to him, was killed by a bullet in the brain. It was a terrible thing: Jew against Jew. When the ship caught fire, my husband jumped into the sea and swam ashore. The moment he arrived on shore, a Hagganah soldier arrested him and threw him into jail. After he was released he joined the IDF to fight the Arabs.

A couple of years later, Menachem Begin came to Cuba to meet my fiancé and the other boys who had volunteered for the Irgun. I had the privilege of meeting him then; he was a very nice person.

Many years later, when we were already living in Detroit, my husband and I attended a dinner for former members of the Irgun. Throughout the meal, my husband kept glancing at someone sitting at another table. "I know that guy," he whispered to me, before going over to speak with him. He tapped him on the shoulder and asked, "Do you remember me?" But the man had no idea who he was. So my husband enlightened him: "When I came out of the water after escaping the *Altalena*, you put your gun to my head!" That man was the Hagganah soldier who had arrested my husband!

In Cuba, my husband had been a salesman. In America, however, he didn't speak the language fluently and was unable to find work. He tried his hand at all sorts of trades, but was never really successful. Then, when he was just thirty-nine, he lost his leg to complications of smoking.

After that, he wasn't able to work. We had three small children and no money. We were very, very poor; it was a real struggle just to put food on the table.

A friend of mine — she meant well, she really did — tried to convince me to stop being so "old-fashioned" and to purchase non-kosher chickens instead of the kosher ones that I always bought. "Just *kasher* them yourselves, like you used to do in Cuba," she urged me. "It'll come out much cheaper that way." Her suggestion made a lot of sense. With the few dollars I'd save, I could buy more food for the family.

Gladys' daughter, Esther, remembers, "After my Mom put the non-kosher chicken in the shopping cart, she looked as if she was going to be sick. Then she turned to my sister and me and said, 'I just can't do it. We'll eat more tuna casseroles, but I just can't do it.' She put the non-kosher chicken back. I cannot tell what an impression this made on me."

Although Gladys had studied bookkeeping in Cuba, language difficulties made it hard for her to find a job in her profession. A friend of hers suggested that she learn to give medical manicures and pedicures. Despite the fact that English is not her native tongue, she managed to complete the rigorous, 500-hour course in a quarter of the usual time and passed the State licensing exam with flying colors.

Our family was always traditional, but I had never really learned anything about my religion. I just kept what I knew. Now that I had to support the family, I started working on Shabbos. I really thought I had no choice, but I hated doing it. One day, however, I decided, "That's it! No more! I won't work on Shabbos." When I told my boss about my decision, he did not fire me! I was able to continue working and still keep Shabbos!

I became completely *shomer* Torah and mitzvos at the age of sixty. Rebbe Akiva started at age forty; I started twenty years later. I was just following in my children's footsteps. But I was always *frum* in the sense that I believed in Hashem and in the Torah, and kept whatever I knew. The problem was that I didn't know very much.

Once I started learning, I had wonderful rabbis to help me, and am still in contact with many of them. When a person learns something, he wants to change. It's a slow, gradual process.

> *Gladys speaks so matter-of-factly, as if it's a given that every middle-aged person is open to change and growth. It's easy to accept something intellectually, but much more difficult to act upon it.*

I moved to Israel at age 74. My biggest challenge is learning Hebrew. The first time I started *ulpan*, I fell in the bathtub about two weeks into the course. For six months I was in terrible pain. I needed a walker to get around and I couldn't sit properly. It took the doctors close to a year to figure out that I had ruptured a muscle in my hip. Once I started physical therapy, it slowly started getting better. But I ended up missing an entire year of *ulpan*!

The following year, I started *ulpan* a second time. But then I broke my foot on Purim. With my foot encased in a heavy cast, I couldn't maneuver on and off buses and had to stop attending *ulpan*. This year, I started *ulpan* a third time. Then I had a mild heart attack. I decided that, no matter what, I'm going to continue. Almost immediately after I was discharged from the hospital, I returned to classes.

I really love living in Israel, although I do miss those children and grandchildren who still live in the States. I get emotional just talking about it. I feel so close to Hashem here. Yes, of course we should feel close to Hashem wherever we are — but here, it's special. There's that special connection.

Baruch Hashem, most of my children and grandchildren live in Israel. Last year, I made a big Chanukah party for them. By this year, it was already a "tradition." We were close to thirty adults, plus eight great-grandchildren — the oldest three and a half, the youngest just six weeks old!

Gladys' life has been far from easy. As a young married woman she fled Cuba to start life anew in a foreign country. When her husband was sick, and later after he passed away, she became the family's sole breadwinner. When I mentioned this to Gladys, however, her response was, for me, a lesson in emunah:

I have no complaints — none whatsoever. If a person wants to complain, he'll always find something to complain about. But that's not what we're supposed to do. We're supposed to look for, and discover, the gifts, while using the challenges as tools for personal growth.

ONE DAY AT A TIME

"How did I cope with these illogical emotions? I ate. I buried my pain in food."

Bracha (a pseudonym)

As mothers, we often underestimate our own importance. After all, it's the mothers who mold their children's inner world. Those first few years of security and trust provide our children with foundations of emotional stability. Bracha's story underscores how a lack of security can impact a person's life.

It's difficult for me to speak about my past. I was born in Belgium, in 1943, the midst of the Holocaust. My family went into hiding. They couldn't remain together; my four older siblings were sent to live on two neighboring farms, while my parents hid with a non-Jewish family. Although my mother was in hiding, I was born in a regular hospital. Somehow, the people involved with helping our family arranged it so that none of the medical staff realized that she was Jewish; or, perhaps they did know, but were compassionate enough to keep their knowledge to themselves. Upon leaving the hospital, my mother returned to her hiding place and I was handed over to a non-Jewish couple. They cared for me as if I was their own beloved child.

But my mother couldn't bear the separation. My father endangered his own life to take me from the family that was raising me and bring me to my mother. But I couldn't stay; it was far too dangerous for the non-Jewish family to hide a newborn baby as well as my parents. So I was placed with a different family. This scenario repeated itself four times during the first one-and-a-half years of my life. Four times, my father — who was a total stranger to me — appeared out of nowhere and abruptly removed me from the one person that I had bonded with. Four times, he took me away from my real mother — whom I didn't know and hadn't bonded with — to leave me alone in a stranger's home.

I only found out about the trauma many years later, when I was an adult. While I was growing up, no one discussed the war years. I didn't even have an inkling that I had been hidden by gentiles until after my own children were grown — but I'm getting ahead of myself.

I had a — quote, unquote — very normal childhood. I loved sports and was able to behave like everyone else. But I always felt different, as if I were an outsider. It was as if I was observing myself, looking at myself through a window.

My mother was very loving. She took us on plenty of outings. We'd go on beautiful picnics in the forest. Yet I always felt that she wasn't really interested in me as a person. And for some strange reason I actually feared my father. It's not as if he wasn't a good father. He was very nice and loving. But I dreaded being with him. It was a deep, inexplicable gut-feeling that came from within. Since it was an illogical fear, I couldn't battle it. Deep in the recesses of my mind, I was still afraid that my father would abruptly take me away — again — from the one person I loved. And for that reason, I was never able to relate — on a deep, *neshamah* level — with anyone. Unconsciously, I was afraid of being taken away to a place that I didn't know.

How did I cope with these illogical emotions? I ate. I buried my pain in food. Then, when I was in high school and my older siblings got married, I suddenly found myself in the position of an only child. I became terribly depressed. Instead of addressing the problem, my parents bought me a dog to alleviate my sense of loneliness. But the dog didn't last long. It was a real terror, fighting with all the other dogs in the neighborhood, and we soon had to get rid of it.

In those days, only "weird" people went for psychological help. Our family was perfect. A smile was constantly plastered on my face. Only "*nebachs*" had problems, not successful people like me! To give you an extreme example, after I was married I hurt my back and had to remain in traction for close to three months. The doctor explained that although medically there was nothing to be done except wait for my body to heal itself, he would give me medicine to alleviate the excruciating pain. Of course, I refused. Me? Take something for pain? Pain relief was for weaklings. I was strong. I was perfect. I couldn't let a silly thing like pain get in my way.

Perfect people never show emotions. They remain calm, cool, and collected under all circumstances. When my sister's one-year-old daughter — and my parents' first grandchild — was killed in a terrible accident no one cried at the funeral. During the *shivah*, everybody spoke about anything except the one thing they were supposed to speak about — the pain and tragedy of the young life that had been so suddenly snuffed out.

I kept my churning emotions from bubbling to the surface until, at age twenty-eight — after the birth of my fourth child — I fell into a deep depression. I would sit on the sofa the entire day, staring at the walls, wondering what would be the best way to put an en end to my misery. When I acted on my thoughts and tried to injure myself, I was admitted to a mental hospital. The psychiatrist doing the intake asked me lots of questions, which I answered to the best of my ability. At one point he looked me straight in the eye and said, "You are speaking as if you were one of the children who were hidden during the war." When he said those words, I felt as if I had just been handed the missing piece of a puzzle.

When I asked my mother about this, she refused to talk about it. I assumed that the memories were too painful. Speaking about those years would open a Pandora's Box — and then, who knew what might come out? My father was no longer alive, so I asked my older sister. That was when, for the first time, I heard the story of my first eighteen months of life. Suddenly, so many things seemed to fall into place: my sense of being different, my strange fear of my father, and my inability to connect with people in a deep, meaningful way.

But although I understood the source of my condition, I had no idea how to conquer it. I binged constantly to quell my emotions, and then tried to punish myself by throwing up eight or nine times a day. My whole life revolved around food. Because I had found a way to control my weight, I remained slim and beautiful — and weak and miserable! My youngest son, who is now in his mid-thirties, remembers me as being locked up in my own world, unable to reach out and connect with anyone, especially not my children. I believed that if I could hide my pain and try to appear normal, the pain would disappear and no one would realize that I had a problem. After all, having a problem was the worst thing possible .... If I wasn't perfect, then at least I had to *appear* perfect. Maybe, if the world *thought* I was perfect, I would actually be that way.

Eventually I lost so much weight that my life was in danger. When the doctor asked why I was so thin, I told him about my endless binges; how I would eat everything in sight, and then force myself to vomit to keep myself from gaining weight. I wanted to stop. I hated myself for what I was doing. But I couldn't control myself. It had become a compulsion.

I ended up in the hospital and was sent to a residential treatment center for eating disorders. There, I was placed with a group of anorexic young women. This was thirty-eight years ago and no one had ever heard of bulimia. I think I invented the disease.

I really had a great time at the residential center! I had no responsibilities. I was served good, healthy food. But I didn't recover. Although when I returned home my symptoms were much less severe, I was still bulimic. Instead of forcing myself to vomit several times a day, I did it several times a week.

My husband remembers those years as a blur of pain and terror. He never knew what he'd find when he returned home at the end of the day. When I was in the hospital, he was plunged into the role of single father. And then there was the shame. Neither of us wanted anyone in the community to know how we were suffering, so we put up a good front while keeping it securely concealed behind closed doors. After all, we had to look perfect.

During this time, I started painting, especially portraits. At first it was just a hobby, a way of relaxing and expressing my inner self. It was really the one bright ray of sunlight in my dark, drab existence. Eventually collectors found out about my work and it turned into a business.

Bracha shows me a charcoal portrait of a gaunt, angular woman with a haunted, worn-out look about her.

That's me. I was a lot thinner then. I thought being thin was beautiful, but I wasn't beautiful. I was exhausted and barely able to cope.

My husband retired six years ago. Now that we weren't tied down, we decided to fulfill our lifelong dream and move to Israel. Although I appeared to be functioning normally, I was still unable to control my food. I was forcing myself to vomit regularly and then berating myself for it. I was still careening between a somewhat normal existence and deep depression. But no one knew. We maintained a good front.

About half a year after making *aliyah*, someone brought me to a twelve-step food-addiction meeting. People there spoke openly of their disease. I met other women — *frum*, normal women — who were battling a compulsion. Women like myself who did ugly things to feed their addiction. Things like, late at night, binging on several tubs of ice cream that I had warned everyone not to touch since it had been bought for Shabbos, or stuffing my mouth with everything on the dessert table when I hoped no one was looking. And then, to purge my guilt, forcing myself to vomit.

Food addiction is a strange disease. For some of the women at the meetings — the grossly obese or those who'd succeeded in losing enormous amounts of weight — the problem was obvious. But there were others, like myself, who were either anorexic or used vomiting as a way of controlling their weight, and who appeared to be normal. We remained oblivious to the terrible toll our addiction was taking on our physical and mental health until it was almost too late.

Today, I realize the heavy price I paid to keep up a good front. I was so busy trying to make a good impression that I never really took care of myself or developed myself properly. Since I had to be "perfect," I felt a need to constantly be in control and viewed a lack of control as a sign of weakness. Today, although I do my *hishtadlus*, once I've done what I have to do I let go and let Hashem. It's His world; He runs the show, not me.

I can't say that I'm fully recovered. Every day is a struggle, and every day that I eat normally without forcing myself to vomit is a victory. I am conquering my disease, one day at a time.

RAISED IN THE CHURCH

"I pushed my way through the crowds to get close to the Wall. As I touched those warm stones, I felt as if I was standing there on behalf of my Jewish ancestors — our family's sole representative."

Ruth (a pseudonym)

When my friend Gita emailed me that she had just spoken with a woman whom I absolutely MUST interview, I picked up the phone and called the number she'd included in the email. A woman with a strong English accent answered the phone. Yes, she would love to tell me her story — which she did, that same afternoon.

We were a normal, middle-class family living in a small town in the south of England. My father was a bank manager, my mother, a teacher. We attended church every Sunday, just like many of the other families in our town.

The only sign that we weren't like everyone else was our last name. My aunts did some genealogical research and discovered that my great-great-great-great-grandfather was Jewish. But that, of course, didn't make me a Jew. I really didn't give much thought to religion, or to the fact that we'd had Jewish ancestors — other than feeling embarrassed by that information.

Just a funny side story: One day, a Jewish man made an appointment to speak with my father at work. It was obvious from the conversation that he assumed my father was Jewish. His parting words were, "Don't worry. I won't tell anyone your little secret."

My parents didn't push religion down my throat. But we were expected to make religion a serious personal experience; I really wanted to experience that much-talked-about spiritual light, but I wasn't successful.

After high school, I graduated University with a BA in history. During my three years at the University I continued my spiritual searching. I was looking for *emes*, and trying many different — and unconventional — venues to find it. But whatever I tried rang hollow.

After graduation, I moved to London where, as my father joked, I worked in drains. I was part of the civil service and responsible for approving grants for drainage and flood defense. During my two years in London I came to the realization that I had a talent for music and that I wanted to pursue that talent.

So I attended a different university to study music. After graduating with a BA in music, I was accepted into a postgraduate program where I received my Ph.D. in composition at the age of thirty-two. Music was my emotional and spiritual outlet.

Baruch Hashem, my career in music was really beginning to take off. But despite my professional success, I felt that there was something missing in my life. I was still searching, but that elusive truth seemed to be just beyond my reach. I knew it was there, but I couldn't find it.

I started going to church again, and became a devout Christian. I felt that in doing so I was giving my soul over to God. But somehow, I never felt that I was able to really make the connection I needed.

But despite these misgivings, the Church continued to pull me. I was drawn to the warm, wonderful, and welcoming people that I met there. I loved the music and the community worship. I felt appreciated and accepted and very much at home. But I was unable to believe their concept of God. The Bible says He is One, so how could He possibly be three?

Our group was evangelistic, which meant that we were supposed to evangelize and convert others to our beliefs. I tried it once, but couldn't continue because I knew that, deep down inside of me, I didn't believe in what I was saying. This created an internal conflict.

Around that time, my father was diagnosed with a brain tumor. He passed away ten months later. We were very, very close. I did my best to help him and comfort him during his final illness. I also spoke with him about Christianity and its beliefs, but even as we spoke, I knew that my words were false. G-d is real; Christian theology is not.

It was during this time that I began investigating our family's Jewish roots. I visited the Bevis Marks Synagogue in London, also known as Kahal Shaar HaShamayim. The synagogue was founded in 1701 to serve the Spanish and Portuguese congregation, and is still in use for daily services. I wanted to see where my great-great-great-great-great-grandfather had prayed.

After my father passed away in 2000, I found myself increasingly interested in my Jewish roots. I was overwhelmed with emotion when I realized that, had England been invaded during the Second World War, those roots — as tenuous as they were — may have been enough to have sent us to Auschwitz. I also realized that the reason I had always been afraid to tell people about these roots was because of my fear of anti-Semitism.

The first time I came to Israel was in September of 2002. It was Succos. I was drawn to the Kotel; it was like a magnet. The first time I went was for *Birkas Kohanim*. I had no idea what it was all about, but I found the experience intense and moving. I pushed my way through the crowds to get close to the Wall. As I touched those warm stones, I felt as if I was standing there on behalf of my Jewish ancestors — our family's sole representative. During that week in Israel I spent hours at the Kotel, mesmerized and overwhelmed by its *kedushah*.

I left Israel on Simchas Torah morning. The night before I left, I went to the Kotel without realizing that it was a Jewish holiday. I was surprised to find circles of men holding Torahs and dancing with tremendous *deveikus*. I had never seen anything like that before and was completely bowled over by it.

Back in England I looked up Jewish synagogues in the phone book and found a Reform temple. I started attending Friday night services there.

Although I was in England, I couldn't stop thinking about Israel. I felt drawn to the Land like a bee to honey, and returned again in May. Someone brought me to a Jewish wedding, and I loved it. I spent hours reading books on Judaism — yet I was still a believing Christian! People kept assuring me that I could remain a nice non-Jew, and that there was no need for me to become Jewish.

I traveled back to Israel for my summer vacation. I ate the Shabbos meals with the Machlis family in Maalot Dafna. They're an amazing family hosting over a hundred people each Shabbos! I also attended classes at the Diaspora Yeshivah and at the OU's Israel Center. I visited Chevron the day after the #2 bus returning from the Kotel was bombed. I remember entering the Avraham Avinu Synagogue and feeling that strange sense of connection. After all, although I wasn't Jewish, Avraham Avinu was also my ancestor. As I *davened* Minchah, I found myself asking Hashem to reconnect me to my ancestor, Avraham Avinu.

When I returned to England at the end of the summer, I did some research and learned that when a person converts to Judaism, he becomes a son (or daughter) of Avraham Avinu and Sara Imeinu. The word *Chevron* is rooted in the word *chibur*, connection, because going to Chevron connects us to our Patriarchs and Matriarchs. I felt that Hashem was leading me somewhere — but I wasn't exactly sure where.

Back in London, I really missed Jerusalem and longed to return. But since I couldn't return right away — after all, I had a job and other responsibilities — I did the next best thing: I went to Golder's Green! I would eat at a kosher restaurant and make sure to *bentch* afterward. Then I would go to the kosher supermarket and stock up on kosher foods. I also lit Shabbos candles each week.

But although I was drawn to Judaism — and was in so many ways acting like a Jew — I was still a Christian. I kept on vacillating between the two faiths.

I returned to Israel in December 2003, which was Chanukah. On the first night of Chanukah, I attended a celebration at a *kiruv* center overlooking the Kotel. Everyone recited the *Shema* together. I knew the first one and a half paragraphs by heart and was able to say it in Hebrew along with everyone else. As I stood with all the people in the room, proclaiming Hashem's Oneness, I felt extremely connected to the Jewish people and the Torah.

I made an appointment to speak with Rabbi Asher Wade. Today he's an Orthodox rabbi, but before converting to Judaism he was a Christian minister. With his background, I hoped that he would understand my struggles and be able to guide me. He suggested that I read Rabbi Fuch's book, *Halichos Bas Yisrael: A Woman's Guide to Jewish Observance.* To be honest, my immediate reaction was that this book was obviously written by a man and I did not want the yoke of keeping all those laws! But, on second thought, I realized that it wasn't about what *I* want; it was about what Hashem wants of me. The problem was that I really wasn't sure what Hashem wanted from me.

I began to sense where all this was taking me — and I was frightened. Back in England, I went to speak with an Orthodox rabbi. He told me to return to Israel. Later on, when I was in the process of converting, he wrote me that after our initial conversation he had no doubt that I would eventually become Jewish.

I returned to Israel in April, 2004. I felt squashed by a tremendous weight. I desired Hashem; I wanted to be part of His people — but my upbringing, and my entire background, still pulled me to Christianity.

I traveled to Chevron and *davened* at Ruth's tomb. Standing at the tomb, I thought about Ruth and Naomi, and committed myself to follow in Naomi's daughter-in-law's path, to make Ruth's people my people. That Shabbos when I ate at the Machlis family home in Maalot Dafna, I found myself crying during the meal. I knew that I had to make all the *kedushah* that I was feeling an integral part of me. I could no longer remain a stranger, looking in.

I returned to England and notified my employer that I would be leaving. Then I told my family and friends. My Mum was really upset at my decision. But I knew that my soul needed to be in Israel.

That summer I returned to Israel to attend a conversion course. I rented a small apartment in Jerusalem and found myself immersed in a warm, supportive Orthodox community. Then Hashem really made a miracle for me: Someone gave me a piano! Now I could make music again. That was my passion, my life.

I couldn't wait to convert and start building my life as a *frum* Jewish woman. After all, I was already in my forties and hoped to settle down and build a Jewish home. On a practical level I was running out of money, but I couldn't commit to a real job until after the conversion. So I learned, and I learned, and I learned some more. Whenever I wasn't at the conversion course, I was attending *shiurim*. During the sixteen months that I spent preparing to convert, I felt that Hashem was refining my soul, that I was becoming a totally different person — a Jew.

When I stood in front of the *beis din* to convert, the rabbis asked me such questions as, "On Shabbos Chanukah, which candles are lit first — the Chanukah candles or the Shabbos candles?" or "What is *Tefillas Haderech*?" *Baruch Hashem,* I knew the answers to all their questions. They also asked me what the fundamentals of Christian belief mean to me.

Before I immersed in the mikveh, one of the rabbis asked me if I believe in One G-d. I answered so emphatically that the *rabbanim* and the attendant all burst out laughing. Upon emerging from the mikveh, I felt as if I had received a new soul. Later on, in the anteroom, one of the rabbanim pulled out a bottle of liquor and said, "I got this at my bar mitzvah and was waiting for a very special occasion to open it. This is it!" We all made a *l'chayim*. It was very, very special.

Baruch Hashem, nearly two years later I was introduced to my husband. He had become *frum* in his early twenties, spent years learning in yeshivah, and has *semichah*. We were married ten months ago. My husband is presently studying full time in a *kollel*. I am grateful to be married to a *talmid chacham* and building a *bayis ne'eman b'Yisrael*.

Where do you see yourself headed from here?

I love writing and teaching music, and would like to use my talents to encourage creativity among *frum* women. I also want to get some more Jewish learning, to become more knowledgeable about my heritage. I would really love to have my own family, but that's in Hashem's hands. I am praying that He will bestow that *berachah* on me.

I have experienced such tremendous *hashgachah pratis* on this spiritual journey toward Judaism, and really feel that Hashem is guiding me, step by step. He is bringing me closer to Him, making me whole and bringing me under His wing. I can only say thank you, Hashem, for bringing me here to Yerushalayim and for returning me to my heritage, the Jewish people.

A friend of mine who was in the process of converting encountered many difficult bureaucratic obstacles such as missing visas and changing laws that delayed her from taking the final step for many, many months. Trying to empathize with the challenges she was facing, I said, "Sarah, it must be so difficult to wait so long to become Jewish." Her response: "Anything I have to do is nothing, absolutely nothing, compared to the zechus of being a member of the Chosen People!"

WAR AND PEACE

"It was amazing to see how the boys transformed themselves from long-haired hippies to yeshivah *bachurim*."

Rebbetzin Sheindel Weinbach

I was born in Belgium on June 26, 1941, at the beginning of World War II. In 1942 the Nazis rounded up my family — my parents, Abraham Israel Lamm and Rachel Rapaport, my six-month-old brother, and myself — and sent us to the Mechelen transit camp. I was two years old at the time.

The Mechelen transit camp was located in a single three-story building — a converted military barracks — in the city of Mechelen. The Germans chose this location because it was midway between Antwerp and Brussels, where most of Belgium Jewry lived, and because of its good railroad connections to the east.

The transit camp opened on July 27, 1942, when the first transport of Jews arrived from Antwerp. Between August and December of that same year, each week two transports of 1,000 Jews left the camp for Auschwitz. In the years between 1942 and 1944, 24,916 Jews and 351 gypsies were transported to the east. Most were gassed upon arrival.

On January 13, 1944, I was liberated from the camp and taken to an orphanage. Two days later, on January 15, 1944, my parents and younger brother were shipped to Auschwitz, where we assume that they were gassed upon arrival. I have no idea who arranged for me to be removed from the camp or why I, out of all the thousands of children who were interred in that camp, was chosen for life. Perhaps my aunt and uncle who raised me knew, but when I was growing up in New York these things were not talked about. People were too busy trying to forge a life for themselves to think about the horrors of their past. Today, of course, it's too late.

Between January 13, 1944 and September 1945 I was shuffled between different hiding places. I have vague memories of briefly being told about staying in a convent — but again, because these things were hardly spoken about after the war, I cannot be sure. I arrived in America on *Tishah B'Av* 5706 (August 6, 1946). I was five years old.

At first I lived with my paternal grandparents, who had also come to America right after the war. But half a year later, when my grandfather passed away, I went to live with my aunt and uncle, also survivors. We were three children; I had an older sister and a younger brother. I view my aunt and uncle as my parents and their children as my siblings; I say *Yizkor* for them and observe their *yahrtzeits*. It's in their merit that I became who I am today.

My parents had tremendous *mesirus nefesh* for *Yiddishkeit*. We lived in Kew Gardens. My mother was one of the handful of Orthodox women there who covered her hair. Although my parents were poor refugees who worked hard for every penny, they never scrimped when it came to our *chinuch*. Day school, Bais Yaakov, summer camp — all these things cost money, while public school was free. Yet they had their priorities straight and understood the eternal importance of a Torah education. Their self-sacrifice made a big impression on me, and guided me in setting my own priorities later on in life.

For high school, I traveled across New York, from Kew Gardens to Williamsburg, to attend Rebbetzin Kaplan's Bais Yaakov. Although I wasn't *zocheh* to have Rebbetzin Kaplan as my teacher, we felt her presence. She was there: at assemblies, walking through the halls, sitting in her office. She radiated calmness and serenity and an otherworldly holiness. Although she never spoke above a whisper, she was always heard. She was not at all pretentious; she looked like a typical Mama, caring and loving.

The girls who attended Bais Yaakov in those days came from diverse backgrounds. I loved to spend Shabbosos at my friends' homes, to experience the different New York Jewish communities — Washington Heights, the Bronx, Borough Park, Williamsburg, Spring Valley. Although we came from different types of homes — *Yekkeshe, Chassidish, Litvish* — we were unified in that we were all strongly committed to a life of Torah and mitzvos.

After graduating high school, I attended Rebbetzin Kaplan's seminary. Finally, I was *zocheh* to have her as my teacher!

I got engaged while still in seminary. My husband and I spent our first two years of married life in Williamsburg. My husband learned in the morning, served as the rabbi of a small congregation, and was English Principal at a yeshivah day school. I taught third-grade girls in the Bais Yaakov of Queens — many of whom I already knew, having been their Bnos leader.

In 1963, when I was expecting our second child, we came to the conclusion that we had to move. We needed something larger that our one-room flat in Williamsburg. Since we weren't able to find anything bigger in Williamsburg and weren't interested in moving to a different neighborhood, we decided to try the *aliyah* option and moved to Eretz Yisrael.

In the beginning, we lived at the far end of Meah Shearim, near Shivtei Yisrael Street. We could see the golden dome of *Har Habayis* from our porch! The border with Jordan literally zigzagged through the city and Jordanian snipers were a constant problem. Coming to Israel was like stepping back in time. It was completely different from what we had been used to in America.

We were homesick, of course, and missed all the little things that we had become used to in America. Even the cooking products were, and in many instances still are, different from what we were used to. Take baking powder for example. In Israel it comes in tiny packets, so how was I supposed to measure two-and-a-half teaspoons? And such staples as tuna fish and peanut butter were unheard of then.

My mother used to send me care packages containing these things, which, to a small extent, assuaged my homesickness.

International phone calls were very expensive. I called home three or four times a year, but then I would be so overwhelmed that I didn't know what to say. We did, however, exchange letters several times a week. I'm sorry I didn't save those letters; they would have made a beautiful book. My mother was really poetic; she had a very special *neshamah* that appreciated everything. A lot of interesting things were going on in her life at that time and she would tell me about them in her letters.

I gave birth to my second child in Eretz Yisrael. It was so different then! After delivery, I was hospitalized in an enormous ward together with twenty-five other women. Without curtains around the beds, we had no privacy. So instead of remaining for an entire week, as was done in those days, I just picked myself up and returned home, much to everyone's shock!

By the time the Six-Day War broke out in 1967, we were already living in our own apartment in the newly-constructed neighborhood of Mattersdorf. Although today Mattersdorf is centrally located, when we bought it for pennies we were taking an enormous risk, as the buildings bordered on no-man's land. At first there were no buses, and the only grocery store was in the very non-religious Romema neighborhood up the hill. We were really cut off from everything.

Unlike the Yom Kippur War, which came as a total shock, before the Six-Day War we were very aware that there was going to be another war and tried, as much as possible to prepare for it. My neighbors and I spent hours sewing huge canvas bags, which the men filled with sand and which were used to fortify the windows. People were really afraid that this would be another Holocaust — that the Arabs, who lived across the valley from us, would invade our homes and murder us in our beds. (Just to give you an idea of how close we were to the Arabs, today it takes us just an hour to hike to Ramot, which, prior to the Six-Day War, was a Jordanian stronghold.)

On Sunday, June 5, 1967, my husband left the house in the morning to take the bus to yeshivah, just like every other morning. When he got to the bus stop, the soldiers ordered him to return home. He raced to the children's nursery school, grabbed our two daughters and ran home. The building next to ours was hit with the first shelling. The shrapnel flew down to us, making neat holes in our windows. We raced down to the shelter and remained there for two full days. Most of us were young families with several small children. With each family allocated only two mattresses, conditions were extremely crowded! At one point the electricity was cut off; people ran up to their apartments to bring down whatever they had in the fridge to share it with their neighbors. Of course, there was no air-conditioning (who had ever heard of air-conditioning back then?) or fans. The shelter was hot and stuffy and it smelled horrible.

People who went outside reported that it was possible to watch the two armies firing at each other. At night, some people (we thought they were crazy) climbed up to the roof to get a better view of the war. But most of us remained ensconced in the shelter in (relative) safety. Our only connection with what was going on around us was through transistor radios. It was very frightening: The Israeli radio reported victories for Israel, while the Jordanian English-language station reported that we were losing. We didn't know whom to believe.

By the third day of the War, Jerusalem was in Israeli hands and we were able to leave the shelters. People were literally dancing in the streets. We had looked death in the eye and come away victorious!

We weren't permitted to enter the Old City until the Israeli soldiers cleared the mines and make sure that everything was safe. The first time people were allowed to go to the *Kosel* was on Shavuos. With our four small children, walking that far was impossible. So on the day after Shavous, we took a bus to just outside Old City and started walking — a real *aliyah l'regel*. There were hundreds of people walking together with us. We felt so connected to history! It was an extremely emotional experience to stand in front of the *Kosel* for the first time.

After the war, we thought that all the Jews would do *teshuvah* and *Mashiach* would come to rebuild the *Beis HaMikdash*. There were incredible miracles: Within the first four minutes of the war,

Israeli forces knocked out the entire Egyptian air force! It was like *Krias Yam Suf*, when Hashem's hand was so obvious! At first, people spoke with awe about the miracles, but most people didn't act on their initial *hisorerus*. Eventually, they spoke about the might of the Israeli Air Force and forgot Who had really won the war.

> *Rabbi Moshe Goldstein, a Middle East Studies professor residing in Baltimore, wrote: "It can even be said the inspiration rising from the Six Day War fueled the beginnings of the baal teshuvah movement." Even the most unaffiliated Jew identified with Israel's plight. The Holocaust was still fresh in people's memories and there was a real fear that this would be a repeat performance. And then, Hashem turned our fear into joy — and we were ecstatic! Everyone — the non-Jews, the unaffiliated Jews and the religious — realized that it was a modern-day miracle. Some took that knowledge one step further and turned it into a catalyst for life-changing decisions. Others allowed common sense to overcome their initial amazement and continued on with their lives as if nothing had happened.*

My husband, Rav Mendel Weinbach, *shlitah*, is one of the pioneers of the *teshuvah* movement. In 1966, together with Rav Nota Schiller, *shlitah*, and Rav Noach Weinberg, *ztz"l*, he opened a *ba'al teshuvah* yeshivah called Mevasseret Yerushalayim. In those days, Reb Meir Schuster was already at work in the Central Bus Station (the *Kosel* was still in Jordanian hands) trying to get young American backpackers to experience a real Shabbos. But when all the students left the country prior to the Six-Day War, the yeshivah closed.

A few year later, my husband, Rav Nota Schiller *shlitah*, Rav Noach Weinberg, *ztz"l*, and Rabbi Rosenberg, *shlitah*, established Shema Yisrael, which eventually was changed to Ohr Sameyach, named after Rav Meir Simchah, the Ohr Sameyach, who had no children.

Shema Yisrael/Ohr Sameyach started out with just six boys, and slowly grew. Today we have branches throughout the world, as well as many different programs catering to various populations: retired professionals, boys with no background whatsoever, boys with a day-school background, dropouts making a comeback, and so on.

Over the years we've met a lot of interesting characters. One boy — today a rebbe in a Brooklyn *cheder* — started becoming *frum* while in the United States. He needed a *succah* for Succos, but his parents said there was no room in the backyard to build one. So he bought an old telephone booth, removed the roof, plopped it down in the backyard, and converted it into a *succah*. It was the minimum size necessary for a kosher *succah*. He came to us for the Pesach Seder, and in trying to eat the *matzos* within the halachically-required amount of time he crunched through them like a beaver, keeping the food in his cheeks before — whoop! — swallowing the whole thing at one go! It really was hysterical. Another one of our guests taught us the Arabic version of *Chad Gadyah*, which has become a family tradition. We still sing it each year!

It was amazing to see how the boys transformed themselves from long-haired hippies to yeshivah *bachurim*. One of my husband's students came to us straight from a mental hospital. His parents had institutionalized him after they saw him doing such weird things as talking to the wall and refusing to turn on the lights on Saturday. It took him three months to convince the doctors there that he was not crazy. After he was discharged, he came directly to Eretz Yisrael. Although he definitely did not look like a typical yeshivah *bachur* — he wore his hair in a bushy Afro — he was completely committed to a life of Torah and mitzvos. Today he's a noted *talmid chacham* and a *Rosh Yeshivah* — and his parents have come to the realization that he is far from being nuts.

Many years ago, some of the women in Mattersdorf thought it might be a good idea to open a central clearing house for clothes that were not being used. Like many other families, we were getting packages of clothing from abroad, but not everything was suitable for our family. At first, the clearing house — or clothing *gemach,* as we later called it — was open just once a week. Eventually the woman who ran it went back to America and I took over. I started advertising in *The Jewish Press* and *The Jewish Observer*, the two Orthodox English-language periodicals in existence then. As word of the *gemach* spread, we started receiving more and more boxes of absolutely stunning clothes from many different countries, including Australia and South Africa! We expanded our hours, and when we saw that we had still more clothes, we opened a branch in the city.

Women from different areas of Jerusalem asked me to help them establish their own neighborhood *gemachs*. I would help them to set it up and provide them with a month's supply of clothing. Within a few weeks, they were able to cover their rent and other costs, and even make extra money, which would then be donated to *tzedakah*. The *gemach* in Mattersdorf, for example, donates its money to *Chesed Yad L'Yad*, which assists neighborhood women after birth and struggling neighborhood families with small monetary grants. The money earned at the *gemach* that I operate in central Jerusalem is used to purchase blankets and linens for poor brides. In addition, that *gemach* has hired a *shaatnez* checker who is paid by the hour to check clothes. Anyone can walk into the *gemach* to have clothing checked at a greatly reduced price. We are hoping that many people will take advantage of this service and be saved from the transgression of wearing *shaatnez*.

Running a clothing *gemach* can be really nerve-wracking. Very often there's not enough room for all the clothes that people want to donate, so I end up taking them into my house. In the last few weeks I've sent boxes of clothes to Kiryat Sefer, Beitar, Tsfat, Elad, and Teverya. Everything has to be sorted; we don't want to send *shmattes*. It's a lot of work, but *baruch Hashem*, thanks to our many wonderful volunteer workers, our network of clothing *gemachs* enables many families to clothe themselves from head to toe.

The future? I hope to be able to keep on doing what I'm doing now. It's hard work, but there's tremendous satisfaction in it, and one sees *siyata d'Shmaya* at every turn, including the blessings in my personal life.

FROM BERKELEY TO JERUSALEM

"I kashered my kitchen ... because I wanted all my daughter's friends and all my friends to be able to eat in our house — on real plates, not paper!"

Dr. Chana Baruch, a"h

The late Dr. Chana Baruch was a well-known and well-loved Jerusalem pediatrician. Her office was located in the local Kupat Cholim Meuchedet clinic just a few minutes walking distance from my apartment. The first time I met Dr. Chana was when I accompanied my daughter and her one-month-old very colicky baby to the pediatrician's office. I was impressed with the doctor's obvious delight at holding such a young infant, and in her patience in demonstrating to the first-time mother the proper way to burp a child. This was obviously a woman who loved her work!

I was intrigued. I assumed that Dr. Chana was in her late fifties or early sixties, which meant that she'd attended medical school when it was not so common for a woman to do so. As it turned out, Dr. Chana graduated Harvard College and UCSD medical school and practiced pediatrics and clinical genetics near San Francisco, California.

I'm a journalist, and journalists can sense a story! A religious pedia-

trician who left a comfortable lifestyle in Northern California to live in a fourth-story walk-up apartment in Yerushalayim — well, it seemed obvious that Dr. Chana had an interesting tale to tell, and one that my readers would like to hear.

The next day, I popped into Dr. Chana's office to ask her if she could fit me into her schedule. Since she had finished work for the day, I offered to walk her home. As we walked along the pathways of Maalot Dafna, I noticed children smile shyly at her. "Look at those adorable eyes," she commented about one. "That one is the spitting image of her older sister," she said, pointing to another.

A week later, I entered Dr. Chana's office and found her in the midst of finishing some last-minute business. Between phone calls and writing prescriptions, she handed me a child's drawing of a little girl having her blood taken. "Isn't the detail amazing?" she asks. She seemed more like a proud grandmother than a physician.

A few months after I interviewed Dr. Chana, the phone rang just as I was about to drop into bed. "Is this Debbie Shapiro, the writer?" an anonymous voice asked. When I answered in the affirmative, she continued, "Do you remember interviewing Dr. Chana Baruch?" The answer, of course, was "Yes!" How could I forget the doctor's sacrifice to keep mitzvos, as well as her love and dedication for her young patients? The woman, who by now had identified herself as Dr. Chana's neighbor, continued, "Dr. Chana passed away less than a week ago, of pneumonia. It was very sudden and totally unexpected. She was only fifty-eight."

When Dr. Chana's neighbor asked me to email her a copy of the interview to give to the family — "It would mean so much to them" — I realized that it had been a tremendous privilege to be able to interview the doctor and provide her loved ones with a glimpse of the tremendous challenges that she had faced and overcome.

May her family be consoled among the mourners of Tzion.

I am the only child of older parents. I was raised in Brooklyn, New York, in a very beautiful neighborhood opposite the museum and the botanical gardens. Although my family was not religious, culturally they were very Jewish.

I was always in my own religious world. At the age of four, when

I recited the *Mah Nishtanah* at the Seder table, I had no doubt that I could never, ever marry a non-Jew. When I was five or six years old, I attended a Reform Sunday school. One day I returned home from Sunday school and asked my parents, "Why don't we light Shabbos candles?" After that (although the candles were often lit after sunset), every Friday night my mother lit candles and my father made *Kiddush*. So although we weren't *frum*, we felt very connected to our heritage.

I was always drawn to religious practice as a way of reaching Hashem. I think that my attraction to it is partly genetic, since from the time I was very young I was told that I am a descendent of the Baal Shem Tov. Like the Chassidim of old, I have always preferred to pray outside, in nature, rather than in an enclosed room.

I graduated high school in 1965 and was fortunate enough to attend Harvard along with a group of supportive high-school friends. In my senior year I married my former husband. His family was observant, but we were not. The rabbi who married us spoke to us about the importance of Shabbos. Coming from a Reform background, I was familiar with the holidays — but who had ever heard of Shabbos?

After our marriage, my husband and I moved to San Diego, where he had a position as an intern. In those days there were very few Jews, let alone Orthodox Jews, living in San Diego. Although we weren't religious, I would usually light the Shabbos candles, and my husband and I would turn over our kitchen for Pesach and invite all the Jewish medical students to our Seder.

We eventually moved to Berkeley, California, where both my husband and I practiced pediatrics. In addition, I was a consultant in clinical genetics. A year before my daughter entered kindergarten, I investigated all the private and public schools in the area and came to the conclusion that Berkeley's small Jewish Day School was the best place for our daughter. I *kashered* my kitchen a year or so later because I wanted all my daughter's friends and all my friends to be able to eat in our house — on real plates, not paper!

I wanted my daughter to have a close connection with Israel. So when she was eight and a half, we spent the summer in Jerusalem. She loved the freedom of being able to go to the pool with our new neighbors — something that, for security reasons, I would never allow in the United States. Years later, she told me that, that summer, she'd decided it was much more fun to be a kid in Israel! That realization impelled her to return to Israel as a young adult, which ultimately was the reason for my own *aliyah*.

Although my husband remained ambivalent, I was becoming more observant. But our marriage had other problems, and in 1991 we got divorced.

I dreamed of moving to Israel, yet for my daughter's security and happiness I remained in Berkeley and kept the status quo. I did, however, encourage her to have a close connection with Israel.

When my daughter was in eleventh grade, she — all by herself! — made all the arrangements to attend an Israeli high school for part of the last semester of her senior year. It was a wonderful experience, and she returned to the United States determined to go back. After graduating high school, she returned to Israel to continue her studies. Today she is married and lives in Israel with her husband and my gorgeous grandson!

Since my daughter was studying in Israel and both my parents had died, there was no reason for me to remain in the United States. And besides, I wanted to re-marry — and neither Berkeley nor San Francisco are suitable places for finding a *shidduch*!

Although I kept a kosher home, attended an Orthodox shul and was basically *shomer Shabbos*, I certainly did not look Orthodox. I was wary of cults and wanted to be certain that Orthodox Judaism is not another cult.

I arrived in Israel six months after my daughter, and moved in to the University dorm with her. I slept in her bed, while she slept on the floor. My daughter, who was never pushy toward me, kept telling me over and over again, "Mom, you are the type of person who would enjoy the Shabbos hospitality that Jeff Siedel organizes at the *Kosel*." After two weeks of hearing this, I felt that I had no choice but to go!

[The man with the saddle shoes, Jeff Seidel, is a one-man kiruv machine. In addition to running several Jewish kiruv centers, a youth hostel, and heritage tours of Israel and Eastern Europe, he brings secular Jews "off the Wall" to Chareidi families to experience Shabbos hospitality.]

Jeff Seidel arranged for me to eat a Shabbos meal with the Machlis family in Maalot Dafna. I was amazed! There were close to two hundred guests for the meal. I later learned that the Machlises host approximately this number every Shabbos, many of them experiencing Shabbos for the first time. The entire family is involved in preparing and serving the food. There are no limits to what they will do to help another Jew. That one Shabbos impacted me to such an extent that today, after many changes, I am slowly growing in my observance of Torah and mitzvos and define myself as an Orthodox Jew.

The Machlises became my surrogate family. As a divorcee, with a minimal knowledge of Hebrew and very new to the observant way of life, I was extremely vulnerable. They went out of their way to help me in every possible way. My daughter once said, "Mom, the Machlises have probably helped you more than they've helped anyone else." Although this would be a tremendous compliment — after all, it's nice to think of oneself as being special — it was not true. They've helped innumerable people.

Can you give an example?

Here's one. When I applied for new-immigrant status, the clerks at the *Misrad Hapnim* (Ministry of the Interior) requested testimony from three rabbis who could testify that I am Jewish. I brought them letters from three well- known rabbis who, although they had been living in Israel for the last several years, had known me in the United States. The clerks refused to accept these letters. They were not even willing to phone the rabbis to confirm the information, explaining that they needed personal testimony from rabbis who knew me up until the time I came to Israel.

But I didn't know anyone like that! The clerks were totally uncooperative. They did not offer me guidance or advice, and I was running myself ragged trying to find a solution to what appeared to be an insoluble problem.

One morning, I showed up at the Machlis home exhausted and depressed. Rabbi Machlis took one look at me and said to his Rebbetzin, "I must accompany her to the *Misrad Hapnim* — today!"

At the *Misrad Hapnim*, Rabbi Machlis asked the clerks, "So, tell me, what's the problem with this woman?" They replied, "We're concerned that she may have converted to Christianity after the rabbis knew her."

Rabbi Machlis spread his hands, leaned back in his chair, and started to chuckle. It was as if he was saying, "Come now! You know that that's ridiculous. What's the real problem?"

One of the clerks blurted out, "Well ... actually, we lost this woman's file." That same day, I took care of all the bureaucracy — and the next day I received my immigrant papers.

A few years later, Dr. Chana met her husband, David Holland.

I've learned so much about *chesed* from my husband. He's a tremendous *baal chessed*, and that *chesed* has changed my life. Thanks to both him and the Machlises, I'm becoming a different person — much less strict, much more giving and loving.

OFF THE DERECH

"Helplessly, we watched our son change — from the wholesome, *frum, cheder yingelah* we knew so well to a rebellious stranger."

Ruchama (a pseudonym)

Children going "off the derech"; it's such a painful phenomenon, and much, much too prevalent. Each Jewish child is a treasure, the object of his parents' hopes and prayers, the future of Am Yisrael. My friend was kind enough to share her story with me.

In almost every instance, a child goes off the *derech* because of something that happened. Very often it is something that happened outside the house; something that was completely beyond the parents' control.

It's impossible to watch a child twenty-four hours a day. That's why it's so important to do everything possible to create a relationship where the child will feel free and confident enough to confide in his parents, ***no matter what***. There are all kinds of dangers lurking on the street, but we can't warn them about their existence since we don't want them to know that they exist. It's a difficult dance.

When I look back at what happened to our son, I realize that as a young mother I was extremely inexperienced. I had no idea how to create an open, accepting relationship with my children.

When a child experiences something that contradicts everything he'd been taught to believe in, he will either act out, or he will just drop everything. It's a very normal reaction. When we see someone who represents a certain group being dishonest or immoral, we don't want to have anything to do with that group. That's human nature — and our children are also human.

Our son is brilliant. He *was* an excellent student. When he was twelve years old, his teacher (who was later fired) beat him up for not placing his finger on the correct place in the *sefer*! When he came home from school and showed me his bruises, I said all the things that mothers are supposed to say: "What happened?" "That must really hurt. Do you want to tell me about it?" But I really didn't take it seriously until later on that evening, when two different mothers phoned to tell me that their children couldn't sleep because they were so upset by what had happened that morning.

[This incident took place nearly thirty years ago. Today, such behavior is unheard-of. All teachers undergo rigorous professional training, and classroom supervision is much stricter.]

Although I reported the incident to several people in the school, including the principal and *mashgiach*, nothing was done about it until several weeks later, when the teacher hit another child. But being the good parent, and not having experts to advise me, we never told our son that we had taken these steps. We thought that we must side with the school in front of our child. Our son later blamed us for not doing anything to protect him. He blamed the school for not firing the teacher. And he blamed Hashem for letting it happen.

It wasn't long before we noticed a change in our son. He was no longer the delightfully friendly and outgoing boy that we knew. He no longer surprised me with thoughtful presents and homemade cards. His *yarmulke* became smaller and was worn jauntily to the side. He started getting up late and *davening* at home. Then he began smoking. Helplessly, we watched our son change — from the wholesome, *frum, cheder yingela* we knew so well to a rebellious stranger.

You cannot imagine what this did to my self-esteem. I felt like a failure, an absolute failure. I remember going to shul on Rosh Hashanah and thinking that all the other women there were so much better than me; after all, they were able to raise their children properly. I was embarrassed to go to weddings, to be seen in public. I felt as if everyone was wordlessly blaming me for having a rebellious son.

Rabbi Yaakov Horowitz, an expert at helping both parents of children who have gone off the *derech* as well as the children themselves, is careful to write about children who have gone off the *derech* in a way that does not put the blame on anyone. He points out that parents must look for solutions, rather than waste precious time blaming themselves or others. But thirty years ago we were not aware of that. Instead of searching for a solution, we wasted our time trying to discover who was at fault.

I suddenly found myself the object of everyone's advice. But most of the people who were giving me advice had no experience with this problem. I really didn't want to hear platitudes and clichés. I hated being told that I'm a *tzedekes* or, worse, a monster. What I really needed was for people to let me know that they were there for me, and that they were *davening* for my son.

> *Ruchama, when you were going through this I was very careful not to bring up the subject or ask anything that might be construed as impinging on your privacy. I didn't want to cause you more pain. But was there anything that I could have done pro-actively?*

First of all, I really appreciate the fact that you didn't feel that you had to preach to me or tell me how to live my life. And you didn't try to put a band-aid on a gushing wound. On the other hand, as a close friend, you could have quietly said something like, "I realize you're going through a hard time now. I consider myself a close friend, and if there's anything I can do for you, please tell me." And then, of course, ask for my son's name for *tefillah*.

I learned many, many things about parenting from this experience, some of which I would like to share with you. One thing is to make sure that your children know what you expect of them, what you consider to be right or wrong. At a parenting group I attend, the facilitator gave an extreme example that really hit home. A youngster who had fallen to such an extent that he was taking drugs, turned to his mother and said, "Ma, I just want to ask you one thing. Do you allow me to use drugs?" The mother was flabbergasted, and replied, "Of course not!" The boy looked at her and said, "But you never told me." After that, he stopped taking drugs!

How did your son's going off the derech impact the other members of the family?

It affected everyone, from the oldest to the youngest. My oldest son was having trouble getting into a yeshivah. My younger children were upset that their older brother was getting away with things that they couldn't get away with.

In an attempt to stop the downward spiral, we treated our son with kid gloves. We bought him treats and gave him privileges that we couldn't afford to give the other children. This undermined the entire *chinuch* in our home. Although I explained to the other children what was going on and why we were more lenient with their brother, they were jealous. Logically, they understood what we told them. But, emotionally — well, a kid is a kid!

Eventually our son left home. It was better for him and better for the other children. He continued to come home for special occasions and family parties, and when he did, he behaved himself and tried to blend in with the rest of us. But the pain, his pain and our pain, was always there.

One Succos, over a decade after the incident with his teacher, he opened up and told us how angry he was at us for not standing up for him when the teacher hit him. He said that he would never forgive us for that. For the first time, I told him about all the phone calls that I had made, of how I had complained to both the principal and the *mashgiach*, and how nothing was done until several weeks later, when another parent reported a similar incident. Then I started crying and he started crying, and my husband started crying. We cried in a way that we had never cried before. That was the beginning of our healing.

Today? Our son is married and lives on a secular kibbutz. We are friendly. Although his wedding was on the kibbutz and was not the type of *simchah* that we had hoped and prayed for, our entire family was there to celebrate with him. He brought in special, glatt-kosher food just for us, which showed us how important it was for him that we be there at such an important moment in his life. Although it wasn't easy, we were glad that we went.

Every Friday afternoon, he calls us to wish us a *Gut Shabbos*. When he and his wife come to our *simchos*, they dress appropriately. Of course we would have liked it to be different, but we are grateful for this relationship, and pray that this will be the path upon which he and his family will eventually return home.

As parents, what can we do to prevent our children from going off the derech?

First of all, *shalom bayis* is of the utmost importance. When the home is a good place to be, the children won't want to leave it. Also, never, ever, ever, blame: not the child, not yourself and not your spouse! Make a concerted effort to look for anything good that the child is doing, even if it is something as minor as putting his dirty sock in the hamper. This is important for all children, but especially for a child who is rebelling. Remember that he's a viable human being who's going through a difficult time. Love him. He's your child, your flesh and blood!

Children don't like to be different. When our children were growing up, we were very poor and unable to provide them with many things that they needed. So, for example, while all the other children in my son's *cheder* wore hooded jackets in the winter, he wore a second-hand beige trench coat — and was the laughingstock of his class. At the time, we didn't realize that there is such a thing as emotional necessities and that, for our son's emotional health, he needed to wear clothes that were similar to what the other kids wore.

I mentioned before the importance of creating a warm relationship with our children. I discovered that cooking with my kids is a great way to develop that relationship. Somehow, working together in the kitchen sets the atmosphere for talking and sharing feelings. My eleven-year-old son makes the greatest pizza — from scratch! Of course I insist that the kids clean up after themselves.

For the last several years, instead of sleeping or going to a *shiur*, I devote Shabbos afternoon to playing games with my children. It's not always easy — I'd much rather catch up on my sleep — but we have gained so much from that time spent together, talking, noshing, and just being a warm, loving family.

For those who are blessed with children who are all on the straight and narrow, please, please, *please* don't shun me or look down on me and my family. Be *mekarev* my other children. They're going through a very difficult time, and they shouldn't be lumped together with their wayward sibling. I understand that you don't want your kids to come to my house for fear that they might be influenced by my non-religious son. Instead, please invite my children to your home. Accept them for their own worth. They are not to blame for their older brother's behavior.

> *When I was a young teenager and our family was going through a very difficult time, our neighbors opened their home, and hearts, to me. They succeeded in making me feel that I was an integral part of their warm and wonderful family. Instead of judging and blaming me for the problems at home, they accepted me for who I was. Thanks to them, I was able to weather that emotionally difficult time and become the person I am today.*
>
> *Years later, when I thanked the family for everything they had done for me, they sort of shrugged their shoulders and said, "You were just one of the gang."*
>
> *I'm sure that having me around so much of the time must have been a real hassle. After all, fourteen-year-old girls can be quite difficult! But that chesed literally saved my life. Today, when my children's friends make themselves a bit too much at home in our house, I think back to my neighbors and remember the impact they had on my life. After being the recipient of such kindness, how can I not pass it along?*

DREAMS COME TRUE

"In the winter, the dorm was freezing cold; sometimes we'd wake up in the morning to find our *negel vasser* iced over! But we were pioneers. The Gateshead Sem was only ten years old and the whole concept of a girls' seminary was revolutionary."

Rina Fisch (a pseudonym)

Rina was one of the first people I met after we moved into our new neighborhood. One of my former neighbors made a Kiddush for her son's bar mitzvah at a yeshivah just up the block from me. At the Kiddush, I mentioned to my friend's sister that I was feeling somewhat lonely and disorientated in my new home. After all, Ramot was a small, cohesive community, whereas the city is just that: a cosmopolitan hub, without the close neighborhood connection. "My mechatenester lives next door to you," said my friend's sister. "Stop in to introduce yourself. She's a lovely person and I'm sure she'll be thrilled to have an English-speaking neighbor."

I followed her advice, and was delighted that I had. Although neither Rina nor I have large chunks of time to spend developing a deep relationship (for that, you need young children and sandboxes!), we have become much more than nodding acquaintances. I was thrilled at the opportunity to interview Rina and find out more about her life.

I am originally from France. Both my parents were born in Alsace, the portion of France that shares borders with Switzerland and Germany. When they were born and while they were growing up, Alsace was part of Germany. But by the time they married, in the 1920s, Alsace had been returned to France.

[In 1871, after the French were defeated in the Franco-Prussian War, Otto von Bismark annexed Alsace and North Lorraine to the German Empire. In 1919, after Germany was defeated in the First World War, the region reverted to France as part of the Treaty of Versailles.]

The Germans took over Alsace in 1939. My father, along with the other Jewish professionals, was forced to leave his teaching job. Afraid of what would happen next, my parents and older siblings fled south, to what was then unoccupied France. That's where I was born, in 1941, two years later, in Toulouse, a large city in Southern France just a few hundred miles north of the Spanish border.

As you can imagine it was very difficult for my parents to make ends meet. My father somehow managed to survive by giving private lessons in chemistry and physics and occasionally *shechting* chickens for a fee, although he often *shechted* solely for the mitzvah. At that time the Germans were deporting only Jews who were foreign residents, and were leaving the French citizens alone. We felt safe — but it was a false sense of security.

The bubble was shattered after my father was thrown into prison on some trumped-up charge. Although my mother managed to secure his release, it was obvious to us that we were now on the Nazis' wanted list and that our lives were in danger. But we didn't believe that the danger was imminent.

After that, something happened to make us aware that our security was tenuous at best. We were hiding several illegal Jewish refugees in our home. Yes, it was against the law and we were risking our lives. But these were unusual times and my parents were not about to let those Jews be deported — not if they could help it. When the Nazi soldiers banged on our front door to search for illegal refugees, my mother bought time by asking them to please wait for her to awaken the children so as not to frighten them. While the soldiers waited at the front door, the refugees escaped out the back door. Meanwhile, my mother threw anything that might incriminate us into the fireplace. We never heard from the refugees, and assume that they were eventually captured and killed.

My parents had started sheltering illegal refugees in the early thirties, when no one dreamed of a war between Germany and France. At that time, a number of German Jews illegally entered France to seek shelter from the Nazis. One day during *sefiras ha'omer*, when Jewish men refrain from shaving, French soldiers came searchnig for illegal aliens — in other words, Jewish refugees. They were looking for one particular man, who just happened to be staying with us. One of the soldiers showed that man a picture of himself — without a beard — and asked him if he had ever seen that person — himself — before! My father quietly instructed my older brothers, who were very small at the time, to make a lot of noise so that the police would leave quickly.

Around that time, Rabbi Schneerson, a Russian refugee and first cousin to the Lubavitcher Rebbe, was trying to organize a rescue effort. He had plans to establish a farm to train boys in agriculture, to give them the skills they would need to settle Eretz Yisrael. He found an old French castle turned into a farm not far from the Spanish border, which would provide a venue of escape should conditions continue to deteriorate, and was looking for an experienced agronomist to run the program.

My father was a senior professor in physics and chemistry, but in French, the word for "senior" — "*agrege*" — sounds like the French word for agronomist, "*agronom*" — at least to Rabbi Schneerson's foreign ears. So Rabbi Schneerson tried to convince my father, the "farming expert," to take charge of his program.

At first, my father explained — or tried to explain — to Rabbi Schneerson that he was more the absentminded professor type than an agricultural expert. But our brush with death had made it obvious that deportation was only a matter of time. "I told him the truth," he later explained. "I informed him that I'm really not the right person for this job, but he refused to believe me. I'm not a fool; I took the job to save my life." After the war, we learned that the Germans came to deport us to Auschwitz just a few days after we fled.

Rabbi Schneerson's plan for a religious boys' farming school never materialized. We lived on the "farm," and there was even one boy who joined the non-existent school, but other than a few refugees who trickled in, that was basically it. It was as if the Rabbi's plan was created for the sole purpose of saving our family!

I don't remember much of our life on the farm; after all, I was just a baby. Everything I know is based on what I later heard from my parents and older siblings. My mother often said that if it wasn't for the local villagers, we would never have survived. They covered up for us and kept our existence a secret. They also helped us physically. Although I am not aware of all the details, I do know that after my younger sister was born they brought us basic provisions, such as a crib and baby clothes. My older siblings attended the village school together with the local *goyim*. Every day, they would walk two kilometers to the tiny country school where several grades studied together in one large classroom.

One day, a group of German soldiers appeared at our farm. My mother panicked and ordered us to run into the surrounding forest while she stayed with the baby to greet the soldiers. But the soldiers were just out to have a good time and had come to take pictures of the old buildings.

The first year, we were literally starving. On erev Yom Kippur, my parents sold the wine barrels that were in the cellar in order to purchase food. Meanwhile, my older siblings were working hard to cultivate the land. By the second year their labor paid off and there were plenty of vegetables to eat.

Sometimes, despite the danger, my father would go to one of the nearby towns to look for work. Once, a soldier stopped him to check his ID. His official French ID was stamped with a big "J" for Jewish — and the Nazis had already started deporting French-national Jews. So he handed him his reduction card, proof that he was a father of a large family and eligible for a discount on bus fare. The soldier examined the card carefully, turning it over a few times. Although he must have realized that my father was a Jew, he gave it back to him and continued stopping people to check their IDs.

When the war was over, we returned to the city of Colmar, in the Alsace region. Although Jews were no longer being deported to concentration camps, there was a lot of blatant anti-Semitism. The French children used to throw stones at me while screaming that it's too bad Hitler didn't get rid of all the Jews. G-d forbid!

You cannot imagine our joy when De Gaulle announced the government plan to compensate French nationals for loss of income due to the war. We were in such difficult financial straits, trying desperately to make ends meet. This seemed like the answer to our prayers. My parents, like so many others, received a large sum of money. But almost the same day, De Gaulle devalued the franc and the money became worthless. The plan was simply a way for De Gaulle to maintain popularity among the masses!

The Jewish community in Colmar was small. We attended public school, and went to Hebrew school on Shabbos afternoon in addition to Sundays and Thursdays, our days off. Shabbos was a regular school day, but of course we never went. Officially, after Shabbos was over we were supposed to go to our friends' homes to catch up on our homework, but we weren't such serious students!

In addition to our formal Jewish education, my father taught us privately at every possible opportunity. And then, of course, there were lots of *divrei Torah* at the Shabbos table. Summers, we attended Camp Yeshurun. There we met other *frum* young people, including the daughters of such prominent French rabbis as Rabbi Munk and Rabbi Chaiken. It was wonderful to spend time with dedicated, Torah-observant young people — people with whom I could identify and try to emulate.

In 1955, my older sister became unofficially engaged to a boy who was learning in Gateshead Yeshiva. Since he wanted his *kallah* to have a seminary education, she attended the Gateshead Seminary. My parents were so impressed with the sem's impact on my sister that they sent all six of their daughter there!

I went to Gateshead in 1957. We were the first "big" class, all of forty girls (today, there are about two hundred girls in each class)! Conditions were far from luxurious. In the winter, the dorm was freezing cold; sometimes we'd wake up in the morning to find our *negel vasser* iced over! But we were pioneers. The Gateshead Sem was only ten years old and the whole concept of a girls' seminary was revolutionary.

I loved the learning. We had amazing teachers who inspired us and left their imprint on us for the rest of our lives. One teacher, for example, was Rabbi Sternbuch, brother of one of the rabbis in Jerusalem's *Eidah Chareidis*. He taught at the Seminary for close to sixty years, inspiring generations of young women.

As a result of my Gateshead education, I wanted to marry a *ben Torah*. This was extremely unusual in the early sixties. Just to give you an idea, around the same time that I got engaged, my husband's friend, Rabbi Matisyahu Salomon — presently the *mashgiach* of Lakewood Yeshivah — became a *chasan*. His *kallah* was from Manchester. When his future father-in-law's friends discovered that the *chasan* was planning to sit and learn, they told the father that he was insane for agreeing to the *shidduch*!

My husband's family was originally from Germany. They came to England in 1939, when my husband was seven years old, and settled in Gateshead. After we were married, my husband joined the Gateshead *Kollel*. To make ends meet, I babysat and rented out rooms in our three-story house to *bachurim*.

In 1966, we moved to Aix-Les-Bains, France, where my husband became a *maggid shiur* in Rabbi Chaiken's yeshivah. We lived there for seven years, until 1973. I taught in the Jewish school: English to the boys and *limudei kodesh* to the girls. The school was so small that the children were able to come to my house for the lessons. That way, I didn't need to find a babysitter for my youngest.

In 1973, my husband was asked to become *Rosh Kollel* in a small religious community forming in Alsace. We lived there for fifteen years, until 1988, but despite all our efforts the community never really got off the ground and eventually it just collapsed.

By 1988, we were in the midst of marrying off our children and several of them were living in Israel. Just when we realized that we'd have to leave Alsace, one of my husband's former *talmidim* "happened" to meet him and offered him a position teaching at an Israeli yeshivah. We moved to Israel, but the job didn't work out. It was difficult for my husband to understand the Israeli mentality. Then someone suggested that he join a very small *kollel*, which he did — and he loves it!

Baruch Hashem, while my husband sits and learns, I teach in a French seminary. Most of the girls there are from traditional, although not *chareidi*, homes. I love my job! I really enjoy teaching — it's both challenging and rewarding. It's a privilege to be able to give to others something of what I received from my teachers so many years ago.

Every stage in life has its own challenges. When I was newly married, it was living in a foreign country with a husband who could barely speak my language. In Aix-Les-Bains and later on, in Alsace, it was raising children in a virtual vacuum. Here in Israel, it's coping financially. When we moved here we had three married children, and eight still at home. Marrying off the children was a real struggle — balancing the debts while covering the grocery bill — but we managed, and saw tremendous *hashgachah pratis* along the way.

As we go through our lives, we can clearly see that Hashem is holding our hands. When He closes one door, He opens another. When the *kollel* in France closed, my husband met a *talmid* he hadn't spoken to for years, who had a yeshivah and was looking for a *maggid shiur*. Although that position did not work out, it was the catalyst that brought us to Israel. When we first came to Eretz Yisrael, my mother was living with us. We had tremendous *hashgachah* in finding a furnished apartment that was perfect for us: big enough to give her the privacy she needed, while at the same time affordable! Then, on top of that, when the apartment changed hands, the new owners were gracious enough to allow us to continue living there.

After my mother passed away, we purchased our present apartment. The owner of the furnished apartment that we were renting asked us if we'd like take the furniture with us — which is how we ended up having furniture! Then, when five of our dining room chairs broke, we discovered that my grandson's neighbors wanted to get rid of their five chairs, which were almost identical to ours, down to the same upholstery. It was amazing!

We live very simply, and always have. *Baruch Hashem,* we've seen tremendous *nissim* in our lives. We've managed to marry off our children and even purchase an apartment in Jerusalem! What more could we ask?

> *When I was a little girl, my dream in life was to become a writer. Then, when I was older, I dreamed of living in Eretz Yisrael. And when I was even older, I dreamed of marrying a talmid chacham and raising an ehrlicher Jewish family. Baruch Hashem, I can honestly say that all my dreams were fulfilled. As Rina says, "What more could we ask?"*

FROM PHILADELPHIA TO TOLDOS AHARON

"I found myself attracted to the Chassidic lifestyle — a lifestyle rooted in *kedushah* and strong family values. My *neshamah* felt drawn there."

Meira Fink (a pseudonym)

Meira and I have been friends for ages. The first time we met was at the weekly women's get-together for shalosh seudos at Shana's house in Meah Shearim. Shana and Meira are both Toldos Aharon Chassidim — you know, the ladies with black stockings and black tichels. They may look a little different, to some even forbidding, but they are really much like you and me and our friends down the street.

One time, Shana's husband, Aryeh — dressed in his Yerushalmi striped coat, below-the-knee pants, long black stockings, and white knitted yarmulke, was walking down the street when he noticed a tourist about to snap a picture of him. Aryeh turned to the tourist and, with his thick New York accent, asked, "What? You've never seen a Yankee before?"

Meira, can you tell us about your life?

I was born in Philadelphia. My father was an accountant; my mother a teacher, social worker, and school guidance counselor — not all at the same time, of course. When I was little, we were less careful about *halachos*, but over the years our family became more religious.

My paternal grandfather was born in Minsk. As a young boy, he was orphaned and had to work as a *melamed* to support himself and his siblings. In 1917 he made *aliyah* to *Eretz Yisrael* with the *chalutzim*. But he was unable to get along with the *Histadrut* and moved to America, where he opened a grocery store. Interestingly enough, my maternal grandparents also owned a grocery store, so even when things got really rough during the Great Depression, they always had something to eat.

As a young girl, I'd walk on Shabbos morning (and sometimes during the week, too) to my bubby's house down the street to visit my *elter bubby* — my father's bubby, who was living with *my* bubby and zaidy. After we finished playing, my *elter bubby* would *daven* with me, word for word. She only spoke Yiddish, which is how it came to be that Meira, an American girl from an American home, is fluent in Yiddish — the language I speak today.

My mother's parents lived around the corner from us. Their house was my second home. Our strong sense of family was augmented with an intense pride in our roots. My father was a direct descendent of the Baal Shem Tov; my mother, of Rav Shimshon of Ostopol.

I have wonderful parents. They are warm, caring people, really loving and special. They taught us be happy with little. My father, *a"h,* showered my mother with love and respect. When we were small, he would take us kids on trips so that my mother could get some rest. Although we all chose different paths in our *frumkeit* — like the many hues of a rainbow — our family has remained close.

My parents sent me to the local Bais Yaakov, where I became very close friends with the *rav's* daughter. I would become excited over anything having to do with *frumkeit*. It was as if my *neshamah* was craving *Yiddishkeit*. Something deep inside compelled me to search and grow in that direction.

In 1970, our family moved to Israel. I was thirteen years old, the oldest of three siblings (eventually we were four — one was born in Israel). It was really brave of my parents to pick up and leave the United States — they had wonderful jobs; we lived in a beautiful three-story home — but they were really worried about our *chinuch*. There was so much intermarriage in Philadelphia, so many kid turning their backs on all that is holy. They were willing to go to any length to make sure that their grandchildren would be *frum, ehrlicher Yidden*.

The Jewish Agency sent us to the Absorption Center in Katamon, which was then a slummy neighborhood in Jerusalem. Everything was so primitive. No one had telephones or washing machines. We were lucky, however. Just a few years before, refrigerators had been an almost unheard-of luxury. Of course, there were no instant or ready-made foods.

On Shabbos, our family would walk from the Absorption Center in Katamon to the Holy Land Hotel at the bottom of Bayit Vegan to have a look at the model of the *Bais HaMikdash* that is on display there. After that, we'd walk up to Bayit Vegan to eat *shalosh seudos* at the Sefaradi shul. We really enjoyed the singing there.

One of the best things about being in the Absorption Center was meeting and became very close friends with Aryeh and Shana Kohn [a pseudonym], a young couple with two small children. Forty years later, we are still very close. The Kohns eventually moved to a newly-built neighborhood on the outskirts (today, the center) of Meah Shearim, and found their niche with the Toldos Aharon (Reb Ahrelach) *Chassidim*.

I found the transition from America to Israel extremely difficult. When we left America, I was in the middle of eighth grade, so I ended up missing my elementary school graduation. Here in Israel, I started out in the middle of the last year of elementary school, when all the other girls knew each other since preschool. I was the outsider trying — unsuccessfully — to get inside.

My parents are very unusual people. My mother literally seeks out the good in everyone and everything — which is why she never complained about life in the Absorption Center. My father, *a"h,* was what I can only describe as a "*lamed vovnik.*" After suffering a stroke at age sixty-one, he took early retirement and devoted himself to full-time learning. He is always the first one to come to shul in the morning and one of the last to leave.

After the Jewish Agency told my parents that there were no apartments available in Jerusalem, we moved to a *Sochnut* apartment in Ashdod. Today, Ashdod has a large religious community. But in those days, the *frum kehillah* was virtually non-existent. My parents really didn't understand all the fine nuances of Israeli life and sent me to a government religious (actually, not-so-religious) school, assuming it would be similar to the school I had attended in the States. I HATED it! It was completely different from the Bais Yaakov I'd attended in Philadelphia.

After one year in this quasi-religious school, my parents sent away from home to a religious girls' high school in the North. It was a nationalistic, Zionistic school, with a very high scholastic level. Although most of the girls were Israeli, there was a large contingent of Americans, and we had a lot of fun together. I have wonderful memories of my years there — hiking through the country, doing *chesed* for families, staying up all night studying for finals, and having deep, philosophical conversations until the wee hours of the morning. I made some very close friends and today, over thirty years later, we still keep up those friendships.

> *I recently went to a class given by the Toldos Aharon Rebbetzin. She spoke about the importance of respecting other people's "brand" of Yiddishkeit — as long as it conforms to the halachah — while at the same time being proud of who we are and not budging one iota from our minhagim. Although I am not part of Toldos Aharon, I have always been impressed by their tremendous warmth and love toward other Jews even as they battle to maintain the kedushah of Eretz Yisrael. To many it appears to be a paradox, but their battle can only be won if based on true ahavas Yisrael.*

Throughout the years, I remained in close contact with the Kohns, whom we had met at the Absorption Center and who later became Toldos Aharon *Chassidim*. After graduating high school, I enrolled in a teacher's college near Tel Aviv. But the scholastic level was so ridiculously low — at least in comparison to my high school — that I left after just a few weeks. I was accepted to a more challenging teacher's college for the coming September, but that was almost a year away.

I spent that year as a substitute in a non-religious high school. Although I had a lot of trouble with the discipline and came to the conclusion that teaching was not for me, I persevered and taught (or more accurately did not teach, depends how you look at it ...) until the end of the year. Meanwhile, my bubby took sick and my mother traveled to Philadelphia to be with her. As the oldest daughter, I found myself in the position of surrogate mother to my younger siblings.

In high school I had become used to a super-intense schedule. So even though I was teaching part time in addition to taking care of the family, I had plenty of spare time on my hands and would often travel from Ashdod to Jerusalem to visit my friend Shana. I found myself attracted to the Chassidic lifestyle — a lifestyle rooted in *kedushah* and strong family values. My *neshamah* felt drawn there.

Shidduchim were a problem; I didn't fit into any specific niche. I met a couple of *Litvishe* yeshivah *bachurim*, but they weren't what I was looking for. Then a very close friend suggested that I meet a Toldos Aharon *chassid*. It was the lifestyle that I was drawn to — *frumkeit*, *tzenius*, a rich family life within a close and supportive community. My close friends, the Kohns, were, at first, very suspicious. After all, why would a Toldos Aharon family be interested in an American girl from a much more liberal background? But after lots of research they came to the conclusion that the *shidduch* really was above board.

My husband and I met four times before we got engaged, which is almost unheard-of in Toldos Aharon. The family made an exception in my case because of my background. I felt that our *shidduch* was orchestrated by Hashem Himself. I wasn't looking for storybook romance — I was looking for someone I could build with, a full partner in creating a solid, *frum* Torah home. And I love my *chassidus* — of course it's not perfect, but then again (as I always tell my children) nothing is.

I had no difficulty fitting into the very close-knit Toldos Aharon community. My neighbors were, and still are, incredible — so accepting and always willing to help me. When I first joined the community, my husband's friend's wife, a woman with a large family and many small children, really went out of her way to do whatever she could to make my adjustment easier. Although people naturally feel comfortable with me since I'm extremely outgoing and friendly, it wouldn't have been possible without *siyata d'Shemaya*. Hashem really guided me to where my *neshamah* needed to be. Although my background is different from that of most of the women in the community, I don't feel that I am different in any way whatsoever from the other Toldos Aharon wives. I'm completely integrated into the community, and very, very grateful to be part of it.

> *Does your American background ever get into the way of raising a Yerushalmi family?*

I came to Israel when I was only thirteen, so I really grew up here. Although I totally fit in with the culture, I still love to read Torah literature in English. When we were newlyweds, my husband had a problem with that. It took him a while to realize that English books can also be kosher!

I firmly believe that just as Hashem gave children to specific parents, He also gave parents to specific children. Children need to learn to cope with their parents' idiosyncrasies. We're all different, and we all have our own unique *derech* in raising our children. For that reason, I'm against child-raising classes. What works for one person might do exactly the opposite for another. If a person has a difficulty, he should talk it over with a *rav* or *rebbetzin* — privately!

Family is very important to me — my first priority. One afternoon a week, my daughters and grandchildren come to me for an Israeli-style supper — salad, cheese, bread, nothing fancy. It gives the cousins a chance to get to know each other. Yes, of course the floors get dirty, but everyone helps me straighten up, and the fun is worth the mess. On Friday night, all the children stop in to wish me a "*Gut Shabbos*," and on Shabbos afternoon my married daughters come with the grandchildren for *shalosh seudos*.

> *Yerushalmis have a beautiful custom: every Tuesday, the daughters and the grandchildren eat supper at their mother's house. My friend Shana has an English library which is open specifically on Tuesday afternoons ("I know I'll be home then"). Last time I stopped in, the older granddaughters made a "carnival" with Monopoly money that the*

grandchildren (and there were a lot of them!) could use to buy all sorts of treats, including pita-falafel for supper! A few weeks earlier, they set up two large plastic pools in the backyard, one for the girls and the other for the little boys under three! What a celebration of family!

I work part-time — about twenty hours a week — taking care of elderly women. I love it. Although I get tremendous satisfaction from helping (I always dreamed of become a nurse), my focus is on my own family, and on meeting their emotional, spiritual, and physical needs. I am constantly prioritizing, asking myself what does Hashem want of me NOW. When my mother in law was living with us, for example, I stayed home from shul on Shabbos to be with her; she needed me and that was my mitzvah. Today, I still stay home — I don't want my nine-and-a-half-year-old daughter to be alone all Shabbos morning (in Toldos Aharon the girls do not go to shul). And if I don't teach her to *daven* properly, who will?

Someone told me that when I am cooking, my head should be in the *davening*, and not the other way around. As women, we have to remember that our home is our *beis medrash*, and it's our privilege to imbue it with *kedushah*.

THREE LIVES

"I felt as if I was a person without an identity, completely lacking a family history. No one knew me from 'before.'"

Malka Glickstein

For years, I knew Mrs. Glickstein as "Glenda's mother." When I was a young married woman trying to keep my head above water while juggling the many responsibilities of raising a family, I never took the time to get to know her. I'd nod, say hello, and then disappear. After all, she's old enough to be my mother, and when I was younger I viewed anyone over sixty as being ancient — from a totally different world, a world that I could never relate to.

But time marches on. Suddenly, I find myself much closer to sixty than to thirty, or even forty. I'm "my mother's age" and view the world from a different perspective. I've learned that although there is a certain wisdom that comes with age, people remain people. At every stage of the game we're struggling with ourselves, and hopefully continuing to grow and develop. It's that desire to grow and develop that keeps us young at heart.

Mrs. Glickstein is one of those women who will always remain young at heart. Every time I meet her, she has a perceptive remark connecting the spiritual to the mundane. It is my sincere hope that my readers will be as inspired by her story as I was.

Mrs.Glickstein, could you tell me about your life?

If I were to write the story of my life, it would be a trilogy; three separate volumes, because I led three very different lives: Before the War, During the War, and After the War.

I grew up in a Tarnow, Poland. Our family was *Chassidish*, although my father was not connected to any specific rebbe. We were four sisters. When the war broke out, my older sister, Sara — we called her Sala — was about seventeen, I was about fifteen, my two younger sisters, Bashya and Chana Rechel, were approximately thirteen and ten. I was the only one of my family to survive. After the war, when I learned that everyone was dead, I felt as if I was a person without an identity, completely lacking a family history. No one knew me from "before." No one knew who I was or where I came from. For years, I continued to hope that I'd meet someone from my previous life — even a distant neighbor. But I never did.

My family shared a one-bedroom apartment with my grandparents. My zaidie was a *sofer*. Each time he wrote Hashem's Name, he would first immerse in a mikvah. So that the children wouldn't disturb him, he wrote at night, when we were asleep.

Every evening, our big common room was converted into a huge bedroom. Each of the children shared a bed with an adult; I shared mine with my zaidie. The three families who lived on our floor shared one bathroom. But we weren't poor. In prewar Poland everyone lived like that.

As a result of the 1918 flu epidemic, my father was left with a damaged heart and wasn't allowed to work. Instead, he stayed home and learned all day. I can't remember him ever sitting and doing nothing. He took advantage of every moment to grab a bit more *limud Torah*. My mother worked hard to support the family.

My father passed away not long before the start of World War II. At the time, we viewed it as a terrible tragedy. Only later did I realize how lucky he had been to merit a proper Jewish burial.

As a youngster, I attended a regular Polish school. The only Jewish school in Tarnow was not at all religious. I really got my Jewish education through osmosis; after all, we couldn't possibly afford to bring a "rebbetzin" to the house to teach us. After graduating high school, I studied sewing and clothes design — two skills that were to be put to good use both during the war and afterwards.

[Prior to World War II, approximately 25,000 Jews lived in Tarnow — about half the city's population. The German occupation of Tarnow began on September 8, 1939. The synagogues were immediately torched and Jews grabbed off the street for forced labor.

During 1941, life for Tarnow's Jews became increasingly precarious. Jews were forced to hand in their valuables. Roundups became more frequent and arbitrary killings commonplace. In June 1942, approximately 13,500 Jews were sent to the Belzec extermination camp, where they were immediately gassed. During the roundup, hundreds of Jews were also gunned down in the streets, marketplace, cemetery, and nearby woods.]

In the beginning, soldiers grabbed people off the streets for forced labor. Food was sparse; we stood in line for hours to receive our daily portion of bread. Every day there was another regulation: We weren't allowed to walk on the right side of the street; we could only shop at specific hours. It seemed that, minute by minute, our lives were becoming more limited. Eventually we were uprooted from our home and sent to the ghetto.

[After the June deportations, the survivors were ordered into a ghetto. There, the Germans set up factories and workshops to produce goods for the German war effort. Because of the crowded conditions, severe food shortages, and lack of sanitary facilities, many ghetto residents died of disease and starvation.

In September 1942, the approximately eight thousand people without valid work cards were deported to the Belzec extermination camp, where they were all murdered.]

Hashem in His goodness made a miracle for me, and I was able to find a job in a sewing factory. When I got the job, I had no idea that it was the key to life. Had I known, I would have done everything in my power to help my sister find work there, too .... One day, I heard an announcement that the Germans were looking for experienced seamstresses. I had studied sewing and dress design, so I applied for the job. The Nazis issued a work card and told me to report to the factory the following morning. When people heard that I had landed a position, they were flabbergasted that I found such a prize job without having to resort to "*protektzia*" or bribery! It was totally Hashem's doing.

[The sewing factory was owned by Julius Madritsch, who was later honored by Yad V'Shem as a righteous gentile. He worked together with Oscar Schindler to save as many Jews as possible.]

Eventually, the ghetto was divided into two sections. Since I had a job, I was placed in the work camp. One day, while we were in the factory, the second half of the ghetto was liquidated. All the inmates were deported and exterminated.

[In October, 1942, the ghetto was divided into two parts. Section A was organized as a labor camp, with separate quarters for men and women. Section B was a family camp for Jews who were not lucky enough to find work and for Jewish laborers with large families. Individuals were not permitted to move from one section to the other. Two months later, while the inmates of section A were laboring in the workshops, section B was liquidated. Approximately 3,500 Jews were murdered.]

I worked at the sewing factory for a year. We labored twelve hours a day. Pearl Benisch later wrote about the factory in her bestselling book, *To Vanquish the Dragon*. But although I knew the group of Bais Yaakov girls who worked there, my machine was at the other end of the huge hall and I had very little to do with them.

My mother and youngest sister fled the ghetto to my grandparents' home in a small village. They perished together with the other Jews of the town, when the Nazis forced them into the town shul and then torched the building. My other two sisters were sent to Belzec extermination camp, where they were immediately gassed and cremated.

[The Tarnow ghetto was destroyed in September 1943. The surviving 10,000 Jews were deported: 7,000 to Auschwitz and 3,000 to the Plaszow concentration camp in Krakow. By the end of that year, Tarnow was declared Judenrein.]

When the ghetto was liquidated, the entire sewing factory, together with its workers, was shipped to Plaszow. We were housed in huge barracks of over a thousand girls each. Our beds were nothing more than hard wooden boards, with ten girls squeezed onto each one like sardines. I slept on the top bunk. In the winter, our barrack was so cold that the vapor from the girls' breath created a layer of ice on the ceiling. For sustenance, each of us received a bowl of thin soup and a hunk of bread that was supposed to last us the entire day. We became swollen from malnutrition.

I remained in Plaszow for approximately one year. When the sewing factory was no longer needed, the Germans dismantled it and shipped the workers to Auschwitz to await transport to another work camp.

The day I arrived at Auschwitz was boiling hot. I was terribly thirsty and bent down to drink some water from a puddle. The moment it touched my tongue, I realized that it was contaminated and forced myself to spit it out. Our group of about two thousand girls was immediately processed and admitted to the work camp. Like animals, our body hair was shaved and our arms tattooed. I still have the number — A21485 — on my left arm. No amount of scrubbing will ever get rid of it. It's an eternal memorial to my experience in Auschwitz.

We couldn't recognize each other with our shaved heads. It was as if the Germans were taking away our individuality and turning us into a herd of animals. After a few weeks in Auschwitz, I dreamed that I was drowning in a sea of bald heads, and was then miraculously pulled out. Shortly afterwards, I was saved from a terrible death and sent to a work camp, where conditions were comparatively better.

During the five weeks I spent in Auschwitz, I had no idea what it was all about. I even asked one of the inmates if my relatives, who been deported before me, were still there. Looking back, I realize that I was pushing reality away; it was the only way I could survive emotionally. I had no idea that Jews were being burnt in the crematoria. After the war, when I finally understood the extent of the Holocaust, I continued to push the horrors out of my mind. But as I grow older, I find it coming back to haunt me, and that is very, very difficult.

But getting back to Auschwitz, the conditions there were designed to degrade and dehumanize us. We wore shapeless dresses with no underclothes. Every five girls were allotted one spoon and one bowl of soup to share between them. It was almost impossible to divide the food fairly. We slept in crowded bunks without even a blanket to cover ourselves.

One Friday morning, it was announced at roll call that my group was to join a transport of several thousand girls being sent to a work camp. The transport was leaving the next morning, on Shabbos. That night I dreamed that I was back home, in Tarnow, with my family. I thought that Shabbos was already over and wanted to go outside to play, but my father said, "*Yetz iz nisht de tzeit* — It's not yet the time." Then I woke up. The dream was so vivid that I was sure my father was trying to tell me something. Suddenly it dawned on me: "*Yetz iz nisht de tzeit* — It's not yet the time." I must not join the transport.

That morning we were marched to the waiting train in groups of five. I told the other four girls in my group about my dream, and we decided to slowly work our way out of the line and then sneak back to the barracks. We later found out that all the girls — thousands of beautiful *Yiddishe maidelach* — were forced onto a ship, which was then sunk. No one survived.

Two days later, on Monday morning, the Nazis announced that they needed volunteers to join a different transport. My four friends and I decided to go. We were shipped to Oederan, Bavaria, where we became slave laborers in an ammunition factory. The conditions there were much better than in Auschwitz. We were even allowed to let our hair grow.

I remember being marched through the town of Oederan on our way to the ammunition factory. The German people there stared at us in wonder. With our strange clothes and shaved heads, we looked like creatures from another planet. In the factory, one of the German civilians who worked with us asked what terrible crime we had committed to receive such a horrible punishment.

Yom Kippur, while I was at work in the ammunition factory, the Germans came to the barracks to shoot a forty-year-old woman with the same name as my own. After all, at forty, she was too old to be of real use to the German war effort. Had I been there, they would have shot me instead of her.

One of the Hungarian girls passed away of natural causes and was buried in the non-Jewish cemetery in Oederan. Although over sixty years have gone by since then, I still wonder if anyone ever returned to the town to exhume her body and inter her in a Jewish cemetery. Maybe one of her friends survived and came back to bury her properly. I would do it myself — I know where she was buried — but I don't have the strength to do anything about it.

I worked at the ammunition factory for approximately one year, until April 1945. By then, it was obvious that the Germans were losing the war. In an attempt to conceal their inhumanity from the Allies, they herded the camp inmates onto cattle cars and shipped us to Theresienstadt. Conditions were so crowded that some of us had to squat on the floor to make room for the others to stand. The experience left its mark on me; to this day I cannot stand being in a crowded place

The German camp-ghetto of Theresienstadt existed for three-and-a-half years, from November 1941 until May 1945. The camp was a temporary stopover for Czech Jews and privileged German and Austrian Jews (mainly veterans and well-known celebrities) until they could be sent east to be exterminated. Toward the end of the war, transports were brought in from other camps and the population swelled. Although conditions there were relatively better than in the other camps, they were still horrible by any standard.

Theresienstadt was a "model camp", serving an important propaganda function. Ostensibly, the Jews were being resettled in the east, where they would be compelled to perform forced labor. Since it seemed implausible for elderly Jews to be taken for forced labor, the Nazis used the Theresienstadt camp-ghetto as a showcase to hide the true nature of the deportations. The Nazis portrayed Theresienstadt as a retirement town for elderly German Jews.

Although Teresienstadt was not an extermination camp, tens of thousand of Jews died there of abuse, starvation, and disease. By 1942, the death rate was so high that the Germans built a crematorium capable of handling almost two hundred bodies per day.

Of the approximately 140,000 Jews transferred to Theresienstadt, nearly 90,000 were deported to points further east and almost certain death. Roughly 33,000 died in Theresienstadt itself.

Our group of about five hundred women arrived in Theresienstadt on April 28, 1945. The war ended ten days later, on May 8. We knew — and they knew, too — that the Allies were going to win. We could see German soldiers running away and the American planes bombing what was left of the German forces.

Upon our arrival in Theresienstadt we were each given a hunk of bread and a bit of sugar. I felt as if my greatest dream had been answered. To this day, whenever I see a thick slice of bread, I recall how I had dreamed of it during the war, and how I felt when I finally received it.

When the Allies liberated the camp on May 8, 1945, the Russians established hospitals to take care of all the sick inmates. After spending some time in the hospital I was strong enough to leave the camp and set out to American-controlled Germany to search for my family. The Allies provided the homeless refugees with free transportation.

Before the war, my father's brother (whose wife was an American citizen) had found refuge in America. Since I had no idea how to contact him, I asked one of the American soldiers returning to the United States to assist me. He arranged for the radio to announce my personal details and explain that I was searching for my uncle. My uncle heard the announcement and contacted me. He promised to arrange the necessary papers for me to immigrate to the United States.

At the time, I was living in a large room in an old German army barrack together with several other girls. One girl's father had fled to Australia right before the war and she was planning to join him there. I had a cousin living in Australia, and asked her to look him up when she got there. By the time my cousin contacted me, I was already married.

My husband came from a town not far from Tarnow. His family were Bobover Chassidim, and he grew up in a home very similar to my own. I remember him describing the delicious foods that were served *l'kavod Shabbos kodesh,* and how they would all sing together at the Shabbos table.

After the war there were many mismatched couples. People wanted to get married and start building a family, and they were often in such a rush that they didn't bother to make sure they were compatible. But Hashem in His kindness found me the perfect husband. I was truly blessed.

The war had left my husband with a damaged heart. He told me about it when we first met. I knew that he might not be able to work to support his family, but it didn't matter. I still wanted to marry him. We were absolutely perfect for each other and I had no doubt that he was my *bashert*. After we were married, many couples asked us to walk them down the aisle. Everyone could see that we were very happy together, and they wanted that same happiness for themselves.

My cousin sent immigration papers for me, my husband, and my husband's unmarried brother to come to Australia. Since they arrived before the American immigration papers, we ended up moving to Australia. I gave birth to my first child shortly after arriving there; it's a miracle that he wasn't born on the way, in India or some other strange place.

When we arrived in Australia in 1948, we were penniless refugees. *Baruch Hashem,* before the war I had studied sewing, so I now borrowed a sewing machine and began working. At first, I did piecework, bringing things home from the factories. Somehow we managed to slide by; in those days rent was only twelve dollars a week and the cost of living was cheap. Then I started designing clothes and sewing them. Eventually, my one sewing machine turned into a small, home-based (actually, living-room-based!) factory. My husband and brother-in-law also found jobs, and together we were able to establish ourselves financially.

Our apartment was about a twenty-minute walk from the nearest shul. We joined the shul and were warmly welcomed. When our son was born, the shul organized his *pidyon haben*. It was very simple: a big challah, some drinks, and lots and lots of good wishes.

Later on, we moved to a different neighborhood that did not have a shul, so we organized a *minyan* in our house. During the week, our living room was a factory, and on Shabbos it became a shul! My husband was the *chazzan* — he had a beautiful voice — and the homemade *Kiddush* was a big attraction. My husband later hired a teacher and organized an afternoon Talmud Torah.

My husband passed away in 1954, after only eight years of marriage. My son was seven years old, my daughter only two. My husband's brother became like a father to my two children.

I told you that my life was colorful, but I never described it as being rosy-pink! Hashem was very good to me; I merited marrying my husband and giving birth to two children before he was taken away from me.

When my son was fifteen, the *rav* of our shul suggested that I send him to study at Telshe Yeshiva, in Cleveland, Ohio. I had no doubt that, had my husband been alive, he would have wanted him to go. It was very difficult to send such a young child so far away — a different continent! — but I wanted him to grow in Torah and at the time that was the only real option.

I remarried in 1960. My second husband was also a survivor. Originally from Poland, he spent the war years in Siberia. He became like a father to my two children.

My son continued learning in Telshe. After his wedding, he learned in the Telshe *Kollel*. Eventually he got a rabbinical position in Cleveland, and has been there ever since. My daughter married and moved to Israel.

Once the children left home, I became a housemother for a girl's seminary. I took advantage of my position to participate in all the classes. Although I attended the same series of classes for nine years, I was constantly gaining new insights. Whenever the principal, Rabbi Groner, would bring visitors to see the school, he would point to me and say, "This is our mature student!" I would often joke that Rebbe Akiva was ***just*** forty when he started learning. I was much older. After spending so many years working around the clock to survive, it was a real pleasure to be learning, and an even greater pleasure to be learning Torah.

My husband and I visited Israel on several different occasions. Each time, we enjoyed seeing our gorgeous children and grandchildren. One time my daughter said, "Mom, I'm never jealous of my friends, except when they tell me that they're going to their mothers' for Shabbos. I wish you were closer and could get to know the grandchildren better." Those words clinched it for us. We were definitely moving to Israel! I wanted to be part of my grandchildren's lives as they grew up, rather than a bubby who speaks to them twice a year on the telephone.

After my husband retired in 1986, we took the big step and made *aliyah*. It's been wonderful to live so close to my daughter and to watch my grandchildren grow up.

(Mrs. Glickstein pauses for a moment before continuing ...)

Hodu l'Hashem ki tov! Hashem has been so wonderful to me! I was privileged to marry a special husband and have two beautiful children. After he passed away, I was granted a loving and caring second husband. And then, I was privileged to move to Israel and live close to my children and grandchildren!

> *Until about a year and a half ago, Mrs. Glickstein would travel to the Kosel every morning, to daven with the neitz minyan. For years, she took a group of women in her car, and on the way there they'd stop first at the kever of Rochel Imeinu or Shimon Hatzaddik. When she was no longer able to drive, she organized a daily taxi to the Kosel and returned home by bus. In addition, every Thursday she went with a group of women to daven at Kever Shmuel HaNavi.*

When a person goes to a *tzaddik* for so many years, he develops a real closeness to that *tzaddik*. Every Thursday, I would go to Shmuel *HaNavi* and have a heart-to-heart talk. We had developed that type of relationship.

Today, once a month a taxi picks me up at three-thirty in the morning to take me to the *Kosel*. I like to get there early so I can *daven* slowly. I push myself to go — it's not easy at my age, I'm already in my eighties, but I'm just so grateful that I can. *Baruch Hashem,* I am able to do what I'm able to do. Hashem is really leading me in the way that I want to go.

THRIVING IN MEAH SHEARIM

"Today I am so grateful that we had those first few years of *mesirus nefesh* for Torah. It laid a strong foundation for the type of home we were able to create, *baruch Hashem*."

Mrs. Udel Frank

I first met Mrs. Frank close to forty years ago, when I was learning in Machon Sara Schneirer, the forerunner of BJJ. I don't remember why I went to speak to her, but I do remember feeling as if I had stumbled into another world. The Franks live in a simple, two-room apartment in the center of Meah Shearim. Simplicity would be an understatement. Yet although they were living, and still are living, with what most of us would consider less than the bare minimum, they are far from poor.

Until the age of eight, our family lived in the Old City of Jerusalem. In 1948, after the British left Palestine and the Hagganah and the Arab Legions were fighting over Jerusalem, my mother gave birth to a baby boy. His *bris* took place in the midst of heavy shelling. When it was over and everyone left, the shul received a direct hit and collapsed. Thank G-d, there were no injuries.

After the Jewish quarter surrendered to the Jordanian Army, all the Jewish residents fled to Zion Gate, which is right outside the Jewish Quarter. I'll never forget the night we spent there. The Arab Legion soldiers kept their guns trained upon us as we lay on the cold stones, shaking in fear while listening to the Arab soldiers threaten to murder us. Their field guns were located right there, so the ground below us shook and our ears felt as if they were about to explode each time they shelled the city. Without food and water, and prohibited to walk about, all we could do was lie there, quaking in fear.

Eventually, the Arabs agreed to allow the women and children to leave the Old City. But the men were taken captive and sent to Jordan, where they remained interned for close to a year. When the Arabs took my father, they didn't realize that he was holding my brother, who was two years old at the time. When they did notice him, they wanted to leave him to die of hunger and thirst in the desert. Of course, my father was not about to let the Arabs kill his son. Somehow, he managed to alert the United Nations, which got involved and returned him to the family.

In all the confusion of leaving the Old City, my mother dropped her newborn baby. You have to understand: The mobs were threatening to kill us, the Jewish quarter was in flames, bombs were falling, and we were a mass of petrified women and children rushing to escape the only place we had ever called home. My mother was just after birth and trying her best to take care of her four small children (the fifth one, my two-year-old brother, was with my father on his way to Jordan) without anyone to help her. The baby somehow slipped out of the blanket and onto the stones. My mother continued clutching the blanket without realizing that the baby was gone, until a soldier came running up to us and asked if anyone was missing a baby.

After the evacuation, we — my mother, my four siblings, and I, along with all the other residents of the Old City — were resettled in Katamon. Before 1948, Katamon was a wealthy Arab neighborhood, but with the onset of hostilities the residents had fled, leaving everything behind. When we arrived there, dazed from the experiences of the previous night, someone pointed to one of the buildings and said, "There's an available apartment — take it." Which we did! It was a large, airy apartment with two big rooms, a roomy hallway, and a tiny kitchen.

Our family loved it there. Living in Katamon was like living on a small kibbutz. We were like one family: We ate our meals together, all the children played together, and everyone shared everything with everyone else. We were all very, very poor. Because there was not enough food to eat and there was a real danger of starvation, the *Rabbanim* ruled that the children should eat the government-distributed rations, which consisted of soup, porridge, and strained vegetables, although the *kashrus* was not up to our normal standards. After all, it was either that or nothing, and the food was definitely not *treif*. In addition, every week the government handed out a box of non-perishables. Eventually a woman in the neighborhood — a real *tzadekes* — opened a small grocery store. She often sent our family free food. I don't know what we would have done without her. Don't forget, my father was taken hostage by the Jordanians and we had no idea when, and if, he'd return.

My mother was very handy. Instead of buying new material to sew clothes, for example, she would recycle old *shmattes*, cutting them down and turning them inside out to make beautiful outfits for her children.

Yes, we were very poor, but there were people even poorer than us — for example, the *koveses* (washer-woman). Once a week, the *koveses* spent eight or nine hours sitting on a low stool in our courtyard or kitchen, washing all of our clothes. Since there was no laundry detergent (or washing machines, for that matter) she rubbed the clothes clean with large chunks of soap. Citric acid was used to get out the stains.

There had been no plumbing in the Old City. Water was purchased from a truck that came around every day or two. Although we had modern plumbing in Katamon, we continued to value every drop of water — something that we should really do today, considering the precarious water situation in Israel. Although the *koveses* used the same water for all the family's laundry, everything came out sparkling clean. Using one big tub of water, she'd first wash the whites, then the colored, and finally the dark clothes. Afterward we used that same soapy water for washing the floors!

My father, Reb Shmuel Shapiro, was a *tzaddik*. He devoted almost every second of his day to learning and *davening*. Every night, he'd return from Ma'ariv, eat a light supper, and then go straight to sleep. At midnight, he'd get up, say *tikkun chatzos*, recite *Tehillim*, and learn until it was time for Shacharis. Then, after a simple breakfast of bread, margarine, and boiled water, he would sit and learn until it was time to *daven* Minchah. When we children were small and would wake up often in the middle of the night, he'd get up at *chatzos* to take over for my mother. But he didn't waste a moment; after rocking a crying infant back to sleep, he would immediately return to his *davening* and learning.

> *The Chazon Ish once told a man who had come to Bnei Brak from Jerusalem to ask him for a berachah, "Why are you coming to me? You're from Yerushalayim. Reb Shmuel Shapiro lives there. Ask him for a berachah!"*

My father was very careful about *shmiras einayim*, guarding the eyes. Although in his later years women used to come to him for advice and blessings, he never looked at them. When walking through the streets, he would keep his eyes focused on his shoes. When we lived in the Old City, my older brother, who was two years old at the time, wandered off into the narrow, winding streets of the Arab Quarter. An Arab policeman found him and, seeing that he was a Jewish boy, asked, "Who's your father?" He answered, "Tatty," and started walking while staring down at his feet. The policeman immediately knew that this was Reb Shmuel's son.

Some time after my father returned home from Jordan, my younger sister was hospitalized with polio. Despite the danger from Jordanian sniper fire, every night he would go out into one of the fields surrounding Jerusalem to beg Hashem to send her a *refuah sheleimah*. Policemen would occasionally accompany him to the field to protect him!

My father was once on his way in the middle of the night to pray in a secluded place for my sister's welfare, when a couple of young nurses on their way to work stopped him. The nurses were afraid to be walking about so late at night, and asked him to accompany them to the hospital - which he did, although it was quite a distance. Had anyone been up at such a late hour they would have been shocked (to say the least) to see my father, the *tzaddik* of Jerusalem, walking together with two non-religious nurses!

My father's father passed away at age forty-three, leaving his wife a young *almanah* with ten small children to care for. In those days, it was almost unheard-of for people to remarry after such a tragedy, and my grandmother remained alone for the rest of her life. My father would visit her often. The famous *tzaddik*, Rav Aryeh Levine, was my great-uncle, which means that Rav Elyashiv is my second cousin.

My father grew up in a very Litvish home. He was drawn to *Chassidus* in his early twenties. Although his mother did not know of his Chassidic leanings, our neighbor, Rav Dovid Schechter, the father of the well-known Jerusalem *tzaddik* Rav Yaakov Meir Schechter, did. He suggested a *shidduch* with my mother, Fraida Kreshevsky, the daughter of the famous *tzaddik*, Rav Yosef Kadish Kreshevsky. My mother grew up in a very, very Litvish home and, like my father, was attracted to *Chassidus* as a teenager. It was a perfect *shidduch*!

> *We're mechutanim with this family in more ways than one. My daughter, Faigie, is married to Udel's nephew, Reb Shmuel's grandson. Since she kept her last name – Shapiro — everyone assumes she's my daughter-in-law! My youngest daughter, Malky, is married to Reb Shmuel's nephew, Reb Shmuel's brother's grandson. My son-in-law's grandfather, Reb Shmuel's brother, is a Litvish rav.*

My father was really what you'd call a "*kodesh*." For the first fifteen years of his marriage, he never slept in a bed. Instead, he would doze off for a few hours over his Gemara, and when he woke up he'd go straight back to his learning. When he was older and did sleep in a bed, he refused to cover himself with a warm quilt, explaining that if he was too comfortable he would have difficulty getting up on time!

As kids, and even more so as adults, we were in absolute awe of our father. But although he was so strict with himself, so *kadosh*, he adored us and pampered us. He was extremely devoted to my mother and treated her like royalty — which she reciprocated in kind. After he passed away, we noticed that she always kept a chair next to her bed. When we asked her about it, she explained that my father would place food and drink on it so that if she woke up at night she'd have something at her bedside to eat. In the morning, he would race out of shul to prepare her cup of coffee and bring her a fresh roll, both of them waiting for her, right next to her bed, as soon as she washed *negel vasser!* If he noticed that she was tired, he'd insist (over her protests) that she go to bed. He'd shoo us into the other room and make sure that we didn't disturb her. I still remember him whispering, "Be quiet now! Mommy has to get some rest."

In his later years, many people came to him for a *berachah*. He'd tell them, "I'm not a rebbe. I'm a plain, ordinary *Yid*. Go to someone else for a *berachah*." After they left, with tears in his eyes he'd turn to my brother and ask him why Hashem was testing him with all this *kavod*!

I married at the age of seventeen. As a teenager, my husband had been very, very attached to my father; he'd looked upon him as his mentor. At first, I found married life very difficult. My husband was always *davening* and learning. He would rush into the house for supper, and then, after a few minutes, he'd rush out again to learn and I wouldn't see him again until the following day. I was lonely and wanted my husband to spend more time with me. My father convinced me to accept this — to give my husband the freedom he needed to grow spiritually. Once our family started growing and I needed his help around the house, I saw much more of him. Today I am so grateful that we had those first few years of *mesirus nefesh* for Torah. It laid a strong foundation for the type of home we were able to create, *baruch Hashem*.

Udel raised thirteen children in a tiny, two-room apartment in Meah Shearim. Today, her home is constantly filled with children, grandchildren, and great-grandchildren. In the course of this interview, several women popped in to say hello or ask her advice about something, a great-grandchild was sleeping in the living room, and a granddaughter was busy in the kitchen. On Shabbos, her dining room resembles a simchah hall, with dozens of people, mainly family members, partici-

pating in the meals. It's a home where the kedushah is almost tangible; a kedushah that was created through Udel and her husband's mesirus nefesh for Torah.

My husband's family was very, very poor. Even on Shabbos, they ate plain, dark bread. Someone once gave his mother a fresh, warm challah *l'kavod Shabbos Kodesh*. When my husband — who was a little boy then — and his sister came home, they couldn't resist the temptation and ate the entire loaf in one sitting. Afterward they hid under the bed, hoping their mother wouldn't find them!

Although we were never as poor as my in-laws, there were times when we really had nothing in the house. But I never asked my husband how we would we manage. We lived frugally and trusted in the Almighty to sustain us.

If I needed something, I would either make it myself or buy it used. When I needed curtains for our living room — which faces Meah Shearim Street, so that without curtains everyone can see right in — I made them out of some old skirts. I prepared delicious vegetable soups from half-rotted vegetables that I either received for free or bought for pennies. Our beds, our cupboards — everything was all secondhand. But it didn't matter. We were happy with what we had and felt privileged to be living a life of *kedushah* in Eretz Yisrael. Now, when everyone has so much more than they did back then, people say that the "situation is difficult" — but back then we never thought of it as difficult. We made do with what we had.

Everyone would be so much happier if they could learn to live within their means instead of going into debt. We're constantly bombarded with advertisements trying to convince us to buy things we don't need, and that end up making our lives so much more confusing. My husband and I don't own a credit card. We don't use checks. We pay cash for everything. We live with what we have, rather than with what we don't have.

Udel runs a huge clothing gemach in a storage room underneath her house. Except for Shabbos and Yom Tov, it's always open and people are constantly going in to take clothes for their families.

My mother-in-law used to volunteer at a clothing *gemach*. After she passed away, I decided to open a new clothing *gemach* in her memory. At first it was just a few items that we kept in a corner of our living room. When it got bigger, we moved it to the patio outside. Then, one erev Pesach, it suddenly started to rain. We quickly brought all the bags of used clothes into the house and piled them into one corner of the living room. What a mess!

That erev Pesach, my married son stopped in with a friend of his, a well-to-do American, to show him a typical home in Meah Shearim. The man was amazed that I had raised thirteen children in two rooms, and asked about the big garbage bags piled in the corner. I explained that they were for the clothing *gemach* and that I had no place to store them.

Beneath our apartment was a water cistern that had been used to store rainwater before the days of modern plumbing. I had plans to empty it and convert it into a *gemach* store, but we never had the funds to do so. My son's friend offered to pay the cost of emptying the cistern and converting it into a store.

After a contractor emptied the cistern — which, by the way, contained sparkling-clean water! — we climbed down to see it and were amazed. It was huge! The contractor opened an entrance on the side and divided the area into two stories, the bottom floor for sorting the clothes and storing what was out of season, the top floor for the actual *gemach* — one room for women's clothes, the other for men's. We even made a chute that goes from the outside directly to the sorting area, so that people can bring clothes at all hours of the day and night without disturbing us.

Once a week, I spend an entire day sorting clothes at the *gemach*. The other days I'm available if people need me. Tuesdays, all my married daughters come here and we eat breakfast and lunch together. It's a lot of fun; we schmooze, say *Tehillim*, and just enjoy being a family. I also work for two hours a day as an escort on a girl's school bus, one hour in the morning and one hour in the afternoon. And then, of course, my children and grandchildren — and neighbors — are always popping in to visit.

As we are talking, Udel grabs her shawl and runs out to catch the school bus before it begins its rounds. "Close the door after you," she calls as she disappears. As I let myself out of her apartment, I no-

tice that lunch is on the stove, ready to be eaten upon her return. Everything is spotless — so typical of the Yerushalmis who take such tremendous pride in their homes. I feel as if I've stepped into another world, a simpler, purer one. And hope that I will be able to take something of that world into my own.

FINDING HASHEM IN THE PHILIPPINES

"In the prison, I asked for a glass of water and then, after ascertaining that the guards were Jewish, asked them to please respond with an '*Amein*' to my *berachah*. The policemen reverently placed their hands on their heads in lieu of a *kippah* as they responded to my blessing. I prayed that the angels that had been created would help me get out of this mess."

Shira Devorah (a pseudonym)

My neighbor in Ramot Polin was Shira Devorah's kallah teacher. Every time I spoke with her, she'd tell me about her very special and wonderful student. So when I met Shira Devorah for the first time at the sheva berachos that my neighbor made in the young couple's honor, I felt as if I already knew her. My neighbor was not exaggerating. Shira Devorah is an incredible young woman, an inspiration for all who know her. My husband and I are often privileged to have Shira Devorah and her husband, Amram, as our Shabbos guests. Each time they come, I am amazed anew at their mesirus nefesh for Torah and their devotion to finding emes.

Shira Devorah, can you tell me about your life?

I was born in raised in the Philippines, in a rural area outside the city of Davao, which is located on Mindanao, the Philippine's southernmost island. We were five children — three girls and two boys. When I was twelve years old, my older brother passed away from meningitis. He was just two years older than I, so we were very close. My family — my parents, my younger sisters, and my one surviving brother — cried for weeks. He passed away right before the winter holiday season, so while we were mourning everyone around us was celebrating — which, of course, only accentuated my family's pain. People tried to console my mother by reminding her that she had other children, but one child can never replace another. My brother's death left a gaping hole in her heart, and in our entire family's heart

We were Roman Catholic. As long as I can remember, I was drawn to religion; I even dreamed of becoming a nun! I wanted to devote my life to serving the Almighty. In high school, for example, when one of my teachers asked us to list our New Year's resolutions, I wrote that I wanted to serve God and to help people.

One of my closest friends was a Baptist. She argued that Catholicism is idol worship. Her words planted the first seeds of doubt in my mind. I was searching for truth. I wanted to do the right thing, but of course I still had no idea what that was. Although I had learned that the Jews were Hashem's chosen people, I had never met a Jew and had no idea what they believed in.

After graduating high school, I worked as a waitress and attended college at night. It was a Christian college, the Assumption College of Davao, and most of the teachers were nuns. Since commuting was not practical, I boarded with my uncle's family and returned home every weekend. My mother broke down and cried each time I left home to return to my uncle's house. It was difficult for both of us; but now, in retrospect, I realize that this was Hashem's way of preparing both her and me for the future, when the only contact we have is by telephone.

I continued seeking the truth in religion, and eventually joined a group of people who didn't believe in the divinity of Catholicism's "savior." Instead, we viewed him as some type of prophet. We tried to serve God as best we could by keeping what is written the Bible. I stopped eating pork and shellfish, which, in the Philippines, are real staples.

Once, while visiting my family in Davao, I decided to remove a statue from our living room. I had already come to the realization that worshipping his statue is idol worship, and that idol worship is wrong. I took the statue out of its niche in the wall and moved the closet so that it covered the hole that was left behind. I threw the statue under our house (in the Philippines, the houses are built on stilts) until I'd have a chance to destroy it.

When my father returned home and discovered what I had done, he was furious! "Why can't you respect your family's beliefs?" he screamed. I argued that our family believes in the truth of the Bible, and the Bible states that we are not allowed to bow down to idols. "It's wrong!" I cried. "It's just a piece of stone made to look like a person. I am going to destroy it!" My father was livid, but my mother managed to calm him down. "Instead of destroying the statue," she suggested, "let's give it to my cousin" — which is what we did.

My mother tried to accommodate my religious beliefs. After I stopped eating pork and shellfish, she prepared special food for me. I was once in the midst of ladling vegetable soup into a bowl when my mother saw me and yelled, "Elizabeth, that soup is not for you! There's pork in it." I really appreciated that. My father, however, had a lot of difficulty accepting the fact that I was so different. One time, my brother asked him, "Tattay [Daddy], why can't you accept Elizabeth the way she is? Isn't this better than her becoming a drug addict?"

It's hard to believe, but yes, there really are people who would prefer that their children become drug addicts to being frum.

Rabbi Tzvi Aryeh Rosenfeld was active in kiruv for close to thirty years, until he passed away in 1978. One of the boys attending his class was heavily involved in drugs. Under Rabbi Rosenfeld's influence, the boy was slowly weaned away from his dependency. But the boy's mother was not happy about her son becoming religious and forbade him to attend the class. When someone tried to convince her to let him continue, she commented that even drugs are preferable to being religous. The boy passed away from a drug overdose a year later.

Eventually I wanted to become a member of Hashem's chosen people; I wanted to be Jewish. Someone in my group knew of a family in Israel that was looking for a Filipino woman to help with the housework. I wrote to them, explaining that I hoped to come to Israel to learn about Judaism, and that I was willing to work during the day so that I could study at night.

It was another eight months before I heard from them. Meanwhile, I decided to travel to Manila, where there was an Orthodox shul, to begin exploring Judaism.

[Manila is home to over eleven million people, and the Philippines' national capital. As one of Southeast Asia's economic centers, its towering skyscrapers, and business and financial districts are a far cry from the rural village where Shira Devorah grew up.]

I traveled to Manila by boat, on a third-class ticket. It was a three-day journey. We were hundreds of people — men, women and children, all together — sleeping on double-decker bunks in one large room. Before boarding the ship, I had prayed that there would only be women in the surrounding bunks. Hashem heard my prayers!

Manila is a very dangerous city, especially for a young woman without family. It is a known fact that criminals abduct the naive women who come from the provinces and sell them into slavery. *Baruch Hashem*, my friends in Davao contacted someone in Manila and asked him to meet me at the docks and accompany me to my father's cousin's house.

My father's cousin had no idea that I was coming. At first he thought that I was just a stranger, trying to take advantage of his generosity. It took a lot of persuasion on my part before he was willing to let me into the house!

The morning after I arrived, I took the bus across the city to the Orthodox shul. I told the man running the office that I want to convert, and requested permission to attend services. But he was not at all agreeable. "You're not Jewish," he said, "so you cannot enter our shul. It's prohibited."

At that point I broke down in tears. I had traveled so far, gone through so much, and now that I had finally arrived, I was being turned away. At the time, I didn't know that a potential convert is to be turned away three times, and that only if he persists is he finally accepted. I really thought this was the end of the road — that I had come to a hurdle that I could never be able to overcome. I would remain a non-Jew for the rest of my life.

Just then, the door opened and the rabbi's wife appeared. "Why are you crying?" she asked. After hearing me out, she told me that I could come to shul, but only if I'd agree to wear a modest dress instead of my pants and T-shirt. Of course I agreed.

On my first Shabbos in shul, there were not enough men to make a *minyan,* so there was no *krias HaTorah*. I was very disappointed. At the *kiddush* after services, one of the ladies asked me why I had come to shul. I explained that I wanted to convert. She introduced me to the rabbi, who told me that since there is no *beis din* in Manila, I would have to convert elsewhere. He suggested that I attend a conversion program in Israel.

As I was about to leave shul, one of the men asked me what I was doing there. When I told him that I wanted to convert, he became livid. "It's hard enough for us Jews to keep the mitzvos," he yelled. "Pack your bags and go back to wherever you came from. There's no way that you can become a Jew. It's impossible!" But we *Yidden* are a stiff-necked people, and his angry words just strengthened my resolve.

That afternoon, at *shalosh seudos*, I met a Philippine family that had converted to Judaism several years earlier. They were very well-off and invited me to stay with them. We became very close and have remained close to this day.

A few months later I received a letter from my mother saying that the family in Israel was interested in my working for them. So I returned to Davao to say goodbye to my parents before traveling to Israel.

It was very difficult for me to say goodbye to my mother. I begged her not to cry. "If you cry, Nannay [Mommy]," I sobbed, "I might end up changing my mind. But I know that you love me and want what's best for me. I need to be in Israel for my spiritual growth. Please don't stop me." The fact that I left home for college, and later on to live in Manila, had prepared both of us for this difficult separation.

In Israel, I worked until three-thirty every afternoon. Then I traveled across town to attend conversion classes from four to eight.

Afterward, I returned home and continued working until late at night. It was a grueling schedule, but I loved it. I was learning Torah!

At the end of the year, when my contract was up, I moved into the seminary dorm. Several wonderful families adopted me as their daughter, taking me into their homes and hearts as they guided me on my path to Torah.

But now that I was not working for an Israeli family, there was a problem with my visa. I placed a request at the Ministry of the Interior to remain in Israel on a conversion visa, but the clerks there told me that, to attain that visa, I'd have to leave the country and then return as a potential convert. My rabbis, however, advised me against it. They said that once I left, I would probably not be allowed to enter again. So I found work cleaning people's homes and requested a foreign worker visa. But since I had already placed a request for a conversion visa, this was now impossible. It was a Catch-22 situation, and it seemed as if there was no solution in sight.

After studying Judaism for three years, I converted in Rabbi Karelitz's *beis din* in Bnei Brak. Prior to the conversion, Rabbi Karelitz explained, "Our *beis din* is unable to provide you with official conversion papers. After you complete the procedure with us, you'll have to go to the Rabbinate to make it official."

I answered, "Rabbi, when I go up to *Shamayim*, Hashem is not going to ask me if I have the right papers. I want to be a Jew."

But although I was Jewish, officially I was still an illegal foreign worker. It was a big bureaucratic mess, and although lots of important people got involved in trying to help me — including one member of the Knesset — no one was able to straighten it out.

A few days before Rosh Hashanah, the police stopped me on the street to check my papers. When they saw that I didn't have any, they imprisoned me for being in the country illegally. A few weeks earlier, one of my friends had contacted Rabbi Amnon Yitzchak to request that he get involved in my case. Now she contacted him again and he asked his lawyer to take on my case.

I was brought to a prison just outside of Jerusalem. I sat in my cell sobbing as I recited *Tehillim*. One of the guards saw that I was *davening* and came over to me. "Are you Jewish?" he asked. I can understand his confusion; after all, I certainly don't look Jewish!

A few days before I was stopped by the police, I had heard a *shiur* about the power of answering *Amein*. I'd learned that our "*ameins*" create *malachim* that will assist us in our times of need. So now, in the prison, I asked for a glass of water and then, after ascertaining that the guards were Jewish, asked them to please respond with an "*Amein*" to my *berachah*. The policemen reverently placed their hands on their heads in lieu of a *kippah* as they responded to my blessing. I prayed that the angels that had been created would help me get out of this mess.

I was taken from Jerusalem straight to Ben Gurion Airport, to be placed on a plane and deported to the Philippines. At the very last moment, the lawyer that Rabbi Amnon Yitzchak had arranged to take my case managed to have me sent to the Beer Sheva prison instead. By then it was already erev Rosh Hashanah. I was so grateful that I hadn't been forced to desecrate Yom Tov.

A friend in Jerusalem arranged for someone in Beer Sheva to bring me *glatt* kosher food, as well as the special foods for Rosh Hashanah, a *machzor*, and a clean dress for Yom Tov. I didn't want to *daven* in the prison ward with the other women, all of them foreign workers awaiting deportation. It wasn't exactly conducive to proper concentration. So I requested — and was granted — permission to *daven* and eat my meals in the prison office.

I lit the Yom Tov candles and *davened* in the small prison office. A female guard stood watching me, to make sure that I wouldn't escape. It was so degrading. I felt like a common criminal and kept bursting into tears as I prayed.

After I finished *davening*, I asked the guards if they were planning to make *Kiddush*. "Yes, of course," they replied. "We're also Jewish, and we also celebrate the holidays. Would you like to join us?" They covered their heads with their hands as one of the guards recited *Kiddush* for the entire group. I shared my *simanim* with them. They were all very curious. They had never met a *frum* Filipino before!

One of the guards asked me why I'd decided to become Jewish. I answered, "Instead of asking me, why don't you ask yourself? If I was so attracted to Torah that I felt compelled to travel around the world to convert, then obviously the Torah contains something special. Ask yourself what that is. You are so lucky. You were born Jewish! You were given this wonderful gift. Why don't you find out about it and discover its beauty?" But he just walked away.

I cried that entire night. I was sure that I'd be shipped back to the Philippines, and never be able to return. That Rosh Hashanah — my first Rosh Hashanah as a Jew — I prayed as I had never prayed before.

On Tzom Gedalia, I was informed that I was scheduled to appear in court. I called my adopted mother in Jerusalem and requested that she arrange for my friends to recite *Tehillim* on my behalf.

I told the judge my story. "Now that I'm a Jew," I concluded, "why can't I remain here, in my home? This is where I belong." My story must have touched the judge's heart (and the True Judge's heart), because she ruled that I could stay.

When I returned to the prison to get my belongings, the guards asked me to bless them. I felt a little silly. After all, who am I to give a blessing? But I did.

> *After hearing this story, I asked Shira Devorah to bless me too. It's rare to meet a person with such mesirus nefesh for Torah.*

Not long after that, a close friend of mine introduced me to my husband, a full-time yeshivah student. After we got engaged, my friends literally married me off like one of their own children. They took care of everything — the wedding, the gown, the appliances, furniture, clothes, even jewelry! I had volunteered to take care of an elderly Belzer woman; now her children were taking care of me!

The wedding itself was beautiful. It was a small affair in a synagogue basement. Rabbi Amnon Yitzchak was there — he gave us a *berachah* under the *chuppah*. The Belzer Rebbetzin was there; I even danced with her! Afterwards, my friends prepared beautiful *Sheva Berachos* for me.

After the wedding, I found work helping elderly women and cleaning for families. *Baruch Hashem,* my husband studies in *kollel* the entire day and works a few hours in the evening selling books.

It is my true hope that my husband will be able to continue learning, and that we will be able to continue growing in our *Yiddishkeit*. It is my dream to build a real Jewish home, with Jewish children and grandchildren, *b'ezras Hashem*.

It's easier for Europeans and Americans to convert. Their origins are not written all over their faces, the way mine are. But is it my fault that I was born in the Philippines? Please, accept me for who I am — a Jew — and not for who I once was, but am not anymore.

From the experiences that I went through on my path to Torah, I learned that although our lives are full of hardships, we must never give up! Hashem is here, literally here with us. He is holding our hands. He never turns His back on His beloved people.

THE STORY BEHIND THE STORY

"In second grade, the teacher asked us what we'd like to be when we grow up. All the other girls responded that they want to become either a nurse or a teacher or a ballerina. But I wanted to be a writer! Everyone thought I was a nerd — and they were right!"

Debbie Shapiro

On several occasions during the last few months, after being introduced to people and affirming that, yes, I am the Debbie Shapiro who writes for the newspaper, I am told, "Everyone wonders who you are." So, ladies (and gentlemen, if there are any reading this book), I decided to interview myself.

There are lots of advantages to interviewing myself. First of all, I'm always available, so I don't have to wait until three o'clock in the morning when the person I am planning to interview that week has time to speak with me. Secondly, I am not about to say something I don't want printed. You cannot imagine how frustrating it is to listen patiently to someone's story for over an hour and then be told, "You know, come to think about it, I really don't want this published." Didn't their mothers ever teach them to think before they speak?

And, thirdly, I will not phone myself while I am in the midst of eating supper and say, "Debbie, could you please change this ... and this and this and this ...." Why don't people just say it right to begin with?

Could you tell the readers a bit about your background?

I was born in Montreal, Canada, the youngest of six kids. But I don't remember much about Montreal because we moved to Los Angeles when I was three years old. In Los Angeles, my father manufactured hula-hoops. (Remember those? They were a fad in the late fifties). His specialty was the ones that glowed in the dark and had marbles inside that swished when you swiggled. When I was six years old, someone torched our hula-hoop factory on the same day that a large shipment of raw plastic arrived — just hours before the insurance was scheduled to kick in and cover it. We became poor overnight. After the fire, I remember my parents sitting in the kitchen laughing hysterically over some silly thing that had happened amid all the chaos. It was their way of dealing with the pain.

Shortly after the fire, we moved to San Francisco, where my father worked as a salesman. Eventually he opened his own business, the Asher Paper Company, and slowly began reestablishing himself financially. It wasn't easy.

My mother was a pro at managing with nothing. We always had lots of guests. At different times, various cousins who were experiencing difficulties with their own families came to stay with us, and my sister's best friend lived with us for four years while attending San Francisco State College. With just a pound of meat, my mother would somehow make a delicious supper for eight, nine, or even ten people. I dreamed of owning a pair of patent-leather shoes. Believe it or not, when I was in second or third grade I had just one dress. I still remember it. It was a checkered shirtwaist, with puffy sleeves and a squared neckline.

One of my fondest memories of those years was taking a walk with my grandfather after the Seder. He would speak about the apple orchard that he had planted in Russia, and then proudly describe the budding Yishuv in Eretz Yisrael. He visited Israel in 1968 and passed away there of a heart attack. He's buried on Har Hamenuchos, in Jerusalem, which I know is something he always wanted.

Why you decide to move to Israel?

Part of it has to do with my grandfather. He loved Israel and tried to instill that love in me.

When I was a kid, I used to ask a lot of questions, much of it having to do with "Why the Jews?" Although my family was not religious, we were very Jewish. We were taught to be very proud of our ancestry, and that being Jewish is something special. To tell you the truth, it really didn't make much sense to me. I would ask my parents what makes the Jews different. Why, throughout so many generations, were we persecuted and blamed for the world's problems, and slaughtered without reason? (Don't forget, I am part of the post-Holocaust generation.) Why are we always the brainy ones, the accomplished ones, the world's Einsteins? Deep down, I knew that my Judaism was very, very precious to me and that I, too, would choose death over conversion. But I had no idea why I felt that way, and no one had a reasonable explanation to offer me.

My next-door neighbor and best friend got me involved in a Zionist youth group. But now the question of "What makes the Jews different" became "What makes the country of Israel different?" Secular Zionism just didn't make any sense to me.

When I was thirteen and fourteen, I would read anything I could find on either the Jews or the Holocaust. I was especially moved by descriptions of *mesirus nefesh* to keep the mitzvos under such horrible conditions. My *neshamah* sensed that there was something there, below the surface, that would resolve my questions. After all the horrors that they experienced under the Nazis, why did so many survivors fight to move to Eretz Yisrael, which was struggling (and is still struggling) for its very existence? Wouldn't it have been much easier for them to move to the United States and lose their identity in the American melting pot?

To make a long story very, very short, by the time I was sixteen I realized that the answer lies in Torah, and I soon found myself enrolled in a Bais Yaakov High School. (In those days, the *frum* schools were thrilled to accept students like me!) I came to Israel a few days short of my eighteenth birthday, and ended up studying in Bais Yaakov Yerushalayim (BJJ). I love *Eretz Hakodesh* and feel that it is a real privilege — as well as a responsibility — to live here.

When did you start writing?

Even as a little girl, I dreamed of becoming a writer. In second grade, the teacher asked us what we'd like to be when we grow up. All the other girls responded that they want to become either a nurse or a teacher or a ballerina. But I wanted to be a writer! Everyone thought I was a nerd — and they were right!

Actually, as a young girl my dream was to have many children and become a writer. When I grew older, the dream had expanded to include marrying a *talmid chacham* and living in Eretz Yisrael. I can honestly say that all my dreams have come true. I have a lot to be grateful for.

In high school I wrote a lot of poetry. I was even the literary editor of my high-school yearbook. But when I got married and started having a family, I completely forgot about writing. In those days there was no outlet for religious writers — no magazines or newspapers, and except for Marcus Lehman and the classic story of Avraham ben Avraham, *frum* books were basically nonexistent. The idea of making a living through writing seemed as far-fetched as the idea of establishing a yeshivah in Moscow or Berlin!

So how did you begin writing professionally?

For years, I worked with preschool children. First I ran a preschool in my living room, and later, I operated a home-based government-subsidized daycare center. The work was very difficult. I took care of six children, ranging in age from three months to three years, from seven in the morning until four in the afternoon. Then, at four, when the kids left, I would quickly turn the daycare center back into a house, tend to my own children, and prepare the following day's meals for both my family and the daycare children. One year I had a couple of extremely difficult children — one little girl screamed hysterically whenever she wasn't held, which, of course, with five other children to take care of, was most of the day. At the end of the year I decided that I couldn't continue, and closed the daycare center. It was a very frightening step. We needed the money I earned to pay the grocery bill. I was very worried that I would never find another job.

But salvation comes in the blink of an eye! A close friend, an extraordinary writer and editor, heard of an opening with an Israeli writing company that supplies articles to American newspapers. She suggested that I apply for the job. Much to my amazement, I was hired! Each week I researched and wrote a *yahrtzeit* article about a prominent Chassidic rebbe. It was like writing a major term paper every week! I learned a tremendous amount — both about writing and about rebbes. But after a year or so I experienced burnout. I just couldn't face writing another biography.

That first job really put me into the ball game. I had gained confidence in my writing skills and discovered that I could cope with the pressure (and, believe me, it really is pressure!) of meeting deadlines. Since then, I've had hundreds of articles published, translated over a dozen books and written several books of my own. But although I've written a lot, I'm not the type of writer who breezily composes something and then submits it. I go over everything I write at least a dozen times — usually, much more. And then, when I look at it again a few weeks later, I always catch lots of things that should have been written differently. Writing is a process that takes a lot of patience and, most important of all, *siyata d'Shemaya*.

What are your plans for the future?

To continue writing. I really love it! It's not a job, it's a passion. I would also like to go into laughter therapy (!). This winter, after doing the research for an article that I wrote on laughter therapy, I ended up hosting an impromptu session with a large group of ladies. It was a roaring success. Another dream is to learn more about my city, Yerushalayim, and eventually give neighborhood tours. One of my hobbies is walking through the old neighborhoods, exploring the courtyards, and seeing the many different communities that live here. And, of course I would like to spend more time with my grandchildren. After all, what Bubby doesn't?

Well, getting to know myself has certainly been interesting. I believe it's a lifelong endeavor. May it be a long and healthy one!

GLOSSARY

Acharonim — authoritative Torah commentators after the 16th century.

agunah (pl. *agunot*) — woman unable to remarry because she has neither a divorce nor evidence of her missing husband's demise.

a"h — acronym for "*alav hashalom,*" peace be upon him; used in referring to a deceased person.

ahavas Yisrael — lit., love of Israel; i.e., love of one's fellow Jew.

Aish — lit., fire; refers to Aish HaTorah, a prominent *kiruv* yeshivah in Jerusalem.

alef-beis — the 22 letters of the Hebrew alphabet.

aliyah — immigration to Eretz Yisrael.

aliyah l'regel — the thrice-yearly pilgrimage to the Temple Mount in Jerusalem during the festivals of Pesach, Shavuos, and Succos.

almanah — widow.

am hanivchar — the chosen nation.

am Yisrael — the Jewish nation.

amein — lit., so be it. Recited after hearing a blessing or *kaddish*, it expresses agreement with the message.

av beis din — chief justice of a Jewish rabbinical court.

avreich (pl. *avreichim*) — kollel student.

ayin tovah — lit., a good eye. This refers to the positive character trait of seeing the good in others.

Baal Shem Tov — lit.. Master of the Good Name — Name given to Rabbi Yisrael, founder of the Chassidic movement.

baal teshuvah (m.), (m. pl. *baalei teshuvah*) *baalas teshuvah* (f.) (f. pl. *baalos teshuvah*) — a penitent returnee to Jewish life, observance, and study.

baalei batim — laymen.

bachur (pl. *bachurim*) — youth; especially used in reference to a student in a yeshivah.

balabusta (Yid.) — the quintessential Jewish homemaker.

baruch Hashem — Blessed is Hashem.

bashert (Yid.) — 1. predestined spouse. 2. destined to be.

bayis ne'eman b'Yisrael —a Torah-true Jewish household.

bechirah — free choice; free will.

bedikas chometz — the search for leaven conducted on the eve of the day before Pesach.

bein hazmanim — intersession.

beis din — Jewish court.

beis hachaim — cemetery.

beis medrash — communal study hall, usually for Talmudic study.

beketcheh (Yid.) — satin frock coat.

ben Torah — a yeshivah student; a knowledgeably observant Jew.

bentched (Yid.) — gave a blessing; see *berachah* 2.

berachah (pl. *berachos*) — 1. blessing recited before performing a mitzvah and before and after eating. 2. an invocation of Divine favor — as in a blessing given by one person to another.

Birkas Kohanim — the priestly blessing recited during prayers, daily in Israel, on holidays in the Diaspora.

bli ayin hara — lit., without an evil eye; an expression used to ward off harmful influences.

bnei bayis — members of a household.

bourekas — filled pastries.

bris milah — circumcision ceremony and/or celebration thereof.

bubby (Yid.) — grandmother.

Chabad — acryonym for *Chochmah, Binah, Daas* — refers to Lubavitch Chassidus.

Chad Gadya — liturgical parable recited at the conclusion of Passover Seder.

chalav Yisrael — dairy products which have been under rabbinic supervision from the time of milking.

challah (pl. challos) — braided loaf of bread used at Sabbath and holiday meals.

chalutzim — pioneers.

chareidi — one who is strictly observant.

chasan Torah — an honorific given to the man called to the final Torah reading on Simchas Torah.

chassid (pl. Chasidim) — 1. follower of a Chassidic leader (Rebbe). 2. a pious individual.

chassidishe — pertaining to the Chassidic culture or community.

Chassidus — the Chassidic movement.

chatzos — midnight.

chavrusa (pl. *chavrusos*) (Aramaic) — study partner.

chazaras hashatz — oral repetition of the *Shemoneh Esrei* by the one leading the prayers.

chazzan — cantor; one who leads the prayers.

cheder — Jewish elementary school.

chesed — kindness; acts of beneficence.

Chevrah Kadisha (Aramaic) — burial society.

chinuch — Jewish education.

chizuk — encouragement.

Chol HaMoed — intermediate days of the festivals of Pesach and Succos.

cholent (Yid.) —stew, cooked overnight and eaten at the Sabbath day meal.

Chumash — Five Books of Moses; one of the first five books of the Bible.

chumrah — stringency.

daven (Yid.) — pray.

davening (Yid). — prayer service.

dayan (pl. *dayanim*) — judge; member of the beis din.

deveikus — the ecstatic state of cleaving to G-d.

derashah — sermon or discourse.

derech — lit., path; path of Jewish life; manner; approach.

Devarim — last of the Five Books of Moses

dvar Torah (pl. *divrei Torah*) — discourse or conversation on Torah subjects; a Torah thought expressed orally or in writing.

ehrlicher (Yid.) — an upright, honest person.

Eidah HaChareidis — A body of Torah sages who espouse the stringent observance of halachah.

Ein K'Elokeinu — lit., there is none like our G-d. Words found in Shacharis prayers.

eiruv — a legal device that permits carrying out-of-doors on the Sabbath.

eishes chayil — a woman of valor; a dedicated wife.

eitzah (pl. *eitzos*) — advice.
elter bubby (Yid.) — great-grandmother.
em kol chai — mother of all mankind.
emes — truth.
emunah peshutah — simple (basic) faith.
erev — eve of; the day before Sabbath or holidays.
erev Rosh Chodesh Sivan — the day prior to the first day of the month of Sivan.
Eretz Yisrael — the Land of Israel.
esrog — citron; one of the four species taken in hand during the festival of Succos.
ezer k'negdo — lit., a helpmeet opposite him, term applied to a Jewish wife; it implies that a good wife will stand at her husband's side to assist him but will oppose him when necessary.
ezras nashim — women's section in a synagogue.
freilich (Yid.) — happy, joyous.
frum (Yid.) — religious; Torah observant.
frumkeit (Yid.) — religious observance.
gashmiyus — materialism.
gedolei hador — the primary spiritual leaders of the generation.
gefilte fish — ground fish balls; traditional Sabbath delicacy.
gemach — acronym for *gemilas chassadim* (acts of kindness). Any organization that provides interest-free loans or services.
Gemara — Talmud.
ger (pl. *gerim)* — a convert.
get (pl. *gittin*) — divorce; a bill of divorce.
goy (pl. *goyim*) — gentile; non-Jew.
Gut Shabbos (Yid.) — traditional Sabbath-day greeting.
hachnassas orchim — hospitality.
Hagah — Israel Civil Defense Unit.
halachic — pertaining to Jewish law.
halachah (pl. halachos) — 1. the body of Jewish law. 2. a Jewish law.
Har Habayis — the Temple Mount.
Har Hamenuchos — mountain on the outskirts of Jerusalem, which serves as a burial ground.
Hashem — lit., the Name, a way of referring to G-d without pronouncing the Sacred Name.
hashgachah pratis — Divine Providence at a personal level.
hashkafah — Jewish philosophy; outlook; worldview.
hatzlachah — success.
hechsher — Rabbinic certification (on food).
heilige Yiddishe neshamah (pl. *heilige Yiddishe neshamos*) — holy Jewish soul.
heter mechirah — a rabbinic dispensation regarding using the land during the Sabbatical year.
hishtadlus — effort.
hisorerus — fervor; enthusiasm.
histadrut — the labor movement in Israel.
Hodu l'Hashem ki tov — Praise Hashem for He is good.
Ibn Ezra — a medieval Torah sage.
iluy atzum — an exceptionally brilliant student of the Talmud.
Imeinu — our Matriarch, refers to one of the four Matriarchs: Sarah, Rivkah, Rachel, and Leah.
ishah l'dugmah — an exemplary woman; i.e., one to emulate.
kadosh (pl. *kedoshim*) — individuals who have given their lives in sanctification of G-d's Name.
kallah (pl. *kallahs*) — a bride.
kasher — a procedure whereby one can make utensils halachically kosher.
kashrus — Jewish dietary laws.
kavod — honor; respect; recognition.
kedushah — 1. holiness; sanctity. 2. a prayer recited in the presence of a

minyan during the repetition of the *Shemoneh Esrei* prayer.
kefirah — heresy.
kehillah (pl. *kehillos*) — community; congregation.
kein ayin hara — see *bli ayin hara.*
kesubah — marriage contract.
kever — grave; burial site.
kibbutz — commune.
kiddush — 1. blessing recited over wine on the Sabbath and festivals. 2. a festive gathering during which kiddush is recited.
kippah — skullcap.
kiruv — outreach; drawing non-observant Jews closer to Torah Judaism.
klal — group; community.
Kol Nidrei — opening prayer of the Yom Kippur services.
kollel — post-graduate study program for married students.
korban (pl. *korbanos*) — lit., sacrifice; in this book, a child whose religious heritage was uprooted by the Zionists.
Kosel, Kotel — the Western Wall, the holiest accessible site.
kosher — adhering to the Jewish dietary laws.
Krias Shema al HaMittah — the bedtime Shema prayer.
Krias Yam Suf — Splitting of the Reed Sea.
l'kavod Shabbos kodesh — in honor of the holy Sabbath.
l'shem Shomayim — for the sake of Heaven.
lamed vovnik — one of the 36 hidden *tzaddikim* in each generation.
lashon kodesh — lit., the holy tongue; i.e., Hebrew.
leichter (Yid.) — candlesticks.
levayah — funeral.
limud Torah — Torah study.
limudei kodesh — Torah studies.
lira — former Israeli monetary unit, predecessor of the *shekel.*
Litvak (Yid.) — of Lithuanian descent; non-Chassidic.
lulav — palm branch; one of the four species taken in hand during the festival of Succos.
Ma'ariv — the evening prayer service.
maaser — tithe.
maabarot — transit camps.
machzor — prayer book used for the Jewish holidays.
madrichah (pl. *madrichot*) — woman student advisor often in charge of the dorm.
maggid shiur — Torah lecturer.
Mah Nishtanah — The Four Questions asked at the Passover Seder.
Mah tovu ohalecha Yaakov — "How goodly are your tents O Israel" — words expressed upon entering the synagogue for prayer services.
maidel (pl. *maidelach*) — (Yid.) girl.
makom Torah — a place where Torah is dominant.
malachim — angels.
manhig — spiritual leader.
Mashgiach — dean of students in a yeshivah who also serves as a guide and advisor.
Mashiach — the Messiah.
masmid (pl. *masmidim*) — exceptionally diligent Torah student.
matzah (pl. matzos) — unleavened bread, eaten on Pesach.
matzliach — successful.
matzos meyuchados — matzos baked under conditions of special scrutiny.
Me K'Elokeinu — lit., Who is like our G-d; words found in Shacharis prayers.
mechalel Shabbos — one who desecrates the Sabbath.
mechanech (m.) *mechaneches* (f.), (f. pl. *mechanchot*) — educator.
mechazek — to strengthen; to give *chizuk.*
mechitzah — a dividing curtain used in the synagogue or at large gatherings

to separate men's and women's sections.

mechutanim — the parents-in-law of one's child.

mechutenester — child's mother-in-law.

mehadrin — lit., to beautify; an exalted level of religious observance.

mein kindt (Yid.) — my child.

melamed — school teacher or tutor.

menachem — console, esp. to console a mourner.

mentchlichkeit (Yid.) — decency.

menuchas hanefesh — peace of mind.

meshulach (pl. *meshulachim*) — itinerant fundraiser.

mesirus nefesh — self-sacrifice; unusual effort or devotion.

metziah — lit., a find; i.e., a bargain; an exceptional value.

middos — character traits; usually used to connote good character.

mikdash me'at — a miniature sanctuary; used to connote a synagogue or study hall; also a home where the Shechinah dwells.

mikveh — ritualarium.

milchig (Yid.) — dairy.

Minchah — the afternoon prayer service.

minhag — custom.

minyan — quorum of ten men necessary for communal prayer.

mishpachah — family.

mitzvah (pl. mitzvos) — a commandment; a good deed.

Modeh Ani — prayer recited upon awakening, expressing gratitude for life.

mohel — person who performs ritual circumcision.

moser nefesh — one who puts unusual effort or devotion into his service of G-d.

moshav — agricultural settlement.

Motza'ei Shabbos — Saturday night; time of the departure of the Sabbath.

Nefesh b'Nefesh — an organization that facilitates immigration to Israel.

negel vasser (Yid.) — ritual washing of the hands upon awakening.

neshamah (pl. *neshamos*) — soul.

Neve Yerushalayim — noted *kiruv* yeshivah.

Nevi'im — Prophets; Biblical Books of the Prophets.

niftar — deceased.

nisayon — test; challenge; trial.

nissim — miracles; wonders.

Ohr Sameyach — noted *kiruv* yeshivah.

Olam HaEmes — lit., the World of Truth; euphemism for the afterlife.

parashah — a Torah portion read on Shabbos.

parnassah — livelihood; income.

pashtus — simplicity.

pasken shailos (Yid.) — to render a rabbinic decision on a halachic query.

pasuk — 1. a verse of Scripture 2. a sentence.

peiros — fruits.

penimiyus — one's internal emotional state.

Perek Shirah — hymn of praise to G-d.

petirah — demise.

peyos — sidecurls; earlocks.

pidyon haben — ritual ceremony of the redemption of a woman's firstborn son.

Pirkei Avos — *Ethics of the Fathers*; a section of the Mishnah dealing with moral and ethical teachings.

pirkei Tehillim — chapters of *Psalms*.

rav (pl. *rabbeim*) — rabbi.

rachmanus — mercy; compassion.

Rashi — primary medieval Torah scholar.

rebbetzin (Yid.) — wife of a rabbi.

refuah sheleimah — a total recovery.

Rishonim — medieval commentators on the Torah.

Rosh Kollel — head of an institute of higher learning.

Rosh Chodesh — one or two quasi-festive days at the beginning of a Jewish month.

rosh yeshivah (pl. *roshei yeshivah*) — dean of a Torah academy

Seder — traditional festive meal celebrated on the first two nights of Passover.

sefer (pl. *sefarim*) — book.

Sefer (pl. *Sifrei*) *Torah* — Torah Scroll.

sefer Yeshayahu — the book of *Isaiah.*

sefiras ha'omer — also called *sefirah*; the 49-day period between Passover and Shavuos.

semichah — rabbinic ordination.

seudah — meal, esp. a festive meal.

Shaar Shechem — Damascus Gate.

shaatnez — Biblically forbidden blend of wool and linen.

Shabbaton — convention held over a Sabbath.

Shabbos (pl. Shabbosim, Shabbassos) — the Sabbath.

Shabbos *seudah* — one of the three Sabbath meals.

Shacharis — the morning prayer service.

shadchan — matchmaker.

shalach manos — gifts of food sent to one's fellow Jew on Purim. Also, *mishloach manos.*

shalom — peace.

shalosh seudos — lit., the third meal; the last of the three meals required on the Sabbath. It is eaten before sunset on Sabbath day.

she'eilah — halachic query.

Shechinah — the Divine Presence.

shechitah — ritual slaughter.

shechted — (Yid.) slaughtered.

sheitel (Yid.) — wig.

sheitel macher (Yid.) — wig stylist.

shekel — denomination of Israeli money.

Shelah —noted Torah authority.

Shema Yisrael — prayer expressing one's belief in G-d's Oneness.

shemittah — the sabbatical year during which land in Eretz Yisrael lies fallow.

Shemoneh Esrei — the main prayer of the three daily prayer services.

shemurah matzos — the Pesach matzah made of flour that has been carefully guarded from coming into contact with water.

sheva berachos —festive meal honoring the newlyweds during the week following their wedding.

sheva mitzvos bnei Noach — the seven commandments that are specifically incumbent on gentiles..

shidduch — marriage match.

shiur (pl. *shiurim*) — lecture on a Torah Topic.

shivah — the seven days of mourning.

shlep (Yid.) — drag.

shliach (m.) *shlichah* (f.) — emissary.

shlita — acronym meaning: may he live a long and good life.

shmattes (Yid.) — rags.

shmiras einayim — the practice of guarding one's eyes from improper sights.

shmiras Shabbos — the observance of the Sabbath.

shochet (pl. *shochtim*) — ritual slaughterer.

shomer Shabbos — one who is Sabbath observant.

shtreimel (Yid.) — fur-rimmed hat worn by male Chassidim on the Sabbath and festivals.

shuk — market.

shul (Yid.) — synagogue; house of prayer.

simchah (pl. *simchos*) — 1. a joyous occasion. 2. the joyous atmosphere in a Jewish home.

simchas hachayim — joie de vivre.

siyata d'Shemaya (Aramaic) — the help of Heaven.

Sochnut — Jewish Agency.

sofer — scribe.

succah (pl. *succos*) — booth in which a Jew is commanded to dwell during Succos.

taharah — purity; purification.

tallis — four-cornered prayer shawl with fringes at each corner.

talmid (m.) (m. pl. *talmidim*) *talmidah* (f.). (f. pl. *talmidos*) — student.

talmid chacham — Torah scholar.

Tanach — acronym for *Torah, Neviim, Kesuvim*; the 24 Books of the Bible.

tefillah (pl. *tefillos*) — prayer.

Tefillas Haderech — the traveler's prayer.

tefillin — phylacteries.

Tehillim — the Biblical Book of *Psalms.*

tereifah — term used for any food that is not kosher and/or is ritually unfit for consumption.

teshuvah — 1. repentance; rediscovery of Torah Judaism 2. a response to a halachic query.

tevilah — immersion in a ritualarium; this is one of the components of the conversion process.

tichel (Yid.) — kerchief; a head covering worn by a married Jewish woman.

tikkun chatzos — lament recited at midnight, commemorating the exile of the Divine presence from Its abode in the Holy Temple.

Tishah B'Av — the Ninth of Av; a day of mourning and fasting that commemorates the destruction of the First and Second Temples.

Toras Yisrael — the Torah of the Jewish people.

tzaddik (m.) (m. pl. *tzaddikim*), *tzadekes* (f.) — righteous individual.

tzedakah — charity.

tzena — the period of dire poverty and austerity in Israel during the late 40s and early 50s just after the establishment of the State of Israel.

tzeniyus — modesty.

tzetel (Yid.) — lit., note; a request written on a slip of paper and given to a Rebbe requesting his blessing.

tzibbur — congregation; gathering of people.

tzitzis — fringed garment worn by Jewish men and boys.

ulpan — study program to learn the Hebrew language.

upsherin (Yid.) — ceremony marking the first haircut of a boy, usually on his third birthday or on Lag B'Omer.

yarmulke (Yid.) — skullcap.

ye'ush — despair.

Yekkish — Germanic.

yemach shemo — may his name be erased.

Yid (pl. *Yidden*) (Yid.) — a Jew.

Yiddish — Jewish; the Jewish language.

Yiddishe maidelach (Yid.) — Jewish girls.

Yiddishkeit — Judaism; Jewish way of life.

Yishuv — 1. (*u.c.*) settlement of the Holy Land 2. (*l.c.*) community; settlement.

Yom Tov — Jewish holiday.

zechus — the merit of a good deed, esp. deserving a spiritual reward.

zeide, zeidy (Yid.) — grandfather.

zemiros — songs of praise, specifically those sung at the Sabbath and festive meals.

ztz"l — acronym for *zecher tzaddik livrachah*, appended to the name of a deceased righteous individual.